Treasons,
Stratagems,
And
Spoils

TREASONS, STRATAGEMS,

AND

SPOILS

*How Leaders Make Practical Use of
Values and Beliefs*

F. G. BAILEY

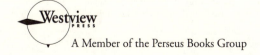

A Member of the Perseus Books Group

Westview Press books are available at special discounts for bulk purchase in the United States by corporations, institutions, and other organizations. For more information, please contact the Special Markets Department at The Perseus Books Group, 11 Cambridge Center, Cambridge, MA 02142, or call (617) 252-5298.

Published in 2001 in the United States of America by Westview Press, 5500 Central Avenue, Boulder, Colorado 80301–2877, and in the United Kingdom by Westview Press, 12 Hid's Copse Road, Cumnor Hill, Oxford OX2 9JJ

Find us on the World Wide Web at www.westviewpress.com

Library of Congress Cataloging-in-Publication Data

Bailey, F. G. (Fredrick George)
  Treasons, stratagems, and spoils : how leaders make practical use of values and beliefs / by F. G. Bailey
    p.   cm.
  Includes bibliographical references and index.
  ISBN 0-8133-3904-9 (pbk); 0-8133-3941-3 (hc)
  1. Political leadership.   I. Title.

JC330.3 .B 35   2001
303.3'4—dc21   2001022032

The paper used in this publication meets the requirements of the American National Standard for Permanence of Paper for Printed Library Materials Z39.48–1984.

10   9   8   7   6   5   4   3   2   1

That man that hath no music in himself,
Nor is not moved by concord of sweet sounds,
Is fit for treasons, stratagems, and spoils;
The motions of his spirit are dull as night,
And his affections dark as Erebus.
Let no such man be trusted.

—**Shakespeare,**
The Merchant of Venice

Contents

PART THREE
HOW TO WIN: LEADERS AND OPPONENTS

Preface

Heraclitus said: "You cannot step into the same river twice, for fresh waters are ever flowing in upon you." But he also said, enigmatically: "We step and do not step into the same river: we are and we are not." In fact, we cannot be sure what he actually said, for all that has come down to us are reports by other philosophers, principal among them Plato, who was keen to prove Heraclitus wrong. Where Plato saw fixity, Heraclitus saw movement. Heraclitus saw the water flowing; Plato saw the category *river*. The apparent contradiction in "We step and do not step into the same river" is not a contradiction at all: It is not about what exists but about different ways to make sense of experience—different ways to model the world. Plato favors the inert model of *structure*: Heraclitus prefers *process*, which portrays movement. Models are tools, and a chisel does not contradict a hammer; both have their uses. This book is about ideas of structure and of process as they are used to make sense of politics, and about a third tool, which is agency or strategy—what we do purposefully in the process of making and unmaking structures.

I am stepping again, thirty years later, into the river that was *Stratagems and Spoils*, a self-defined "handbook" written for students to help them think about politics and political leaders both in their own and in other cultures. That book provided programs—sets of propositions and questions—to be used on narratives of political events. Programs are tools that can be tested and improved by applying them to different situations, and *Stratagems and Spoils* was written with that procedure in mind; so is this book. Heraclitus was right: Things move, and every program, every set of questions, every sequence of investigative operations, when applied to particular political situations, inevitably reveals itself as ready for amendment, ready to give way to something more effective.

I have stayed close to the main frame of *Stratagems and Spoils* and have used a few of the same narratives, selecting those that, colleagues told me, resonated in the minds of student readers. In the intervening years I have written other books about politics, and some ideas from them (and several narratives) are also deployed here. The guiding inquiry in this book is into the use that leaders make of values and beliefs to control their followers and to defeat their opponents. *Treason*, the new word in the title, indicates a touch more attention to *morality*—to ideas of duty and conscience—as a foil to *rational calculations of advantage*, which dominated the earlier book. That shift in emphasis perhaps reflects the experience of thirty more years peering into the Erebus—the dark and shadowed place of politics and politicians—and finding there a politics of conscience (more often than I had thought) at war with a politics of advantage.

Definitions are variable things, selected according to the needs of the inquiry. The first two chapters sort through various meanings that have been attached to the word *politics* and pick out those that will contribute to understanding political processes and their associated strategies, specifically those that leaders use to attract and keep a following (Chapters 3–6) and to contend with one another (Chapters 7–12). A strategy is effective when it is deployed appropriately, and much of the book is taken up with describing the contextual variables that decide which strategies work in which situations.

A word about tone. Looking into that Erebus, I find it difficult to maintain a posture of scientific dispassion, still less of academic solemnity. There are politicians who are downright evil. There are also many who are so stuffed with self-importance, so unaware that they are ridiculous, and sometimes so obtusely unperceptive of the world around them and the consequences of what they are saying and doing, that mockery is the inescapable reaction. Alternatively, political institutions themselves are stupidly constructed and best portrayed in tales of the picaresque. Folly, however, does not entirely fill the stage. There are politicians who deserve to be thought tragic—greatness felled by adversity—and whose lives evoke a sadness that things should turn out that way. The drama of politics is filled with ambiguities, and very complicated; one and the same person, in the same performance, may wear the mask of villain, bumbler, trickster, and tragic hero—you will meet one such player in Chapters 9 and 10.

The political world, so often grim and disagreeable, is best tolerated by looking first for its absurdity, and then for its irony. Irony enters because the systems that we *design* to make our politics orderly are often trumped by patterns of events that emerge *spontaneously*. What we do intentionally to create an orderly society does not necessarily have the consequences that we anticipated; to that extent our reason fails us (although it is often possible to work out, afterward, why things turned out the way they did). Similarly, the strategies that we construct to gain our own particular ends, whether or not they fail us, in their aggregate contribute to the natural patterns that sometimes disturb or defy our would-be rationally designed order of society; things may even fall apart. My focus will be on strategies, but the story would be unanchored if it did not thread through the chapters that follow the complex interplay among designed order, individual initiatives, and a natural order.

Part ONE

How to Understand: The Basics

In politics nothing is contemptible.
—Disraeli

- The practice of politics concerns the orderly distribution of power; and power is the capacity to make someone do something, whether they want to or not, whether they know what is happening or not. The word "orderly" is a trickster because, as I said in the preface, it covers two very different situations: an order that is rationally designed as against a pattern that evolves on its own, that is natural and spontaneous, that can be described and to some extent understood after the event, but was not planned.
- The first chapter—on the basic features of political ideas and actions (as I choose to see them)—has three parts that arise out of that distinction.
  - The first is a tension between dutiful action and self-interest, which produces the contradiction between an intended order (legal, constitutional, to some extent customary) and a natural order that evolves out of the initiatives taken by people eager to gain power or to avoid having it wielded over them.
  - Second, the designed order is limited because reason has only a limited role to play in political arenas. People react off the cuff, without thinking things through; more than that, there is a limit to rationality and some matters, always

and everywhere, precede reason and must be taken on faith.

- Third, the intended institution-based order is precarious in politics because self-interested actors may profit when they circumvent it—hence "In politics nothing is contemptible." At the same time, the slide into chaos is countered by the natural tendency of power to expand into spaces where freedom once existed.

- Successful politicians need to comprehend not only the normative order of the political arena in which they operate—etiquette, customs, rules, and regulations—but also its unintended and unforeseen patterns. In other words, they must try to make sense of political events scientifically, seeing these events as parts of a natural system. That kind of understanding is also the goal of this book. For this purpose a method is required. Its basic elements and assumptions are outlined in Chapter 2.

1

The Aroma of Politics

- This introductory chapter highlights three features that are found in political arenas everywhere:
  - first, a tussle between the public weal and private interests;
  - second, mindlessness; and
  - third, an ever-present risk of collapse either into chaos or into excessive regimentation.
- In each of these, like a perfume hiding a disagreeable odor, a respectable theme masks something that is less presentable: duty fronts for self-interest; reason cloaks mindlessness; and behind order lurks chaos or, facing about, freedom falls prey to despotism.

The Public Weal, Private Interests, and *Realpolitik*

People with political power rarely admit that they enjoy it, and never say that they use it to benefit themselves. In the past they said that God appointed them and gave them a divine mandate to govern, and whatever they did, they did for God's glory. (That voice is heard now from ayatollas in Iran and fundamentalist Christians in the United States.) A generation or two back—and still sometimes today—politicians invoked the Fatherland or the Motherland or the Nation or the Race and proclaimed their devotion to it. In the United States, nowadays, they prefer a common touch and speak about service to "the

American people" and their duty to exercise responsibly the authority entrusted to them. Their rivals say that such claims are false and hypocritical and that only they themselves are the people's true and sincere servants. Cynical persons, outside the political game, declare that power inevitably corrupts; if you want to understand how politics work, find out who has a piece of the action and ask what is the payoff to being in power.

Situations are rarely so transparent that you can decide without hesitation where truth lies. Look at this example; it reeks with ambiguity. Many years back, over a period of several weeks in March and April, I watched a man in a village in India being—metaphorically—crucified. His name was Tuta. He was a man of low caste (a Washerman) who, through hard work and some good luck, had become richer than the village leaders thought he should be (they were of high caste) and they were able, by judicial means, to wrest away some of his wealth and put it into the public purse; they fined him. I thought at the time—I still think—that at least some of them were politically motivated: They were thinking about power and at the same time looking for a chance to get their hands on his money. They wanted to cut him down to size, and they knew he did not have the means to fight back effectively. But this was a judicial matter, the case was argued in a series of meetings of the village *panchayat* (council), and they could hardly make his prosperity the basis for an indictment and a fine. Instead they accused him of harboring a spirit—what they call a *devata*—which served him and made him rich; but it had run amok and killed an adolescent girl in a neighbor's house. Tuta was only one of half a dozen people in the village who kept a *devata*, and they were all uncovered by means of an elaborate divination. All except Tuta were penalized with small fines. He, since his was the *devata* that, according to the divination, had done the killing, was fined thirty times as much as any other offender—equivalent at that time to the income that a reasonably comfortable household could expect to receive over a period of two months. Tuta's money was supposed to pay the cost of the divination.

I wrote a book about that incident and called it *The Witch-Hunt*, because what the villagers did seemed to me to have precisely the flavor of the dictionary's definition of a witch-hunt: "a single-minded and uncompromising campaign against people with unacceptable views or behaviour, one regarded as unfair or malicious persecution."

The clique in the village council that engineered the prosecution did not, of course, present the affair in that way; if challenged they would have said (and probably believed) that they were acting in the public interest by ridding the community of a dangerous presence. Nor did most other people (I met two skeptics) consider the indictment to be unfair or malicious. But I saw the incident as essentially political: It had to do with power. Powerful people were seizing the opportunity, occasioned by the girl's sudden and unexpected death, to put an upstart back in his place. I think most villagers had a more clinical definition of the situation; the issue for them was public health and public safety, not power.

From another aspect their concern might have been judged political. We use that word not only to talk about the exercise of power and its distribution but also with reference to the purposes for which power is exercised. In this sense politics is the art and science of government: Political institutions look to the good order and well-being of the city or the state or whatever constitutes the body politic. Tuta and his *devata* were a cause for apprehension, a threat to the community, and a public menace. Those who punished him were doing their civic duty.

In what might seem to be free association but is not, I saw Michael Dukakis, the Democratic contender in the 1988 presidential election in the United States, as another Tuta, a man put down by a witch-hunt. Tuta and Dukakis differ along virtually any dimension that I can think of, except one. In what certainly seemed to me an act of "unfair or malicious persecution," Dukakis was nailed by totally fabricated rumors about mental illness and by that infamous Willie Horton message on television. Horton, a violent criminal, was released from a Massachusetts jail under a parole scheme. Dukakis was then the state's governor. While on parole Horton committed another violent crime. The ad, as I recall it, was macabre and shadowy, showing a turnstile gate revolving as dark figures in jail clothing moved in and out. The message was clear: Dukakis, governor of a state and a would-be president, far from being the keeper of good order and the guardian of the public interest, favored policies that were a cause for apprehension. He was himself a public menace.

These two cases suggest that there are different ways to think about politics. The traditional way—the one that I learned as a student—is in line with the derivation of the word from *polis*, the Greek word for a city. The study of politics is the study of the institutions that we use to manage public affairs, to govern, to keep things orderly. It is the study of persons in authority. We learn about the rights and duties of presidents and prime ministers and dictators, about legislatures, about law courts and other judicial institutions, about rules of succession, about elections, about state and local government, and so on. Politics focus on public affairs and public institutions. One studies political forms and constructs a chart that shows how different institutions are connected with one another and how the tasks of government are divided between them. Then one sets the chart in motion, so to speak, and asks what actions are taken in the course of managing public affairs, that is, to what use is power put and what checks on the abuse of power regulate the system. The grand assumption behind this model is legitimacy; politics is public service. On balance power is exercised in a responsible and statesmanlike manner through institutions that are accepted as legitimate; otherwise we would not have survived. The body politic, as that metaphor suggests, consists of functionally integrated members. Attention is directed toward institutions and institutionalized roles. Leaders, in that scheme, are modeled less as politicians than as statesmen, who do their duty by serving the public interest before they serve themselves.

There are very few political leaders, now or in the past, who are thought to deserve that accolade, and no one—not even Gandhi, who was morality incarnate—goes unchallenged. The skepticism arises out of the other model of politics, which envisages the body politic not as a well-adjusted organism but as an arena in which politicians fight for power, always and everywhere. In this model, the orderly management of public affairs is only half the story, perhaps the lesser half. It may indeed be no more than a façade, a screen that the contestants erect to hide the unsavory things they do to one another (and to the public interest) in the struggle for power. Concern for the public weal is then a cover story. Tuta was punished not because his *devata* had done harm, but because the ruling elite wanted him humbled. The Bush campaign didn't give a hoot about Willie Horton and public safety. They didn't make any effort to do a serious cost-benefit analysis of the Massachusetts jail-parole program. They wanted to frighten the electorate out of voting for Dukakis so that George Bush would become the next president. That is *Realpolitik*, politics that are practiced without concern for morality in public life.

The public-weal model, which is the denial of *Realpolitik*, has always seemed to me either wishful thinking (it too readily assumes that what *should* go on *does* go on) or, in the hands of practical politicians, it is a ruse to conceal their domination over and exploitation of those who do not have the power to resist them. I do not mean that all politicians all the time are totally unconcerned with the well-being of the body politic. Each instance deserves its own evaluation. I do mean that most of them most of the time see themselves in power as a precondition for the general good; their own power is always at least a part of the equation, no matter how much they play it down. "Seek ye first the political kingdom," said Kwame Nkrumah, Ghana's first prime minister, being unusually frank about the matter for a politician. It pays to start with the assumption of *Realpolitik* and see how well it fits the case, for if one starts at the other end, assuming that all concerned are motivated only by a concern for the public interest, there is a temptation to pay exclusive attention to the purposes for which power was used and the results that were (or were not) achieved—Roosevelt and the New Deal, Johnson and the Great Society, Reagan's Evil Empires and Star Wars—and never to ask how the leaders managed to wield power in the first place. The public-weal model is more a design, an ideal, than a description of any political reality. It takes for granted that politicians come to power through elections and exercise it by virtue of the office they hold; it overlooks the many things that politicians do to win an election and the many stratagems that are needed to convert constitutional power—the power of office—into practical power. The political achievements of great men and women are, of course, a legitimate historical study; so also is the study of institutional forms; but neither is a substitute for the analysis of political strategies and the political process.

Reason, Emotion, and Presuppositions

The public-weal way of looking at politics has a distinctively rational view of political behavior. For sure things may go wrong because people may act foolishly and irresponsibly, but by and large the system works well to the extent that the leaders and the led are agreed on the goal and ready to use their minds not only to plan logically about how best to serve justice, create prosperity, and maintain good order, but also to think critically and examine the evidence for and against whatever is proposed. It is assumed, in this scheme, that, since everyone agrees on what the goal is (the public good), reason can play a major part in governing the world. (That point of view is hard to maintain when one thinks about the Willie Horton message. It wasn't addressed to anyone's mind; it was designed to short-circuit logic and fire up emotions, including racist feelings—Willie Horton was black.)

Realpolitik notions also rest on rationality. They suggest that, in order to make sense of politics, you should model successful politicians as cunning, scheming fellows, who may not have read Machiavelli but in truth don't need to, because anything they could have learned from *The Prince* has been acquired in the school of hard experience (if it was not already bred in the bone), otherwise they would not be successful politicians. Rational calculation, in other words, dispassion and cold reason unhindered by moral scruples or emotional commitment, dominate the political arena. Both that judgment and its moral equivalent (that rationality serves the public weal) overlook a significant feature of politics everywhere: Political arenas all the time exhibit behavior that clearly indicates one or another form of mindlessness, both in leaders and among the led. Let us start with the led.

Those who gave George Bush a vote in 1988 solely because the Willie Horton message convinced them that Bush would be the better president were making minimal use of their minds. Rational voters would have wanted evidence that what happened in the Horton case was the norm, or at least part of a statistically significant pattern. They might also want to know what black marks were on record against Bush, who already had a long career in public affairs. Beyond that there is almost an infinity of inquiries that would be needed to make a rational decision about who best deserved to become president.

An "infinity" of inquiries suggests that they are not going to be made. Political strategists seem to assume—I think rightly—that Ordinary Jane and Ordinary Joe are quicker to feel than they are to think; they respond more readily to a message that touches their emotions than to one that requires them to attend to a carefully reasoned argument. Reason does not mobilize support; slogans do. Reasoning is demanding; slogans are comfortably compelling. I will have more to say about this in the chapters on leaders and leadership, but for the moment it is enough to borrow a word from a man talking about

Mussolini's Fascists, and say that all political regimes—democratic, dictatorial, oligarchic, or whatever else—promote *diseducation*. Some do it more discreetly than others, but all leaders, if they are to gain and use power, must at some stage put a stop to their own critical thoughts and doubts and to critical comment from their followers. No action is possible if questions continue to be asked; no regime can govern without some level of faith and trust and consent. Democratic regimes insist that the consent should be "informed," but, as the Willie Horton message suggests, cleverly packaged disinformation can also be an effective persuader. Politicians and political institutions need commitment, which is an unthinking, unquestioning, quasi-religious willingness to accept the regime's fundamental values and beliefs. Leaders want service that comes from the heart, not service doled out according to a cost–benefit reckoning. Of course there is homely wisdom about not being able to fool all of the people all of the time, which may be true if time is taken to mean the longest of long runs. But you can certainly fool enough of the people—"dumb them down"—to get them doing what you want, and to keep up the sham over a long period, sometimes so long that only later generations come to realize what went on behind the smoke and mirrors. That is the tale of any era or any regime or any person when they are viewed from the perspective of a later generation—colonialism, America's "Manifest Destiny," the USSR, the Victorians, even, at present, what Henry Kissinger did or failed to do when he was in a position of power.

Diseducation is a policy. A policy implies a policymaker who decides on it and puts it into practice. That supposes two kinds of people in the political arena: those who do the persuading and ruling, and those who are ruled and persuaded. Policymakers, unlike their victims, must—at some stage—use their minds. But rationality is not a simple on/off matter; the word "reason," like many words that refer to human behavior, has several meanings. A Swedish statesman, Count Oxiensterna, wrote, in a letter to his son in 1648, *Nescis, mi fili, quantilla ratione mundus regatur*—"You do not understand, my son, how small a part reason plays in governing the world." I do not know precisely what he had in mind. It might have been the gullible and diseducated masses, but that seems unlikely in the seventeenth century, when the notion of educated masses would have been a startling oxymoron. He was probably thinking of the foolishness of rulers and of their impassioned natures, which lead them to do stupid things. Or possibly he meant, with Robert Burns, that "the best laid schemes o' mice and men/Gang aft agley." Things go wrong because the planners miscalculate; reason proposes, reality disposes. Much of the tale about governments and governing is about unanticipated difficulties and unintended consequences. All three possibilities suggest that it would be a mistake to try to make sense of politics by focusing *exclusively* on rationality—on people using resources in a calculated way to achieve their goals.

Rationality, however, has to be a part of the picture. We have to begin by assuming it, certainly in the case of those who do the ruling and persuading (and in the case of those who work out how to resist being ruled or persuaded). They are acting purposefully, which is all that rationality means. Rationality, as used by economists (and by me in this book), is the considered allocation of scarce resources to given ends. That does not mean that a rational decision is always a correct one and always delivers the intended outcome (although the word "irrational" is sometimes loosely used to condemn miscalculations of that kind). The Republicans' onslaught on President Clinton during his second term was perfectly rational: They wanted to run him out of office before his term ended, preferably in disgrace, and they had decided that impeachment was the way to do it. They hugely miscalculated: They believed the American people would be horrified by his sexual extravaganzas and would see in his private misbehavior a clear indication of his being unfit for public office—would see him as a public menace. The Republicans did not realize how much people would be turned off by the all-too-obvious and cruelly persistent witch-hunting, by the manifest hypocrisy of the Republican leaders whose own peccadilloes came embarrassingly to light, and by the painfully inept and repetitious performance of the House politician-prosecutors in the impeachment hearings. Yet these miscalculations do not make their actions irrational. The Republicans were rational: They had a target in their sights. But unlike the men who brought Tuta to his knees, or the contrivers of the Bush campaign against Dukakis, they did not correctly estimate the way the political cross-winds were blowing.

Nor can leaders—or anyone else—be constantly and exclusively rational. Rationality, to say it again, is about allocating scarce means to achieve *given* ends; rationality cannot be used to determine ends.

Certainly one can have an end—for example, Clinton's desire, when he first came to office, to establish some kind of national health system—and then discover that it cannot be presently attained. The rational course is to stop the effort and save the resources for some other purpose. But to reach that decision a transcendent end has to be brought into the reasoning, in this case probably Clinton's realization that if he persisted he might, at the very outset of his presidency, turn himself into a lame duck. His presidency—the holding of power—was fundamental: lose that, and everything else collapses. Sooner or later, in any chain of reasoning, the question "For what purpose is this done?" must be answered with "For its own sake. This is the beginning, the foundation." Fundamental values—or beliefs, or desires—stand on their own; they cannot be rationally determined. A conviction becomes a matter of principle or conscience, fixed and unarguable, beyond rationality; and the consequences, whatever they are, are then left to the care of God. The same is true of drives that are psychobiologically given. They are impulses to act directly without ever thinking about the consequences. Such absolutes are a part of every political scene, indeed, of every human life. Drives and convictions, whether despicable or admirable, whether acknowledged or not, set the goals and determine the action, and, if reason comes on the scene at all, they are its givens. Clinton's libido, not part of institutional politics, nevertheless was a nonrational given in the political equation. So also was the peculiarly reason-inhibiting antipathy that Republican legislators evidently felt toward Clinton, apparently from the outset of his presidency.

Not-to-be-questioned values and beliefs are prejudices, a word that condemns them. But what I label prejudice you may hold sacred, as an eternal verity, an unquestionable truth. Racial and class prejudices work that way; those who hold them are usually quite sincere. (It would be better if they were hypocrites; at least the positions would be negotiable.) We all have such not-for-sale beliefs and values, we even have whole philosophies (like free-market capitalism or the inevitability of revolution or natural selection or any of the many religious creeds); life could not go on if we did not have them to guide us and make us feel secure. There is neither time nor energy to question everything; some things must be taken on trust.

That returns us to the calculating politicians. If they are to be effective they must carry in their heads a map or chart of where these rocklike cultural formations are to be found. They must calculate which they should occupy and which they should avoid, and—here the metaphor founders—they need to know how to create unquestioned beliefs and how to dissolve them. They need the skills and resources, in other words, to be able to define situations in ways that will serve their own purposes. Clinton won the impeachment battle because, among other reasons, his enemies never succeeded in defining fellatio, an indisputably private matter, as a disqualification for holding public office.

The Inherent Instability of Politics and Its Opposite

If you add together the ideas (i) that the public weal often does not coincide with private interests and (ii) that reasoned calculation is inevitably at war with emotion and impulse, then it is hard to imagine how a body politic could function like a well-integrated organism. It must be always in a state of tension, stretched and strained, pulled simultaneously in opposite directions, as in a tug-of-war, and therefore necessarily unstable and liable to collapse in one or the other direction.

Imagine this situation as a line that stretches from *cooperation* at one end, through *competition* in the middle, to outright *chaos* (no-holds-barred fighting) at the other end.

order_____competition_____chaos

The diagram suggests that any continuing political situation can be construed as movement one way or the other along this continuum. *Perfect* order, which features in the politician-as-statesman or public-weal model of politics, is a null category, a box that contains no events but only the rules that prescribe orderly cooperative action intended to produce some agreed state of affairs. The other end of the continuum, also a null category, imagines the opposite: conflict in which there are no rules and the contestants are out to destroy one another—Tennyson's "nature red in tooth and claw." To say it again, both extremes—perfect cooperation and unrestrained conflict—are imagined constructs, neat abstractions, not untidy realities. Reality, which is untidy, lies at neither end but in the space between, where people fight for power but do so with greater or lesser attention to the rules that define a fair fight. This central part of the continuum is competition.

Another way to show that neither end of the continuum has an objective existence as anything more substantial than an idea or an asserted definition is to convert the diagram and explicitly evaluate the positions to read like this:

despotism_____competition_____freedom

What one person sees as *huqomat*, the land where good government and order reign, another will call tyranny. *Yaghestan* is the land of freedom; alternatively it is mere anarchy. Everything in politics is disputable and open to an inverse interpretation; everywhere there is tension.

The public/private opposition likewise produces tension. It is ubiquitous because the distinction occurs at every step in a taxonomy. Public/private is relative. When an individual's interest is set against the joint interests of his or her family, the family's interest is public and the individual's is private. Likewise a family's interest is private when opposed to the interest of the community. The same is true of cliques in university departments, and departments in divisions, and divisions in universities, and universities in the tertiary education sector. Wherever a larger entity encompasses a smaller one, and wherever power is a prize, accusations of "partisan behavior" or "sectarianism" or "factionalism" or plain "self-interest" will surface. Whatever is partisan at a higher level will be seen, at the next lower level, as action taken in the public interest. Heraclitus again: Everything both is and is not, depending on where you choose to stand. The same ambiguity occurs all the way up and down any system of nesting groups; every step is an opportunity to disagree.

How does one make sense of this kind of claim and counterclaim? What seems to be the short and direct question—Where is the truth?—is the least useful, because only on rare occasions does an undisputed truth emerge. When the interests of the encompassed and encompassing entities are opposed, there is an inherent and usually inescapable uncertainty about what to call "the truth." Did Nixon break the law and so act against the public interest, in order to keep himself and his party in power? Most people think that the evidence against him was conclusive, but it could still be argued that he was acting in the nation's best interests, even if he was breaking some of its laws. Were Tuta's accusers after his money, or did they want to humble him, or did they really believe they were protecting the community against a malignant force? All three versions could be true. The lesson seems to be that inquiries about *the* truth are best left to historians, courts of inquiry, or investigative journalists; they are neither a central part of, nor a prerequisite for an analysis of political action and political systems. The right course is to listen to all the stories, with an ear tuned to *Realpolitik*, and work out how the antagonists compete to define the situation.

Competition is unstable because the antagonists manipulate situations and push them in one or the other direction. Those in power have an interest in the particular order that gives them dominance. It pays their rivals to demonstrate that the regime's order is in fact not orderly at all and that the reality is not what the regime says it is. More on this later. Adversary politics can be read as a repertoire of strategies used to demonstrate that one's opponent's definitions of what brings order to the situation are false; one way to do this is to push the encounter in the direction of chaos, and thus show that there is no order.

Even if antagonists did not behave in this way, competition would still lean toward instability, because the competitor who can make a move that his opponent has not anticipated thereby gains an advantage. The rules of fair play set limits on what can be done to win; they specify boundaries and thus they narrow the range of actions and reactions that the antagonists are trying to anticipate. But rules are the outer limits of possible action; they are not precise instructions. They do not indicate specifically what should be done; if they did the encounter would be a ritual, and not a contest. A rule generalizes and situations, including tactical situations, are particular; a rule cannot foresee every contingent situation. The resulting ambiguity leaves room for maneuver and a chance to strike where the opponent may not have anticipated an attack. Moreover, by its very nature the tactic of doing the unexpected is likely to be pushed beyond ingenious interpretations to breaking rules (but in a manner that—the perpetrator hopes—will not be penalized). The antagonist is especially fortunate if he can count on the support of supposedly impartial arbiters. The three judges who selected Starr to direct the prosecution (when his predecessor looked likely to let Clinton off the hook), and several times gave him the go-ahead in expanding his inquisition, were Republicans. In short, in encounters where power is at stake—that is, all political encounters, although not all political interactions—there is an inherent push toward disorder.

Here again, we seem to meet a Machiavellian element of cold rationality, schemers who think about the rules of right conduct only when devising ways to get round them. But this, as I said, cannot be all that is in their minds; none of the scheming makes sense without first identifying whatever mindless convictions, enthusiasms, or dispositions provide the driving force. This is the domain of unreason, of emotion, of action taken heedless of the consequences. All politicians must have in themselves at least a trace of the fanatic, of being possessed by the demon that is hungry for power and quick to find enemies. Politics, if unchecked, drifts toward unreasoned enthusiasm (about both good and evil) and therefore toward chaos.

If that tendency everywhere went unchecked, political systems, which do in fact produce some level of order in the competition for power, could not exist and there would be only Hobbes' version of the state of nature, in which life is solitary, poor, nasty, brutish, and short. What, then, checks the lemming-rush toward disaster? There are three restraints. One is the umpire who is genuinely impartial and penalizes those caught using unfair tactics and so inviting chaos. The American electorate performed this role in 1998 when they voted enough Republicans out of the House of Representatives to cause a crisis in the party's leadership (Gingrich resigned and his designated successor never even got out of the starting gate). The umpire can also be modeled more abstractly, not as a person but as a set of internalized conventions that regulate political conduct and control a political arena's runaway tendencies. (I will talk about Gandhi in that context later.) The other brake is enlightened self-interest, which makes it clear, if not to every enthusiast at least to their allies and supporters, that cavalier disregard for the rules of fair play will engulf them all in disaster, friends and foes alike. That happened in the Clinton affair when the legislators, both Republican and Democrat, voted to end the institution of a special counsel. They did not do so because Starr failed to hit the main target (the removal of Clinton), thus demonstrating that his office was ineffective, but—almost the reverse—because they foresaw an orgy of impeachments and therefore unending chaos if they did not rescind the statute.

The third restraint is of a different order, being a process no less inherent than instability. It is the tendency of authoritative institutions to expand, creeping always in the direction of control, intruding increasingly into the minds of individuals, watching over them, regulating all they do, normalizing them, robotizing them. This was classically described in Foucault's *Discipline and Punish* and later identified by him as a manifestation of "governmentality."[1] The civic-minded see instability and chaos as the danger that hangs over society. Others see the opposite: The real peril is centralization and control. Max Weber had similar ideas about bureaucracy, ever expanding, ever rationalizing until it produced *Entzauberung*, a "disenchantment" of the world, leaving it bereft of spontaneity, originality, creativity, mystery, and all the pleasures of wonderment.[2]

This to-and-fro between public and private, reason and unreason, and control and chaos characterizes the political processes that will be analyzed from Chapter 3 onward. Chapter 2 will outline the methodological assumptions that make this analysis possible.

2

The Toolbox

- This chapter describes three tools for understanding political behavior and political process:
  - first, the method of comparison;
  - second, models of structure, context, and process; and
  - third, models of strategy (also called agency models).
- Both process models and agency models link structures to their contexts.

The Comparative Method:
Universals and Thick Description

Bismarck, the Prusso-German statesman nicknamed the "Iron Chancellor," said that politics was not a science (*Wissenschaft*) but an art (*Kunst*). Science deals with facts that can be communicated; art deals with another kind of knowledge, which is skill, and skill cannot be communicated in the same way. Of course he is right. All the generalized political knowledge that you might cull from Machiavelli's *The Prince* (Bertrand Russel said it was a "handbook for gangsters") or from the fifteen books and 150 wonderfully detailed chapters of Kautilya's *Arthasastra* (a fourth century B.C. Sanskrit treatise on the art of government) would not substitute for political skill. The reason is simple: A handbook provides general rules, and situations are always particular. There is always a gap and the ability to fill it is a measure of political skill. No handbook could, by itself, create a skilled politician, but it can convey a foundation of systematic knowledge about politics, which is required to understand how political skill is exercised. To that extent, there can be a science of politics.

Science looks for underlying patterns and assumes that matters which appear different on the surface may yet have features in common. The imagined ultimate goal is something universal, but universality is a heuristic—a rule to guide the research—not an anticipated result. At the present time, universality in cultural anthropology has a bad name. True universals, it is argued by those who ignore the concept's heuristic use, are biological events or processes like insemination, birth, and death. The associated sociocultural institutions—marriage, rules of descent that allocate a newborn child to one or another group, and rules of succession and inheritance—take many different forms, because they are culturally constructed and not given by nature. Universality resides in the biological facts, not in the sociocultural institutions, which are occasioned by them but are not in any predictable way determined by them.

That instant rejection of universals, and the accompanying disdain for the use of the comparative method, closes off the only way to explain what goes on in social systems, including political systems. Comparison in social science has a function similar to that of the controlled experiment in the hard sciences. An assumption of universality is a logical beginning to any inquiry into social or cultural regularities. You set out with the idea that whatever phenomenon you are investigating is found everywhere, and wait to be proved wrong; then you have a difference to be explained, and that explanation tells you why things are the way they are. The alternative is simple relativism, which is the assumption that each culture must be modeled as sui generis—one on its own. But even a plain description of another culture has to make implicit use of the comparative method, and everyone uses it, including those who profess to disdain it.

I will set out my position by means of examples, and then touch on the methodological and supposedly moral issues that underlie the universals/relativism debates and are said to invalidate the method of comparison.

Being reminded of Tuta's misery by the Willie Horton message was not the only time that my observations in one culture associated themselves with incidents in another. Often the comparative revelation came the other way round and I was struck by differences before I thought about similarities. Ten years after watching Tuta being put in his place and more than thirty years before the Republican pack was loosed on Clinton, I lived for part of a year in Rochester in upstate New York. That was my first visit to the United States and there was much that was different from my native Britain. There were little things, like the light switches: They were all upside down. The language was the same in a general way, although there was a small new vocabulary to learn: Lifts, for instance, were now elevators; suspenders held up trousers, not socks; and the thing on the end of a pencil was, embarrassingly, not a rubber but an eraser. Some words were oddly pronounced: "Poem," for example, had only one syllable. Some phonemes were different too. On Halloween a senior university official whose name was Beadle walked around in a Beatle wig (the pop group was center stage at that time). I missed the pun entirely, because my variety of English distinguishes voiced from unvoiced intervocalic dentals (d-sounds from t-sounds when placed between vowels) and allows them to change meanings. Beadles in England would be heard as a plurality of low-ranking church officials.

People were different too. About to land in Rochester, I heard the pilot announce that the landing gear was stuck, the engineer was trying to free it, and meantime we would circle the airport to use up fuel. On the ground we could see fire trucks drawn up alongside the runway. To my utter astonishment some of my fellow passengers fell to praying, not simply closing their eyes and muttering to themselves, which would not have surprised me, but speaking out loudly and clearly, both men and women. When the engineer succeeded and we landed safely, everyone applauded to show their appreciation for the pilot, the engineer, and, I suppose, for whatever God had answered their prayers. That open and unembarrassed display of emotion astounded me. This was evidently not the land of the stiff upper lip. (I am still taken aback by—and find utterly distasteful—the evident relish with which television cameras zoom into the face of anyone moved to tears.)

There were also manifestations of similarity. One of them, which has stayed in my memory, is like the Tuta–Dukakis connection: It requires quite a high level of abstraction to find a resemblance in the midst of diverse cultural phenomena. During that year, 1963, the U.S. Senate held a televised inquiry into a criminal organization, the Mafia, also called *cosa nostra* ("our thing" or "our business"). The inquiry took hold of me. I had not been much in the habit of watching television and had not realized the dramatic potential of such presentations. The content of what was revealed was truly sensational—murder and mayhem. The principal performer was a man named Valachi, who had been a minor figure in the organization. He spoke matter-of-factly but vividly, even sometimes poetically, about the assassination of crime bosses and the murder of lesser figures, and answered, with good-humored patience, the oft-repeated question of an elderly senator who could not follow the fairly simple Mafia procedures and organization that Valachi described—"Ya get it this time, Senator?" I was also fascinated when I discovered in *cosa nostra*'s affairs a pattern of political action that I had detected in reading about other people in other places. At first I had assumed that disorder must rule over such criminal settings and that life for a Mafioso must be, if not solitary or poor, then certainly nasty, brutish, and short. For many of them life was like that. But it soon became clear from the charts that were used to show the patterns in Valachi's narratives that, in this violence and apparent disorder and unpredictability, order in fact prevailed. Of course, if order had not prevailed, there would have been no continuing organization and no charts to depict its structure. *Cosa nostra* was revealed as a highly structured thing.

Order manifested itself in two ways. The Mafiosi had rules about right conduct and about how their violent game should properly be played, not least being the code of *omertà*, which requires absolute loyalty to the leader and the gang ("family"), and silence about its affairs everywhere (especially on the witness stand); in other words, *cosa nostra* had its own moral code. Second, out of the decisions and actions that individuals took there emerged an unintended regularity, a pattern that was not a moral order but a natural order. One could predict a likely connection between gang wars and changes of leadership in one or the other "family." Succession was patterned, and I had seen the pattern before in a monograph written by Fredrik Barth about the Pathans of Swat in Pakistan.[1] I suspect that I could find something comparable now in the hostile takeover battles between corporations in a capitalist economy or in the manner in which heads rolled in the Republican leadership during the Clinton imbroglio.

Mafiosi and the Pathans have absolutely no connection with one another: They live in totally dissimilar environments, have entirely different economies, and subscribe to different religions. Yet I could see some resemblance in their patterns of political action. I have to unpack this comparison, because it grievously offends against both the creed of the sanctified "Other" and the commandment to refrain from using the model of a natural system to make sense of social processes. The Other is the hapless person (called the "native" in days gone by) who features in anthropological monographs about cultures and societies that are not the anthropologist's own. One can sin against the Other in several ways. Placed in the anthropologist's monograph like a specimen in a museum or—worse—in a laboratory, the Other is not only patronized but also diminished by the very act of comparison, deprived of its humanity and its dignity; differences are "dominated" by enforced "equivalences" and the integrity—the wholeness—of the Other is bent and shaped for comparative purposes into a caricature that is acceptable in the prejudiced ambiance of the anthropologist's own culture.[2]

For sure neither a Pathan nor a Mafioso would feel gratified by a comparison that saw no difference between them; neither of them seem likely to go along with the gentle Gandhi's panhumanist insistence that "all men are brothers." But in fact they would have no reason to feel demeaned, because Pathan and Mafioso are not being compared; the differences between them have not been eliminated. No evaluative judgment has been made of their life-styles or their cultures. The discourse is not about whole peoples and cultures but about an unintended (i.e., a natural) pattern that reveals itself in the ways in which people in these two settings compete for power. But that, the critic might reply, is exactly the point. Pathans and Mafiosi are being reduced to mere *things* in a natural system; they are no longer human beings whose conduct is guided by rules of right and wrong. To compare things is to homogenize them at least with respect to what they have in common; in that process they are deprived of their distinctiveness, their individuality, and, in the case of people, of their moral capacities; in this way they are debased. The correct procedure is "thick" description: The more particulars that can be crammed into the portrayal, the more is justice done to the many-sidedness of the human experience and to the undoubted fact of our moral awareness.

Of course that is the case: To make a comparison and to produce a model of social behavior as a natural (unintended) system is to abstract away the particulars, including (sometimes) our moral capacities. There can be no comparison without abstraction. But to produce the thin abstracted version of a culture in order to compare it with another culture does not somehow do away with the rich and detailed versions of culture, from which the thin versions were drawn. The debate (if it deserves to be called that) arises from a confusion between *description* and *explanation*. To make sense of anything there are two basic questions to be asked. *What is this?* is answered with a *description* of events, or procedures, or organizational forms, or structures, or individuals, or roles, or whatever else. Tuta's story is a description; so are the Valachi hearings; so is my brief and selective account of the attempt to remove Clinton from office; and there will be many others as the book proceeds. The second question asks for an *explanation*: *Why is it like this and not different?* Why did the village bosses turn on Tuta? Why on him and not someone else? Why did the Bush campaign give such prominence to the Willie Horton message? Why does it continue to resonate in American political mythology? Why couldn't the Republican politician-lawyers put on a performance that matched the elegant and persuasive presentations of the professional lawyers who defended Clinton?

The answer to a why question must include a general proposition. Why did the village bosses turn on Tuta? Because they thought he was an upstart. "Upstart" is a general category that applies across different societies and cultures: It denotes persons who usurp the privileges of a rank or status. The word carries with it the suggestion that other people will try to put upstarts back in their places. Once the idea of upstart is stripped of its specifics—once Tuta and the ethnographic particulars of Indian village life and the caste system are left behind— the notion becomes a tool for investigations elsewhere. In other words, it becomes a *question* that one can ask of any political situation. Was Clinton seen as an upstart? Would that explain the self-defeating malevolence of his Republican enemies? Those few cases that I have already given abound with lines of possible investigation that emerge as soon as one generalizes. All of them, for example, raise the issue of fairness and suggest that political competitors are inclined to break the rules of a fair fight—the Willie Horton message, Starr's "persecution" of Monica Lewinsky and others, or the specter of a Mafioso who, like Valachi, breaks the code of *omertà* and "sings" to the authorities. Politics, as I said, has an in-built proclivity for rule-breaking and disorder. In the same way, questions about succession to power and the strategies employed and the processes involved apply to Pathans, Mafiosi, the Republican party, takeover bids in the financial-market arena, and many other particular settings.

A universal, in this scheme of things, is not like the biological events of birth and death that occur everywhere, but rather a notion that what occurs in a particular case may also occur elsewhere. "Universal" does not assert the existence of anything more than the possibility of asking a question; it has to do with heuristic and analytic procedures, not existences.

Models: Structure, Context, and Process

Tuta's main prosecutor—or persecutor, depending on where you want truth to lie—was the Bisoi (headman), who belonged to the dominant Warrior caste. The two of them squared off in a very uneven contest to determine whose definition of what had happened would prevail: either Tuta, through his negligence and greed, had caused an untimely death—or he had not; the girl had died for some other reason. The Bisoi won and his subtext (that Tuta had stepped too far out of a Washerman's proper place) never got into the domain of public discussion. Still less did the possibility that the case was pursued solely to screw sixty rupees out of Tuta.

I lived in Tuta's village—it was called Bisipara—long enough to hear about and sometimes observe events that made it clear that Tuta was not the first person to offend against the establishment version of Bisipara's caste structure. Caste is a complex institution. The simple feature to grasp at the outset is that a caste structure is a hierarchy, which is manifested in the rituals of everyday interaction and made sacrosanct in a mythology that connects rank with the divinity: High castes are nearer to God than are low castes. People of different caste do not intermarry; high castes do not accept cooked food from lower castes; and the intrusion of a low-caste person into the kitchen of a high-caste house or into a temple pollutes it and requires a ritual of purification.

Underpinning the ritual structure is a de facto distribution of wealth and power. High castes tend to be well-to-do and powerful—in Bisipara's agrarian setting they were the landowners. The Bisoi's caste, the Warriors, saw themselves as the only rightful landowners, as

the lords of the village, the body politic itself. Land had been, and to
a degree still was, the main source of wealth. Other castes received a
share in return for specialized services performed for the landowning
Warriors and for each other: They were priests (Brahmans),
Herdsmen, Potters, Barbers, Distillers, Weavers, Washermen, and
others, and at the bottom a caste of Pano Untouchables, who were by
tradition the village scavengers. Panos were leather-workers, the
leather coming from the village's dead cattle, which they took away
and skinned, and—horrified people said—some of them would eat the
meat. The cow is sacred to Hindus and the carcass of a cow or ox or
water buffalo pollutes and is avoided by everyone except
Untouchables. Scavenging and drumming at village festivals were
occasional services; the Pano's main source of income was farm-labor-
ing, each Pano family being attached to a landowning Warrior household. Except for the Brahmans, who stood nearest to God, Warriors
had the highest ritual status and Untouchables the lowest.

Ideally this was a nonmoney, nonmarket economy. Servants of all
categories were paid in grain, and were thought of not as employees,
hired out of a labor pool, but as part of their lord's household or of the
village, the body politic. The metaphor of the body, which functions
as a whole, its members dependent on it, and itself depending on
those members, is a good way to capture the flavor of caste thinking.
So also is the idiom of the family, which we regard as the very inverse
of a market system.

That is a skeletal and idealized description of Bisipara's caste *structure*, a static portrayal of what possibly might have been nearer to reality sometime in the past. The reality that I observed was not so neat
and tidy. Tuta, the village Washerman as of right, conformed entirely
to the ritual requirements of his caste role: He washed clothes for
households higher in caste rank than himself (i.e., most of them
except the Untouchables), he performed various specified rituals
when there was a birth or a death or a marriage in those households,
and he was paid with a measure of rice each time he performed a service, plus an annual allocation of paddy from the patron's harvest and
the privilege of keeping for himself and his family, on ritual occasions,
various garments that had belonged to members of his patron's household. In all of these matters his conduct, with respect to the caste
structure, was exemplary. But he had other sources of income: He
worked for cash in some neighboring villages and for some house-

holds in Bisipara; he ran a small trading business; and he lent money at usurious rates, which was the norm in Bisipara and elsewhere in rural India. In this way, he had become wealthier than a Washerman was expected to be. The witch-hunt was a *process* that brought him down, nearer to what his superiors thought was his proper place in the caste *structure*. Process, in that particular instance, reveals a social system performing like the human body or the air-conditioning system in a house, restoring an equilibrium position (a structure or idealized state of affairs) when something has knocked it out of kilter.

Sometimes the process does not restore the status quo. Tuta, as I said, was not the first person to get out of line with the proper caste structure, as defined by the Bisoi and the Warriors. The Distillers stood, traditionally, not much above the Washermen. Some Distillers were wealthy, and therefore, if I am right in my cynical conjectures about the headman's motives, they should have been ripe for plucking. One of them, indeed, was identified by the divination as owning a *devata*, but his fine was a thirtieth the size of Tuta's. Why was he not cut down to size? There are several answers (besides the fact that the divination did not identify his *devata* as the one that did the damage).

First, he was well enough connected to fight back effectively. Second, he was a Distiller. The whole Distiller caste in the region, owing to a misguided government measure at the turn of the century that banned home-distilling and allowed alcohol sales only through licensed outlets (which Distillers, in accordance with their caste tradition, monopolized), had become rich and had invested their wealth in land. By the time the authorities realized their mistake and brought in total prohibition, the Distillers had become substantial landowners, with an average per capita holding higher than that of the Warriors. They then did what the newly rich generally do: They demanded greater respect. They did so by endeavoring to raise their rank in the caste hierarchy. They forbade their women to work in the fields; they clothed them in the long sari, instead of the knee-length garment worn by other women; they became vegetarians (some of them, some of the time); and they did not (most of them) drink. (Despite prohibition, home-stills were common; a potent liquor was made from *mahua* trees or from toddy palms.) In addition to these generalized signals of respectability, they used an interactive strategy: They would take cooked food only from Brahmans and refused it from other castes that had considered themselves above Distillers, including even the

Warriors. The claim was moot, because none of these other castes would accept food cooked by a Distiller. The result, at the time I was there, had been to put them on hold: Other castes were not sure where to place them.

In short, things worked out differently than in Tuta's case. Distillers were not brought back into line, but neither were they unambiguously promoted. Rank within the caste structure had become uncertain, and there had emerged an element of competition, which is not supposed to happen. There was, however, a civilized, almost gamesmanlike, quality to the way in which the Distillers and the rest of the clean castes in the village competed with one other. No one engineered a showdown to impose a decisive end to the encounter, as they did for Tuta; both parties seemed content with scoring points when they had the chance. Neither side looked for a conclusive outcome. Certainly no one questioned the caste *structure* (as distinct from rank within it) as the appropriate framework in which to conduct village politics.

That revolutionary move was made by the lowest caste, the Pano Untouchables. Confrontations between them and the clean castes were not games; the antagonists were not trying to score points; they wanted a knock-out. On several occasions the struggle edged on violence. The Panos upset the status quo far more effectively than did the Distillers. Why the difference?

The process began with a handful of Pano leaders becoming moderately substantial landowners and, like the Distillers, wanting respect. Initially, I believe, some of them hoped to do what the Distillers had done; they worked within the idiom of caste purity and they used similar public-relations strategies. They built a temple in their own street and made their devotion to Hinduism very public. The leaders urged their caste-fellows (with a conspicuous lack of success) to give up scavenging and to become vegetarian and teetotalers. They set an example by adopting a life-style that would have made clean caste people respected, but in their case it only earned them mockery. The reason was their rank in the caste system: What Distillers could do, Panos could not, because Panos were Untouchables. Untouchability was an insurmountable barrier; it was a defining characteristic in Bisipara's caste structure, not something that clean caste people were ready to negotiate. It was what I earlier called "rocklike."

So the goal shifted, and the Pano leaders became de facto revolutionaries (probably without thinking in such radical terms). They made a bid to change the structure that regulated village politics from caste to citizenship. Caste founds itself on hierarchy; citizenship on equality. They took advantage of a law, which had been enacted some years earlier, requiring that Untouchables have free access to temples. In the honored Gandhian Freedom Fighter style (more on that later) they gave due notice to the village authorities and to government officials and then marched on one of Bisipara's temples and demanded access. The clean castes resisted; the police arrived; officials mediated without much success. Later the Panos went to court claiming that they had been threatened with violence by the Warriors. Judicial inquiries and a civil case followed. The Panos did not win on either occasion, but their capacity to mobilize on their side the (not in the least enthusiastic) local authorities made the clean castes sharply aware that Panos had rights as citizens of India equal to their own. At that time letters were franked with the slogan "Untouchability has been abolished" and Gandhi, from the 1930s on, had made the status of Untouchables his own concern, finding them a name that stuck for several decades—Harijans, "the children of God." In the world of state and national politics (officially, at least), Untouchables were equal to everyone else (in fact headstart-type programs in education, government employment, and reserved seats in the legislatures made them more than equal). Bisipara Panos aimed to make the same true of village politics. The hierarchical structure of caste would be replaced by the democratic egalitarian structure of common citizenship.

If we compare these three events—the minor fracas over Tuta and his *devata*, the long-running and fairly orderly dispute about Distiller ranking, and the nearer-to-chaos imbroglio that set Panos and clean castes at one another—we find first that all of them are small instances of a political process that had been going on in India for some years and which, in its most general form, goes on everywhere all the time. We organize (which means "keep some degree of order and cooperation in") our political interactions by means of structures: a parliamentary structure in Britain; in the United States a presidential structure; Bisipara (until the Panos, Gandhi, and Indian national and state politicians put their oars in) organized its politics through a caste structure; China has a one-party democracy; Iran has a theocracy and at this moment Pakistan has yet another military dictatorship; and so on. Some of these regimes are more stable than others, but even the most rocklike is susceptible to changes in its context, which itself is construed as structures. The model is simple: A *structure* (e.g., a caste hierarchy) and its *context* (e.g., a feudal state or a bureaucratic state) relate to one another as a *system*: Changes in one produce changes in the other. The working of that system is a *process*: If the contextual structures change, so will the dependent structure. Political structures are thus functionally connected with economic structures, religious structures, demographic structures, and whatever else constitutes their context.

The caste system in India has in fact changed over the last two centuries (and probably has always been shifting). What at the opening of the nineteenth century was a set of rules applied to relatively small, separated populations later changed its scale of operations in step with improved communications, a shift in the nation's economy toward industrial capitalism, the unification of India, a nationwide system of government, and, in the twentieth century, the emergence of party politics. Caste usages that fitted well into a feudal and agrarian politico-economy, such as the one that encompassed Bisipara before the British took control of the area in the mid-nineteenth century, were modified under a market-oriented authoritarian bureaucracy. Later, with the coming of elections, national politics became part of the caste system's context and so modified it. In Bisipara, castes that had depended on the landowning elite for their living acquired new sources of wealth and power. Some, like the Distillers, tried to work their way into the existing power structure of the village, which was framed in the culture of caste beliefs and values. The Panos, blocked by the insurmountable ritual barrier of Untouchability, opted for a revolutionary strategy that would remove caste as the organizing structure for village politics.

Models: Agency and Strategy

The process model of structure and context omits one essential feature of social change: People are involved in the process.

Process is simply a description of what happens when one structure (e.g., caste) fends off (or fails to fend off) the attack of a rival structure (e.g., citizenship) or is replaced by it. The blatant reification of that last sentence will serve as a reminder that people—Tuta, the Bisoi, Distillers, Pano leaders, officials, politicians, and so on—are always involved in these situations. We can, if we wish, leave the people out and remain at the impersonal level, modeling politics as a natural system, like evolution or the movements of the planets, which follow their own course without human intervention. Things look tidier that way, and political analysis can concentrate on the logico-mathematical exercises that are found in game theory or in neoclassical economics. Abstract models are sometimes an intellectual delight, but what they have to do with the real world that we experience is often not clear. One way to remedy this and come nearer to the world of experience is to supplement models of structure, context, and process with models of *strategy* (also called *agency* or *action* models).

Tuta and the Bisoi, and the other players in the drama, were *agents*, which means that they sized up the situation, took action, and caused things to happen. The same word, "agency," denotes the roles played by Republican legislators, Judge Starr, President Clinton and his defenders, various officials in the judiciary, journalists, writers of editorials, talk show hosts and their guests and the people who phoned in, and, not least, the voters whose definition of the situation made it clear to Republicans that they were not winning friends. All of these people, well informed or not, acted and re-acted to their opponent's moves with some goal in mind, and one way to make sense of a political arena is to reconstruct what went on in the minds of the antagonists and their allies and supporters, to find out what they thought, and to explain why they thought it. In other words, agents are imagined as thinking in terms of structure, context, and process, and having not only a goal but also a strategy, even if it is only to do what someone else tells them to do, or do whatever they did the last time this kind of situation came up.

To think about agents and their strategies is ipso facto also to think about structure, because a strategy is intended to make one or another structure prevail in some particular situation. Initially it helps to model a structure as something fixed, "rocklike," around which agents have to devise their strategies. Structures, prima facie, determine what strategies can be effectively employed, and unless you are aware of structures, you can make no sense of the strategies that agents use. The constitutional and legal framework of the United States clearly limited Republican strategies when they set out to remove Clinton from the presidency. In theory someone might have taken a Pano-like radical line and argued that the office of president so much encourages illusions of personal invincibility that it would be better to have a titular president, as in India or Israel or Ireland, and a parliamentary system. To have done that would have been to run head-on into the brick wall of the American constitution; it would not have been a realistic strategy. In a similar way, the caste system, Indian legal codes, Hindu beliefs about *devata*, and the lack of medical services (the girl died of a virulent form of malaria, which could probably have been controlled by timely medication) all provide fixed limits within which Tuta and his enemies maneuvered.

I made that point cautiously, using "initially" and "prima facie" to indicate that structure is not literally like a rock. Rather, it remains rocklike only so long as someone can make that definition of the situation stick. To define a situation is to decide which structure will be employed in it. I can think of two events in Tuta's witch-hunt that reveal the uncertainty that precedes or hangs over the definition of a situation. When the girl first fell ill (this form of malaria strikes suddenly and usually kills within twenty-four hours), one man—a half-brother of the Bisoi—insisted vehemently that this was a sickness and no *devata* was involved. If he had made his definition stick, nothing more would have happened: There would have been no witch-hunt. Second, when the case was well along and the divination was being conducted, another man asked me, skeptically, if we had *devata* in England, hinting that all this hullabaloo was a put-up job by the Bisoi. That definition, too, had it been spoken out loud and voiced by enough people, might have ended the case. But the definition was only whispered. Again, nothing happened. Nonetheless, the point is clear: Structures control agency but also are themselves open to being changed by agents. The goal of an agent is to define the situation, to say what structures will organize political interaction.

Process is the keystone of an arch composed of the other three elements—agency, structure, and context. Structure is presented as something fixed, but the presentation of any particular structure is always a claim that is accepted by some people and contested by others. Their contesting is a manifestation of *agency*. To understand why there is a contest, one asks what has changed in the *context* of a *structure* to provoke *agents* into initiating a *strategy* that leads to (or blocks) a change of structure. The events of their contesting and the effect on a structure constitute *process*. Structure and strategy are matters of design; process, by contrast, is a pattern of events that results in part from the actions taken (or not taken) and also from factors that the strategists (agents) failed to take into account. Process is a pattern that can be perceived, described, and sometimes, after the event, understood.

All four elements—structure, context, agency, and process—are needed to understand what goes on in politics.

A Formula

Political strategies are sets of ideas (models) that guide an agent's behavior in cooperative or competitive interactions that concern power. Power is the capacity to make someone do something, whether or not they want to do it, and whether or not they are aware of what is being done to them. That definition is straightforward, and needs no further comment. I will, however, elaborate both on "interactions" and, at more length, on "sets of ideas" or "models."

"Interaction" is a generic term that includes both cooperation and conflict and everything in between. For the noncompetitive forms of interaction, as in alliances or various types of collusion, I will generally use the same term, unless the context makes it necessary to add the adjective "cooperative" or "noncompetitive." Interactions that involve competition will be "confrontations" or "encounters." Given my leaning toward *Realpolitik* and my interest in the *struggle* for power rather than in its orderly distribution (the commonweal or civic approach to politics), the models that I construct to make sense of a political arena will mostly have to do with competition. Models of a perfectly orderly distribution of power would then be simply the proclaimed structural goal (or asserted structural actuality) of one or another competitor. Since this definition implies a pessimistic view of the human condition, I should make clear what a "model" is and, even more, what it is not. A model is not a simple true-or-false description of what exists in the world; it is a tool for understanding what goes on there or for making claims about what should go on there.

For reasons that are already apparent (mindlessness and the tension between *Realpolitik* models and public-weal models) and which will be amplified as we move further along, political arenas are confusing places in which it is sometimes hard to perceive and describe what people are doing, let alone work out why they are doing it. Political contestants are message-senders who have a strong incentive not to tell the truth. The contestant who behaves simply and straightforwardly is also behaving predictably. Those who assume that all the other contestants are as honest and aboveboard as themselves are, other things being equal (and in this case they generally are), certain losers. Think of those among your friends and acquaintances who like to see themselves as powerful and notice how often they prefer not to let their right hand know what their left hand is doing. They are private people, not because they are shy and do not like being at the center of attention, but because they know that to be genuinely open is to be vulnerable. Successful politicians need at least a touch of paranoia, and a political arena is a hotbed of deceit, dissimulation, disingenuousness, intrigue, and every other imaginable form of craftiness. It was said of Austen Chamberlain—by the quick-tongued F. E. Smith—that Austen always played the game (the English idiom for playing fair) and therefore always lost it.

I said earlier that mindlessness is a feature of politics. Strategies require reasoned purposive behavior and are therefore incompatible with mindlessness. In practice, however, the contradiction is less an obstacle than an invitation to think of mindlessness as a variable that ranges from, at one end, knee-jerk action prompted by in-the-bone antipathy or total adoration for a person or a cause to, at the other end, careful tactical calculation, minimally affected by emotion, of the opponents' mind-set, the resources available to them, their likely counterstrategies, and so forth. These calculations are complex.

The way to make sense of this (or any other) complexity is, paradoxical though it sounds, to pretend that it does not exist and to assume that matters are more simple than you know them to be. This is done by translating the raw and incomprehensible reality into ideas, which are elementary categories stripped clean of all the complexities that in reality cling to them. These elements are created through a process of abstraction and then put together in a model that will reveal patterns hidden in the confusion of raw experience. The model is like a template, which, when laid over a higgledy-piggledy reality, makes visible a form or a structure or a process. The diagrams displayed to clarify Valachi's rambling narratives revealed the structure of Mafia families, the process of succession to leadership in them, and the changing contexts that set the process in motion.

Political strategies can be resolved into two sets of elementary categories. One set consists of goals, resources, and constraints: Goals are what the protagonist desires to be the outcome of the situation; resources are the means available to achieve the goals; constraints are whatever stands in the way of achieving them. Each category is a variable and the relationship of one to another can be presented in algebraic form: $S=f(G, R, C)$, or S (strategy) is a function of G (goals), R (resources), and C (constraints). In words: If the goal, or the pattern of resources, or the pattern of constraints is known, then the corresponding strategy can be deduced. Or: If the goal, or the pattern of resources, or the pattern of constraints changes, another strategy will be appropriate. Or: If antagonists are seen to change their strategy, they will have done so because they have perceived a change in the pattern of resources and constraints (their goal remaining the same), or else they have changed the goal, or both.

The second set is composed of three roles: protagonist (p), opponent (o), and umpire (u). The protagonist makes a competitive move; the opponent responds. Since we are assuming competition and not all-out conflict, the moves are constrained by rules and it is the umpire's task to see that rules are observed. All three actors have a repertoire of strategies that are functions of their goals, constraints, and resources. Constraints provided by the rocklike concept of Untouchability made it impossible for the Panos to use the Distiller strategy for caste-climbing. By the same token, Gandhi's campaign against Untouchability and the legislation it stimulated gave the Panos a resource (not available to the Distillers) that caused them to change their goal from advancement within the framework of caste to the removal of that structure altogether from the village political arena.

Matters become more complex when one realizes that p's calculation of resources and constraints must include p's estimate of the goals, resources, and constraints that both o and u build into their own strategies. The formula $pS=f(G, R, C)$ would then have to be supplemented by $pS=f(oS, uS)$: p's strategies are in part a function of what he or she perceives o's and u's strategies to be. Bisipara's clean caste(p) must calculate how aware the Panos(o) are that they have as a resource the special status conferred on Untouchables by the government (for some time they knew nothing about it) and at the same time must make a guess about how enthusiastically government officials(u)

would enforce the regulations. If we then consider that u's and o's strategies in turn include their guesses about p's strategies, we eventually produce the equivalent of an endless series of mirror-images in mirror-images. At one or two removes the formula is generally usable; if it were not, then bluff could play no part in political encounters. But the potential complexity (and the impossibility of knowing conclusively what is in another's mind) are reminders that there are limits to the human capacity to collect data and to compute it, and that in political arenas thinking must be suspended—sooner rather than later—in order to reach a decision and take action.

In a retrospective analysis of the strategies deployed in a past encounter, however, rationality may be pushed to an extreme, not pretending that these are the thoughts that actually went through the actors' heads, but rather working out from the strategies used what values logically should be given to G and R and C. Starr's office, it is generally believed, regularly leaked to the media information and disinformation that they considered would hurt Clinton's case. To do so is against the law. Therefore they must have reckoned that in this particular instance the law, as C, a constraint, was not an important factor, and the Justice Department (acting as u) did not have that law as a high priority in its list of goals. Into that calculation would have gone an assessment of the resources of the Justice Department, its other commitments, its past actions, the personnel who would be involved in a decision about whether or not to prosecute, and . . . the list could go on ad infinitum, producing variable after variable generated by the formula $S=f(G, R, C)$. Nor (in Starr's estimation) did the other u, which was public opinion, set a high priority on the law that forbade the leaking of information. In that instance Starr's office was probably right. If, however, they calculated that the general public would not be offended by the relentless pursuit of Clinton's associates, including Monica Lewinsky, they were wrong: They miscalculated the high intrinsic value that people put on fair play. In this instance too one could produce a list of further inquiries. What did they think Monica Lewinsky's goals were? To get off the hook? To protect Clinton? Publicity? What assessment did they make of her resources to defend herself? Once again the formula $S=f(G, R, C)$ can be used to generate questions and inquiries.

That in fact is its purpose. It is not tested, each time it is used, for truth or falsity. There can be no empirical test, because it is simply a statement of what the concept "strategy" means, and, logically, it is on a par with *area=width × breadth*. Its use is as a tool of inquiry—as I said, a template that, when laid over a confusion of claims, counterclaims, actions, reactions, and consequences, produces a pattern that extracts meaning from the confusion.

We take forward into the next chapter, which begins our analysis of political leaders, the comparative method (the heuristic search for universals) and the models of structure, context, agency, and process, as tools to make sense of what leaders do, why they do it, and what the consequences are.

Part TWO

HOW TO LEAD:
LEADERS AND FOLLOWERS

---

*The first element is that there really do exist rulers
and ruled, leaders and led. The entire science and
art of politics are based on this primordial, and
(given certain general conditions) irreducible fact.*
—*Gramsci, Prison Notebooks*

- In theory, certainly, the distinction between leaders and led is
  clear, but in practice the relationship takes many forms and at
  the margins it may be difficult to separate followers from
  opponents.
- The prime element in this relationship—its pure form, so to
  speak—is faith that the leader can and will provide the service that his followers require, which, I will argue in Chapter
  3, is to make decisions in situations that are not routine.
  Where there is no uncertainty and the followers know what
  to do, there is no need for leadership.
- Leaders range in style from those who are remote and godlike to others who present themselves as "everyone's friend."
  Followers vary from the masses, whose only function is to
  adore the leader and do what they are told, to the entourage
  (various intermediate categories such as cabinet ministers,
  cronies in "kitchen cabinets," civil servants, aides, staff, and
  the like) who advise him/her and put into practice whatever
  he/she commands. Some of them are leaders themselves and
  may become the leader's rivals. These topics, and the strata-

gems available to keep overambitious subordinates in their places, are considered in Chapters 4 and 5.

- All stratagems—whether used to gain the trust of a mass or to rein back on insubordinate members of an entourage—are connected, in a quite complicated way, with a context in which a variety of different and (in varying degrees) contradictory cultures coexist. The connection is complicated not only because there is a plurality of cultures but also because leaders are both constrained by the existing cultures and at the same time are required, as leaders, to make decisions in situations where the cultures give no advice or, more often, conflicting advice. Sometimes leaders must transcend them all, decide on a course that is new, and so run the risk of upsetting everyone. Chapter 6 considers this situation and provides an answer, of sorts, to the claim (voiced in Chapter 3) that no one can enter politics and remain honest.

3

Decisions and Legitimacy

- The first part of this chapter defines leadership by describing the actions and the qualities that distinguish a leader from a follower, and by separating leadership from simple domination. Leaders have legitimacy; they rule not by force but by consent.
- The second part describes situations in which leadership is apparently in abeyance.

What Leaders Do

"You can't adopt politics as a profession and remain honest." That was said by an American diplomat, Louis McHenry Howe, in a speech at Columbia University in 1933, voicing what most Americans still believe about all but a few of their politicians. That attitude is not confined to Americans. General de Gaulle, himself an adroit mover in political arenas, was careful to distance himself from politicians: "Since a politician never believes what he says, he is quite surprised to be taken at his word." Clement Attlee, the prime minister who displaced Churchill as the Second World War ended, in reviewing a book by the general said that de Gaulle was a very good soldier and a very bad politician. De Gaulle wrote him a letter, in which he said: "I have come to the conclusion that politics are too serious a matter to be left to the politicians." (He was playing with an earlier bon mot, attributed to Georges

Clemenceau, the prime minister of France in the First World War: "War is much too serious a thing to be left to the military.")

It is not difficult to find quotations condemning *politicians* wholesale. *Leaders* as a category, however, are seldom dismissed in that way: *Leadership* is a praise word. Particular leaders get their share of opprobrium, but not the whole class. I intend to break with that custom, and take, as my text, a slightly amended version of Louis Howe's aphorism: No one has ever succeeded as a political leader and yet remained honest. You can see at once—probably as the name of Mahatma Gandhi (not Indira or her son Rajiv) leaps to mind—that both the word "honest" and the word "leader" will require some unpacking. *Honest* can wait until more evidence has been presented and the argument properly made; I will begin with *leader*.

The first step is to obey the logic of the word: A leader who has no followers is, by definition, not a leader. Here is Bernard Baruch, an American financier and politician, sometimes called "the adviser of presidents": "A political leader must keep looking over his shoulder all the time to see if the boys are still there. If they aren't still there, he's no longer a political leader." The idea is very simple: To be a leader, a person must have followers. Since that statement is a tautology—a definition of what the word "leader" means—it must hold in any political setting, in any culture (unless there are cultures that have no leaders—more on that later). I register the significance of the leader–follower relationship here at the outset, and emphasize it, because four out of five books about leaders are biographies or histories that concentrate on their meritorious achievements (or on their failures) and sometimes, when the author has an attitude, on their villainy (Pol Pot or Hitler or Nixon or Stalin or any white South African in power during the apartheid regime), but do not have much to say about leadership itself and do not examine the strategies those people used to become leaders in the first place or to make things happen afterward. Achievements and failures do of course come into the picture, because they can make or break a leader; but an account of things accomplished, or of disasters, does not directly address the ways and means of enlisting, retaining, and using followers. The question of what goes on between leaders and their followers (and why it takes one form rather than another) will guide the inquiry and will eventually justify (to the extent that can be done) the claim that there never yet was, nor ever will be, an indisputably immaculate leader.

The next step is to say what essential features define the relationship between leaders and their followers. Many years ago in India I encountered an unpleasant man, an official who was charged with implementing rural development projects that required a measure of enlightened cooperation from his clientele, who were ordinary villagers, uneducated people who had a reputation, very much taken for granted by the administrators, for what in those less label-sensitive days was termed "backwardness." I asked him about his work. Was it going well? "Men," he said, "I can lead. Animals I must drive." Before joining the civil service, he had been an officer in the military. Deplorable as the sentiment is, the distinction it makes between leading and driving—between leadership and domination—is valid. Cattle are driven from behind, with a stick. Leaders go in front, not needing to look over their shoulders. (The point is strengthened, rather than undermined, by a regimental joke that I recall: Lieutenant X, who was slightly built and only five foot tall, led his stalwart six-foot troopers into battle, encouraging them with the cry "On my men! I'm close behind you.")

Without consent from their followers, without some level of mutual trust, leaders cannot lead. It is sometimes difficult to acknowledge that leaders whom history has judged despicable may yet have enjoyed the respect and admiration of their followers. The Romanian dictator Nicolae Ceaucescu, who was promptly put to death when circumstances loosened his control, by his very fate seems to demonstrate that leadership and consent need not be conjoined. But that conclusion misreads the evidence. Nor is it enough to say that he was not a leader at all, but a driver, and drivers by definition do not need consent. That could not have been the case, because those who did the driving for him, the military and the security forces, presumably gave him enough consent to make his fifteen-year rule possible. Baruch's suggestion is the better one: By 1989 "the boys" (his own army) were not "still there" behind him. Until that time he had enjoyed some measure of their trust and consent. Ceaucescu's execution (Mussolini suffered a similar fate) does not prove that he had never enjoyed a consensual following. Mahatma Gandhi himself, respected and even adored by most Hindus, was assassinated in 1948 by right-wing Hindu nationalists.

In any case, the point of the proposition that links consent and leadership is not its truth or falsity—it is a matter of definition—but the question that it prompts one to ask about leaders: What level of legitimacy do followers grant them? Beyond that there is the further question: What resources and constraints can a leader use to keep followers loyal? How does one account for different levels of consent at different times and in different places? That, in turn, produces a richness of derived questions about cultural differences, about structures and processes, about contexts, about difference in situation (e.g., routine occasions versus crises), and about the various strategies available for creating consent. These and other questions will guide the inquiry.

Meanwhile let me take the third step in defining leaders and leadership and ask the question that provides a heading for this section: What do leaders do? The answer is: They make decisions. They dispel, or at least hold at bay, the uncertainties that everywhere pervade both individual life and social life. The human condition includes the never-ending task of coping with problems that arise in life because what we want or need, and what fate deals out for us, are not always the same. From this point of view, life is an unremitting struggle to get the better of circumstances before they get the better of us. This, of course, is again an overly rational way to see things. Sometimes we are not aware of circumstances until they have already humbled us. Sometimes we see what is coming, take action, and it is the wrong action, and circumstances again are the winner. Sometimes we get it right and so arrange matters that what we want in fact happens. The solutions that we arrive at, however, whether right or wrong, are rarely the outcome of up-from-the-ground calculation. They come ready-made from our cultural inheritance; we identify the problem and do what we always do when that problem comes up. It is hard to imagine that there could be any life at all if we did not have that repertoire of ready-made answers.

But no cultural repertoire can cover every eventuality. Problems constantly arise that have no known solution in our culture or, more often, that have several solutions and no obvious way to decide between them. Then indecision postpones action, and the problem is left to solve, or not solve, itself. More than that, if the situation calls for *collective* action, indecision leads to argument and argument again may postpone action, until it is too late. That, par excellence, is the occasion for leadership. The leader decides. Even if the decision turns out to be wrong, the very making of it—of stepping forward with a solution that is not already provided in the cultural repertoire—is the hallmark of leadership.

Of course enough bad decisions (ones that do not produce the desired outcome) will end a leader's career, unless he can convince people that the outcome was not bad at all, or, if bad, was not his fault but someone else's, or unless he can pull off the spectacular gamble that both Gamal Abdel Nasser and Fidel Castro risked and won—following a debacle make a public offer to resign, presumably expecting that the offer would not be accepted. Seasoned politicians, like Winston Churchill, knew all about the post hoc cover-up. Asked what qualified someone to be a politician, he said: "It is the ability to foretell what is going to happen tomorrow, next week, next month, and next year. And to have the ability afterwards to explain why it didn't happen." The legitimacy that a successful leader enjoys is not regulated by hard accounting; legitimacy is like a sponge that mops up the negatives, until eventually it becomes saturated. But "eventually" may turn out to be a very long time. Saddam Hussein, during his entire rule (he seized power in 1979), has led Iraq into one disaster after another; and as I write this, he is still in power, building himself palaces to his own greater glory, despite the miseries that his penchant for making war has visited on his people. Evidently enough of "the boys" are still behind him.

The most damning thing to be said about a leader is that he or she cannot take decisions and stick with them. In 1936, when the British prime minister Stanley Baldwin dithered over rearmament, despite the clearest evidence of Hitler's aggressions and continuing aggressive intentions, Churchill said (about his own government—he and Baldwin were both Conservatives): "So they go on in a strange paradox, decided only to be undecided, resolved to be irresolute, adamant for drift, solid for fluidity, all-powerful to be impotent." Leaders who are undecided and irresolute, who drift where the currents take them, are unfit to lead. Who would be encouraged to follow Warren Harding, the twenty-ninth president of the United States, hearing this message? (Fortunately, it was said in private to a friend. He was complaining about a problem he had with tariffs.)

I listen to one side and they seem right, and then God! I talk to the other side and they seem just as right, and there I am where I started. I know somewhere there is a book that will give me the truth, but Hell, I couldn't read the book. I know somewhere there is an economist who knows the truth, but I don't know where to find him and haven't the sense to know him and trust him when I did find him. God, what a job![1]

One might add: "God, what a leader!" Leaders do not flounder. They decide on one or the other "truth" and then, as Churchill said, get ready to explain later, if they need to, "why it didn't happen." They ride political turbulence and political uncertainty on a raft of intuition, confident that they know the truth (or if not confident, at least appearing to be), certainly not hoping to find it in a book (unless it's the Bible or the Koran or Chairman Mao's Little Red Book). Intuition is the absence of reasoning. In the case of leaders it is more than that; it is defiance of reason, a readiness to gamble against the odds, and the more often the gambles come off, the more the leader gets a reputation for political skill—doing things effectively without being able to explain, in scientific terms, why they succeeded. Henry Brook Adams, an American historian, caught this essential feature of leadership in one short sentence: "Practical politics consists in ignoring facts."[2]

Ignoring facts in practice usually also means ignoring advice. Every leader has advisers at his side, sometimes there by statute, the leader being legally required to get their consent before his decisions are put into effect, and sometimes members of his "kitchen cabinet"—unofficial consultants, usually old friends and companions, and generally believed to have more clout than the official advisers. Advice of either kind gets put aside if the leader's intuition tells him that he is right and they are wrong. Here is Hitler, having successfully re-occupied the Rhineland, explaining in 1936 why he rejected advice not to do so: "I go the way that Providence dictates with the assurance of a sleep-walker." (Not, perhaps, the most reassuring metaphor, given the power that he exercised.) Gandhi, a very different man, was likewise advice-resistant; India's first prime minister, Jawarharlal Nehru, wrote, "Behind all his courteous interest, one has the impression that one is addressing a closed door." Frank Moraes, an Indian journalist, after citing this sentence adds, "It was true of both men." Comparing Nehru with another Indian politician, Krishna Menon, he comes up with an explanation:

> If Nehru grew first in the shadow of his father Motilal and then that of Gandhi, Menon was successively influenced by Annie Besant and Harold Laski. The removal of these influences on both had oddly parallel results. It intensified their sense of innate isolation, their intellectual arrogance and impatience toward those whose ideas ran counter to their own.[3]

Whether the notion that the loss of mentor or father figures leads to arrogance is sound Freudianism, I do not know. The point here is that these three persons—Gandhi, Nehru, and Menon—all had their quota of legitimacy as leaders and all were noticeably ready to disregard advice (and whatever facts were contained in the advice) in favor of doing what their political instincts told them to do.

The point also is that to seek advice is not yet to have made a decision, and to wait for reason to provide the problem's one and only rational solution is to wait forever. A gamble, large or small, is an essential feature of every decision that leaders make. They may try to hide the risk—that depends on the situation, and I will come later to various devices for laying plausible claim to rationality. But to rely solely on rationality is the mark of a manager, not a leader. Sometimes, indeed, there is no way to hide the uncertainty and the fact that the decision has not been rationally made, except to be honest about it and tap straight into the followers' emotions. After the fall of France in June 1940, and the rescue of the remnants of the British army from Dunkirk, a French general, Maxime Weygand, said, "In three weeks England will have her neck wrung like a chicken." That was a perfectly rational assessment; the facts were on his side. The United States had not yet entered the war. The victorious German armies were not yet committed to the campaign against Russia (Russia and Germany had signed a nonaggression pact in 1939), and nothing seemed to stand in the way of their invading and conquering Britain, as they had just conquered France. Churchill, who had become prime minister a few months earlier, in May, made a series of speeches that wholly abandoned reason and voiced only defiance, picking up a theme from his first speech in Parliament after becoming prime minister: "I have nothing to offer but blood, toil, tears, and sweat." (Eighteen months later, speaking in Canada, he quoted Weygand, adding, famously, "Some chicken! Some neck!")

When leaders ignore facts, and are seen to do so, and yet retain a hold on their followers, they demonstrate in the clearest possible fashion that they enjoy what I have variously called *legitimacy* or *consent*— that is, the followers follow without asking what the cost will be, and only because they believe it is the right thing for them to do; they see it not as a matter of expediency but of principle or conscience. Such loyalty is not given to everyone, and it varies from one leader to another, depending on how they conduct themselves. I will return to that topic later. Meanwhile I will consider what circumstances govern the occurrence of decision-needing situations.

All Chiefs and No Indians (and Vice Versa)

That aphorism negates the *Der-Führer*-one-and-only-one-leader notion. I do not know where it began. I first heard it from a detached and cynical academic (there are some) talking about his colleagues, each and every one of whom went his own way so insistently that any coherent program in that department could only have been a happy accident. "Happy" may not be the right word: They were reported to be a quarrelsome lot. No chief was content simply to do his (or her) own thing; all wanted the other chiefs to be loyal and obedient Indians; not one of them showed a moment's doubt about his (or her) own natural superiority. It was a new department in a new university. The outcome was a de facto contentious egalitarianism.

A curious feature of higher-level academic institutions, more common in certain fields than others, and more often the case a generation ago than it is now, marks them off from other formal organizations like the military or monastic orders or communist parties. The philosophy of these latter organizations defines the institution itself as the sole and supreme focus of its members' loyalties. Everyone should pull together for its sake; the collectivity is all that matters; individuals are privileged to serve it. Universities, on the other hand, tend to downplay the collectivity and elevate the individual scholar. Universities exist for the furtherance of knowledge (and, as a by-product, the education of the young). Knowledge is furthered by individual scholars committed, as their first priority, to finding, in whatever is their field, a pattern that had not been known before. In this endeavor the institution is merely a facilitator, nothing more: Time and energy spent on collegial duties are time and energy taken from the proper scholarly endeavor. This state of affairs, if it had ever existed, would have been a true manifestation of anarchy in its good sense. Domination would be absent and everyone would be free to pursue the goals of scholarship, with accountability lying entirely between the scholar and his conscience—true scholars, each their own invigilator.

Of course, that is a castle-in-the-air that nowhere could be a reality, except in the land of scholars with private means, which nowadays is virtually uninhabited. But even there, and even in the most decen-tered scholarly community in which members are tenured for life (such was once the case for dons in Oxbridge colleges), individuals are still accountable before the worldwide jury of their peers in whatever is their branch of scholarship. Moreover, in practice their scholarly work is made possible only by their accepting responsibilities in the institution that supports them. The college has to be administered and—as the world is today—research grants have to be won, results published in journals, and colleagues not angered by having collegial responsibilities off-loaded onto them. Nevertheless, the fantasy of a well-functioning but leaderless community does have a theoretical reality as one end of that same continuum (see Chapter 1) that stretches between tyranny (good order) and freedom (chaos). There are communities in which leadership is relatively unemphasized. There are others in which it is strongly marked. Power differences are everywhere, but not to the same degree. Why should this be?

In certain settings, groups function well enough without anyone giving orders; indeed, nondirected coordination is a feature of every-day life. I watched a team of half a dozen men (grandly called "tree surgeons") prune a large pine in my yard. They had a brief conference before they started, mostly telling me what they were going to do. After that, hardly a word was spoken. Two men climbed the tree, tied the safety lines, fixed rope trusses on long branches so that parts could be cut off one at a time, cut and dropped them piece by piece, while the men on the ground retrieved the fallen branches, trimmed them, gathered the debris, cut the big logs to fireplace size, and piled them up. No orders were shouted, not even a warning when a branch was about to come down. Perfect anarchy (no one seemingly in charge) and yet perfect order! What does that example say? It says they had done it all before; they were practiced; there was no occasion to make decisions, because everything required for perfect coordination had been decided beforehand. Each member of the gang carried in his head a map of what to expect and how to act and react. There was no need for a display of leadership.

About two generations back, social anthropologists exercised their wits on acephalous societies (acephalous means "without a head"), that is, societies that had no government. A book published in 1940, *African Political Systems*, edited by Fortes and Evans-Pritchard, con-tained eight essays (by the two editors and six other contributors) about different African societies. Three of these societies were acephalous; five had centralized political systems, being governed by chiefs and kings. Centralized political institutions, in their many different forms, were familiar enough in the European experience, but acephalous societies had about them a touch of the bizarre. How could a society continue to exist, when the Victorian explorer's standard first-contact demand "Take me to your chief!" was void? The everyday commonsense assumption is that someone must be in charge; otherwise there would be chaos. Thus it seemed only to be expected that the acephalous Nuer tribes of the Sudan, about whom Evans-Pritchard wrote, would be in a continuous state of "unrest," truculently defiant of the colonial rulers, precisely because they had no chiefs. Yet Nuer society had continued to exist in a state of—Evans-Pritchard's phrase—*ordered anarchy*. How did the Nuer do it?

One answer is that they didn't. Evans-Pritchard's essay (and a book published at the same time) did not focus on the reality of Nuer life, but instead provided a highly abstracted account of purported patterns of Nuer thought about their own society. He produced—again his own words—an *imaginative construct* of Nuer society. In this construct his explanation for ordered anarchy is in essence the simple one that explained how the tree pruners did their work. Nuer carried in their heads a map of their own society that enabled them to resolve the meaning of each other's actions and to react appropriately. They had a moral code and a set of understandings that let them get by with a minimal exercise of authority. Evans-Pritchard presents some vivid descriptions of their violence and their extravagant and bellicose egalitarianism, which he much admired: Every Nuer thought himself as good as every other Nuer—all Indians and no chiefs. Yet they did not live in chaos; they lived in ordered anarchy.

That portrayal does not fully square with the reality of Nuer life at the time when Evans-Pritchard lived among them. He describes it in some detail (and in the most elegant prose), but many of the facts that he provides do not at all fit his imaginative construct. Nuer are fiercely egalitarian; but Nuer rebellions against the colonial power were led by powerful "prophets," men inspired by the "Sky-gods." When a prophet died, the divinity, in some cases, passed into his son, thus producing a "hereditary political leadership." Prophets appeared when Arab traders and slave-raiders entered Nuerland. They were, Evans-Pritchard writes, a response to "the new Arab-European menace."

The story of the Nuer and their prophets and my description of the gang of tree pruners suggest that the all-Indians-and-no-chiefs condition is sustainable when the same decisions have been taken many times already, and when the circumstances to which those decisions were adapted have not changed in any significant way. The department in which every faculty member went his or her own way must have been insulated, for whatever reason, from changes in the world around it, from, for example, rebellious students demanding that the faculty get its act together, or from administrative czars wanting more statistics to make a better case to get more money out of the central administration, or from any of those emergencies that make the habit of all-debate-and-no-action a self-destructive luxury. It is not an accident that in my present university, which has a strong tradition of democratic self-rule (flavored with the American frontier mentality of the unconquerably defiant autonomous individual), the only authoritarian heads of department are in the medical school, where negative feedback for delayed or mistaken actions is relatively severe and relatively rapid. They alone do not follow the egalitarian principle of short spells in the driving seat, and their departmental heads typically are autocrats who serve for more than the three-year span that is customary elsewhere in the university. Nor is it an accident that in democratic nations the citizens' democratic prerogatives are curtailed in wartime. In short, crisis and novelty, the uncertain and the unexpected, intensify the need for decision-taking and therefore the need for leadership.

Some further comments are required. First, it is not the case that authoritarian figures (notice that I do not say "leaders") exist *only* in crisis situations. Tyrants are also found where everyone knows more or less what is going to happen and there are no ambiguities that call for the exercise of leadership. English university departments in London and the provinces (not so much Oxbridge)—again about two generations ago—were ruled by god-professors, life-tenured, unshiftable, and characteristically authoritarian in manner. (They are memorialized in *Lucky Jim*, a satirical novel by Kingsley Amis.) Professors in universities on the European continent were even more godlike, with lesser academics being servants—not even acolytes— and certainly not colleagues. Authoritarianism was not in those cases a response to being under siege and the need for decisionmaking; it was simply a tradition. Academic life was highly routinized and required no policy decisions and therefore no leadership; there were no occasions for the genuine decisionmaking that resolves otherwise unresolvable dilemmas. Given this routinization, the authoritarian posturing of the god-professor was only that—posturing. It signaled domination, not leadership. No real decisions were required because, like the tree cutters or the Nuer (in Evans-Pritchard's presentation), they all, professors and their juniors alike, carried in their heads a map of what had to be done and how to do it. When, in the 1960s, that map ceased to be a reliable guide because the universities were politicized by rebellious students, after varying periods of chaos one or another form of effective decisionmaking came into use and put an end to god-professorships.

That leads to a second comment. I have so far set the situation in a simple binary form: all-chiefs (or no chiefs) versus *the* leader. Both of these forms are imaginary constructs. The modal reality is neither the tyrant at one end nor chaos at the other, but a place somewhere on a continuum of intermediary forms of decision-taking: round-table discussions; committees that have chairmen; leaders constrained to consult and take advice and poll opinions; leaders who only go through the motions of seeking advice and consent; and, at the far end, the dictator or monarch surrounded by his cronies. Some of those situations will be considered later. The point here is still that the study of leadership is centrally involved with the study of how decisions are taken.

The third comment also takes a step nearer to reality. Its purpose (as in the conclusion of the previous chapter) is to undo an impression of structural fixity that the discussion so far may have given. Analysis works that way; an inquiry begins by supposing that things are simpler than they are known to be, and then, step by step, builds in more and more complexity. We think of the Nuer people as an example of ordered anarchy and of other peoples described in *African Political Systems*—Zulu or Ankole—as centralized kingdoms. Using models of that kind, we see people constrained by the structure of their society; the life that is described—since the description is simply of rules and principles—is a long way from the lived-in actuality. Nuer, for example, were fiercely egalitarian; but they also knew how to give homage to their prophets. In other words, their conduct is not constrained by the *one* structure that Evans-Pritchard makes central to his analysis. Rather, Nuer can shift between the two structures, their choices depending on the circumstances. That opens up a new field of inquiry: Having described the alternative structures, one can then ask what contextual conditions favor one rather than another structure? One can also ask questions about strategies. For example, what strategies did a Nuer prophet use to tame the fierce egalitarianism of his followers?

Answers to those questions will make clear the connections between leadership, decisionmaking, and power. A decision that sticks is, of course, a manifestation of power. I am saying something different: Decisions in which leadership is manifested are typically decisions about power, about the allocation of resources, or about which principles will be used to come to a decision. Here is an example.

From time to time, as a very junior person, I attended meetings of a newly formed professional association. The god-professor regimes were still at that time more or less intact. The constitutional form of the association (frequency of meetings, eligibility for membership, how to select officials, whom to select, and the like) had not yet hardened. It had, however, as you will see, imported a firm political structure ready-made from the world outside itself. The association's formal purpose was to promote the well-being of the profession. Our seniors, however, took their cues from a subtext that was about the importance—the clout—of their own separate departments. (Whether or not any real power was at stake, I am not sure. Often in academia the fiercest fights are about matters of little consequence.)

The participants came from different colleges and universities. Each contingent was headed by a god-professor accompanied by followers, who were divided roughly into two ranks, a middle rank of seniors who had not made it to a god-professorship, and below them a collection of juniors who were not in the running for that kind of eminence. (In fact the system changed a few years later and many of the Indians wound up as chiefs, though as professors, not god-professors, since by then that role had been written out of the academic opera.) In the course of the three or four days of meetings, I noticed a very clear pattern of forming and re-forming, according to the occasion. In plenary business sessions (those to which the lower deck were admitted) and also in academic sessions when papers were given by individuals, the members of each department sat together, massed in close order in the spirit, if not the actual form, of a Macedonian phalanx. These were occasions on which power and prestige were contested; departmental members formed up as a team in action against other teams in an arena where prizes were to be won or lost. Papers that were given were constructively criticized by members of the reader's department (sometimes even praised), and fiercely attacked by people from rival departments. A similar solidarity was manifested in debates over business and procedural matters. The Indians rallied behind their chiefs, or (to shift the metaphorical venue) the barons (god-professors) led their knights (senior faculty) into battle and behind them marched the humble foot soldiers. These were occasions when decisions about power or its allocation were being made.

Other occasions were not (at least officially) concerned with business. Lunch was eaten together, a part of the host institution's refectory being reserved for those attending the conference. In the evening, before dinner, everyone gathered for drinks. On these occasions departmental solidarity was replaced, more or less, by a rank or generation solidarity. The elite gossiped with each other; the middle ranks stayed together; and so did the junior faculty. You might remark, correctly, that such a formation revealed the distribution of power by seniority in universities, and certainly on those occasions there was no shortage at the junior level of unkind gossip about departmental elites. You might also notice that these ties cut across departmental allegiances and in that way promoted the profession's solidarity. The points that I want to emphasize here are, first, that when decisionmaking and power are not significantly present in a situation, neither is leadership. Second, the one-chief (leadership) versus all-chiefs (equality) distinction is not only a difference between two structural arrangements, but represents a dynamic process, a tension that is a feature of day-to-day and hour-to-hour political interaction.

Once again it helps to imagine a continuum, this time between the poles of one-chief and all-equal, and imagine leaders working out where the situation lies on that continuum, whether to accept it as unshiftable and adjust their leadership strategies accordingly, or, if they think it feasible, deciding how to redesign—that is, redefine—the situation to give them better control over their followers.

Strategies used by leaders to define their relationship with followers will be considered in the next chapter.

4

Controlling Followers

The first part of this chapter describes two ways of bidding for legitimacy and winning the consent of a mass following:

- to be "one of the people";
- to be godlike.

The second part describes strategies used to control overambitious members of an entourage:

- the Machiavellian device of divide and rule;
- the strategy of "the people's friend."

One of Us or Far Above Us?

What must leaders do to make themselves trusted? In essence this is a question about public relations. What qualities do leaders present themselves as having in order to seem trustworthy? What do other people say about their conduct and their qualities? I will consider two modes of self-presentation: the first is fraternal identification, the second is godlike.

When members of formal organizations like the Teamsters' Union in the United States, or a Masonic Lodge, or Catholic monks, or other less organized categories like American Blacks or villagers in

India want to lay stress on mutual and unbreakable trust, they may use the word "brother." Leaders throughout the ages have done so. Here is Henry V at Agincourt on St. Crispin's eve:

We few, we happy few, we band of brothers;
For he to-day that sheds his blood with me
Shall be my brother; be he ne'er so vile
This day shall gentle his condition:

Notice the last two lines: the king and the vilest (humblest) of his subjects are made *equal* in brotherhood.

Politicians do it too, often quite crudely. David Lloyd George made a famous (or notorious) speech in 1909 in Limehouse (a working class area in London). He was justifying a taxation policy and, seemingly with success, working up his audience's emotions:

I am one of the children of the people. [Loud and prolonged cheering, and a voice, "Bravo, David! Stand by the people and they will stand by you."] I was brought up among them. I know their trials; and God forbid that I should add one grain of trouble to the anxiety which they bear with such patience and fortitude.[1]

Colonel Gadhafi, the Libyan leader, sings the same song, but less rambunctiously: "We are not rich people; the parents of the majority of us are living in huts. My parents are still in a tent near Sirte. The interests we represent are genuinely those of the Libyan people."[2] In the 2000 U.S. presidential election, according to newspaper and radio reports, no less than two Republican candidates for the party's nomination identified themselves with janitors—one had once worked as a janitor and the other was the son of a janitor.

They are looking for empathic identification with people who, they assume, probably see themselves as distant from, inferior to, not in touch with, and therefore distrustful of the high and mighty leader. There is a risk in doing this, especially in America, for the message might be interpreted not as "I am one of you," but "Look how far I have risen above you." But even construed that way, there is still a hint of Lloyd George's "I know what it is like to be an ordinary person."

There are some slightly more subtle ways to convey that message, more chummily done and avoiding the heavy theme of class conflict that was loud and clear in Lloyd George's speech. In 1952, Nixon, then vice-president, speaking on television, delivered this mawkish oration:

> Pat and I have the satisfaction that every dime we've got is honestly ours. I should say this—that Pat doesn't have a mink coat. But she does have a respectable Republican cloth coat. And I always tell her that she'd look good in anything. One other thing I probably should tell you, because if I don't, they'll probably be saying this about me too, we did get something—a gift—after the election. . . . It was a little cocker spaniel dog . . . and our little girl—Tricia, the six-year-old—named it Checkers. And you know the kids, like all kids, love the dog and I just want to say this right now, that regardless of what they say about it, we're gonna keep it.[3]

What could be cozier? Everything—the folksy style, the invocation of his wife (Pat) who looks good in anything, his (little) child and their (little) dog—proclaims "I am just like the rest of you. I am not grand!" Yet there is more than that. The speech had a serious intent, which was to deflect the accusation that is still thrown at all but a few holders of elected office in America: They fatten themselves on the job by taking "gifts." The apotropaic device—the shield—that Nixon used in that speech to deflect the charge is not only folksiness but also a self-deprecating humor (with the faintest whiff of the paranoia that surfaced so painfully twenty-two years later). Politicians making fun of themselves invite the audience to laugh not only with them, but also—very slightly—at them.

There are other devices that lessen the gap that must exist between the leader and the led. Leaders will sometimes use a vulgar form of speech if they believe their audience is at home with vulgarity. I have a clear recollection of a prominent politician (male) addressing an audience of longshoremen and referring to a widely reported altercation with a group of women, saying, with a self-congratulatory and knowing grin, "Had to kick a little ass there!" The unspoken notion is to get down to their level and so win their trust. Radio talks help to give leaders a fake one-to-one contact with ordinary people, Franklin Roosevelt being the pioneer with his "fireside chats." A good television presence gives the modern politician an edge over rivals who cannot convincingly fake intimacy in front of a camera. Sometimes—not so often

nowadays—kinship terms come into use: Golda Meir, Israel's prime
minister between 1969 and 1974, was "grandmother;" Gandhi was
bapu, father, or *mabap*, our mother and father. Nicknames or diminu-
tives do the same job: the Roosevelts were Teddy and FDR,
Eisenhower was Ike, Churchill was Winston or Winnie, Lloyd George
(at least on the occasion cited above) was David, Reagan was "the
Gipper," General Montgomery was Monty, and in one memorable
instance that staidest of statesmen, Woodrow Wilson, was startled (and
then gratified) to hear a voice from the audience cry out "Atta boy,
Woody!" But Hitler was never Adolf, except in English political car-
toons and comic writings, Mussolini was never Benito, and both of
them were distanced from and elevated above the common people by
being known, starkly, as "The Leader" (*Der Führer* and *Il Duce*).

Nicknames, however, also have a negative use. With a suitable
adjective attached, they familiarize a leader but at the same time mark
him or her as unworthy of trust or devotion: Nixon was Tricky Dick
and Margaret Thatcher was the Iron Lady. Iron Lady cuts two ways.
It could suggest that nonfloundering, direct-action quality that every
leader needs. Or it could indicate a remote, ruthless, and uncompas-
sionate person who cares only for principle or getting a job done, but
never for people. Remoteness marks the second leadership style: the
leader who is distant, unapproachable, godlike, and therefore to be
worshipped. Some touch of the divine, the magical, must be present
even in the most demotic of leaders, because no leader can afford to
be on the same level and indistinguishable from everyone else.

The magical quality that is part of leadership is inwardly manifested by a colossal and irrational self-confidence, underwriting the
capacity, already described, to make decisions that ignore or defy the
facts. It generally goes along with Nehru's "impatience toward those
whose ideas ran counter to [his] own." Here, for example, is
Nkrumah, Ghana's first president, bluntly sorting out possible critics
and giving a hint of the way his rule would later develop: "All Africans
know that I represent Africa and that I speak in her name. Therefore
no Africans can have an opinion that differs from mine. If any one of
them acts against my better judgment, he must be doing it because he
. . . has been paid."[4] Nkrumah was toppled, exiled, restored, and exiled
again, dying in 1972.

Looked at from the outside, the magic of leadership is the strange
quality that Weber christened *charisma*, which is the capacity to inspire

devotion and enthusiasm: "a certain quality of an individual personality by virtue of which he is considered extraordinary and treated as endowed with supernatural, superhuman, or at least specifically exceptional powers or qualities."[5] The quality is not a single identifiable physical feature of the person like a humped back or blue eyes, but is recognizable only in the devotion that other people bestow on charismatic leaders, in how they act toward and what they say about them. Hyperbole seems to be the style of choice. Here are some of the more extravagant examples. The first is about Hitler.

> With us the Führer and the ideas are one and the same, and every party comrade has to do what the Führer commands, for he embodies the idea and he alone knows its ultimate goal.[6]

The second describes Stalin's superhuman role in the Second World War.

> All operations of the Great Fatherland War were planned by Comrade Stalin and executed under his guidance. There was not a single operation in the working out of which he did not participate.[7]

The third is a pæan for Chairman Mao.

> All rivers flow into the sea and every Red heart turns toward the sun. Oh Chairman Mao, Chairman Mao, the mountains are tall but not as tall as the blue sky. The rivers are deep but not as deep as the ocean. Lamps are bright but not as bright as the sun and moon. Your kindness is taller than the sky, deeper than the ocean, and brighter than the sun and moon. It is possible to count the stars in the highest heavens, but it is not possible to count your contributions to mankind.[8]

Charismatic qualities can be described in more believable ways, always, however, with a hint of something spellbinding in the person ("magnetism" and "mesmerize" are favorite words). Here is Nehru, writing about Gandhi.

> For it was clear that this little man of poor physique had something of steel in him, something rock-like which did not yield to physical powers, how-

ever great they might be . . . there was a royalty and kingliness in him which compelled a willing obeisance from others. Consciously and deliberately meek and humble, yet he was full of power and authority, and he knew it, and at times he was imperious enough, issuing commands which had to be obeyed. . . . Whether his audience consisted of one person or a thousand, the charm and magnetism of the man passed on to it, and each one had a feeling of communion with the speaker. . . . It was the utter sincerity of the man and his personality that gripped; he gave the impression of tremendous inner reserves of power.[9]

It would be hard to find a clearer evocation of leadership qualities: "rocklike," "full of power and authority," "magnetism," "tremendous inner reserves of power," and in particular the capacity to combine in his one person both "kingliness" and the knack of giving every member of a large audience "a feeling of communion with [him]."

Nehru's descriptive analysis deserves further comment. First, although it makes sense to say that Gandhi was born with the dispositions and capacities that Nehru describes, that does not tell the whole story. It also is clear that Gandhi made conscious use of his gift, turning the magnetism on when required and on other occasions resorting to plain domination—"at times he was imperious enough." Second, though Weber is right to speak of "a certain quality of an individual personality," it is clear that the quality only becomes visible in interaction. In a sense, it is not so much a quality in the charismatic person as a sentiment or emotion in the minds of those who are charmed. Third, charisma—the word means "gift" or "grace," the mark of divine favor—is not entirely God's gift. It can be manufactured more or less out of whole cloth by suitable public-relations strategies and the right presentation of self. A very small part of Ronald Reagan's charisma was God's doing; the greater part came from his experience as an actor and from the skill and foresight of his handlers. Charisma, to say it again, does not ultimately reside in the leader but in the relationship between him and his followers, that is, in the way they think and feel about him. The mystique—he can do miracles—exists nowhere except in the minds and hearts of his devotees (and perhaps in his own mind).

That fact—that the gift of charisma is in the hands of devotees—introduces a necessary dynamic into what has so far been mostly a static portrayal of leadership. What can be given, can also be taken away. Nkrumah lost his charisma. As he became increasingly tyranni-cal, Ghanaians changed their mind about him. Churchill's charisma declined markedly as the war drew to its close and British public opin-ion moved in the direction of socialism and the end of empire.

The situation is yet more complex. Just as there can be a shift in and out of charisma, so also there are other forms of domination and lead-ership between which individuals move. There are charismatic lead-ers who fill the political stage by presenting themselves as the exclu-sive locus of all that is valuable and desirable, as in the case of Hitler, who "embodies the idea and he alone knows its ultimate goal." In other cultures (American presidents or British prime ministers) lead-ers would not dare to present themselves in that way, even if they believed—and tried to convey in other ways—that they alone could do whatever had to be done. Sometimes a would-be charismatic leader hitches a ride on a cause for which there already exists a band of devotees. Most Soviet communist leaders—those who did have charisma—achieved it in part by identifying themselves with Marxism and the party. At another extreme are leaders who strive continually to be "one of the boys" and work hard to diminish the distance between themselves and their followers. There are still other ways of exercising power: a following can be bought, and beyond that there is the style of plain domination, driving rather than leading. Neither of these is within my definition of leadership, but they are still ways of exercising power and are available to those who on other occasions conduct themselves like leaders.

This listing of alternatives moves us away from an inert model of power embodied in charismatic leaders or demotic leaders or non-leaders who buy their way into power and toward a model of strate-gies. Charisma, being "one of the boys," representing a cause, and so on are strategies, alternative ways of competing for and exercising power. A particular leader may favor one or another strategy over the rest, but he is unlikely to be effective if that is the only political tool he knows how to use. Leaders need to have at their disposal a collec-tion of strategies that are differently applicable in different situations. The demotic leader should know how to set himself apart as gifted with some quality or ability that his followers neither have nor fully comprehend; they must be made to realize that they lack the ability to take his place. Conversely, those leaders who present themselves as godlike and far removed from ordinary people are the stronger if from time to time they reveal a human face, showing not just mercy, which is a divine prerogative, but also the human quality of compassion and of empathy with the feelings of others, even if it is only a fiction put about by their public-relations experts.

Entourage

Leadership strategies to attract, maintain, and manipulate a mass following are different from those used on an entourage—staff, cronies, and confidants—who stand close to the leader. *Close* refers to the frequency, intensity, and nature of the interactions and the style and content of communication between leaders and followers. Plain domination is the major element in controlling an entourage; conversely, legitimacy is more readily won from a mass of followers than it is from an entourage. The difference, as you will see, has to do with diseducation and access to information: Reality is more easily hidden from the masses than it is from an entourage.

Reality suggests that there is one simple truth that, once known, cannot be ignored or denied. There are such facts, of course: It is, or it is not, Sunday; there was or was not an earthquake earlier this year in Turkey; and so on. But political realities are usually not like that: Political "facts" often turn out to be points of view and plain "reality" dissolves into several competing versions of reality. So what is concealed from the masses is not reality but versions of it other than the one favored by the persuader. The man in the Limehouse audience shouted to Lloyd George, "Bravo, David! Stand by the people and they will stand by you," and in that declaration hugely simplified a complicated situation for Lloyd George because in effect it told him that he was trusted and would not be asked to spell out the possible alternatives to the policy that the Limehouse speech constructs. That there might be difficulties, that there were other proposals, or that there was a contrary case to be made were all buried under the simple message of "Trust me! I am one of you." (The speech was in support of a budget that imposed heavier taxes on the moneyed classes, in particular on landholders. Most of it was taken up with accusing them of greed, unwillingness to pay their fair share, and indifference to the hardships suffered by the poor. The speech introduced into English a new verb, "to Limehouse," the equivalent of rabble-rousing.)

Leadership of a mass cannot be otherwise. There is a double thrust in the direction of diseducation. First, any persuasive argument is based on presuppositions that must be taken for granted; they cannot be rationally justified, only asserted. Even those who go through the motions of presenting all sides of the question still must base their arguments on presuppositions (which rivals will call prejudices), for without presuppositions no case can be made at all. Second, the need to simplify increases with the size and diversity of the audience—diversity of interest, diversity of knowledge, ethnic diversity, class diversity—each new category takes the speaker a step nearer to the simple appeal of "Trust me, because [. . .]." "Because" is followed by a slot into which a leader can offer four basic justifications. Three of them we already have: the demotic appeal ("I am one of the people"); the charismatic appeal ("I am like a God and can work miracles"); and, third, the appeal to duty, as in Churchill's "I have nothing to offer but blood, toil, tears, and sweat" or Kennedy's "Ask not what your country can do for you—ask what you can do for your country." The fourth mode of persuasion is an appeal to self-interest, enlightened or not. That echoed and re-echoed through Lloyd George's Limehouse speech. It appears again in the Democratic Party slogan in the 1952 campaign: "You never had it so good!" These different appeals seem at first sight to be incompatible with each other, but in fact a clever speaker can weave them all into the one message. What cannot normally be revealed to a mass audience is the actual complexity (and often insolubility) of problems that the speaker claims to be able to solve.

The same smoke and mirror tactic—making the problems seem simpler than they are—is not so easily used on an entourage. Indeed it would be counterproductive to do so systematically, because the entourage is the leader's eyes and ears. They are also, in a sense, his hands, for they see to it that his commands are put into effect. An entourage consists of advisers who are taken into the leader's confidence; when consulting with them he is off the record. (Nixon's error was exactly that: He intended to preserve on tape the image of himself as a leader, proud, practical, defiant and resourceful in adversity, and instead wrote himself into history as an unprincipled paranoiac.) Consultations with an entourage are kept private exactly because, if they are to be of any use, they must take account of realities that are concealed from the public.

Those realities—*res tegendae*, things to be hidden—comprise not only the complexity of the problems that must be solved, but also whatever failings and weaknesses the leader may have. Flaws are not broadcast to the mass, even flaws that could reasonably be thought irrelevant: Franklin Roosevelt took care to conceal the damage that polio had done to his body. Rumor had it that Churchill was indefatigable because he had the knack of taking twenty-minute catnaps and waking refreshed. It was left to his doctor, Lord Moran (of course a member of his entourage), to reveal that he needed medication to help him sleep. Hitler, I have read, had only one testicle; if that was the case, the story must have come from someone close to him—or, of course, from his enemies. Gandhi, the ascetic, in middle life became celibate and would test his self-control by sharing his bed with a young woman. When that story was told in a book of reminiscences by his secretary, N. K. Bose, there was a huge outcry, and the book, although not banned, vanished from bookshops and was stolen or withdrawn from libraries.

Such revelations make it hard to imagine that people close to a particular leader, his friends and cronies, are invariably and unswervingly devoted to him; it is even hard to think of any actual leader who did not have among his entourage, if not the shadow of a Judas figure, at least someone whose faith was less than total, someone who from time to time revealed impatience or ambivalence. I have heard a recording of the speech that Nehru made when Gandhi was assassinated in January 1948:

> Friends and comrades, the light has gone out of our lives and there is darkness everywhere. I do not know what to tell you and how to say it. Our beloved leader, Bapu as we called him, the father of the nation, is no more.

No one who heard Nehru speak those words could have doubted the sincerity of his grief. One does not, however, have to search far in Nehru's autobiography to find remarks like the following (he was speaking of the religious element in Gandhi's charismatic presentation of himself):

> It seemed to me sheer revivalism, and clear thinking had not the ghost of a chance against it. All India, or most of it, stared reverently at the Mahatma and expected him to perform miracle after miracle and put an

end to untouchability and get Swaraj [independence] and so on—and did precious little itself! And Gandhi did not encourage others to think; his insistence was only on purity and sacrifice.[10]

Or this:

> As for Gandhiji, he was a very difficult person to understand, and sometimes his language was almost incomprehensible to an average modern. But we felt that we knew him well enough to realize that he was a great and unique man and a glorious leader, and having put our faith in him we gave him almost a blank cheque, for the time being at least. Often we discussed his fads and peculiarities among ourselves, and said, half-humorously, that when Swaraj came these fads must not be encouraged.[11]

That was written in 1936. When independence was won in 1947, most of those "fads" did go into a pending file. Nehru had other ideas about the right political form for free India: It should be unambiguously a secular state.

Saintly qualities are sometimes presented in the propaganda of other leaders—recall the hymn of praise for Chairman Mao—but they rarely appear in the memoirs of those who had (or claimed) intimate knowledge of particular leaders. In them the warts appear. Here again is Frank Moraes, writing in 1973 about Indira Gandhi (Nehru's daughter and, like him, prime minister of India; she was assassinated in 1984 by a member of her bodyguard):

> Mrs. Gandhi has the reputation of never forgetting. More ominously she rarely forgives. She has shown a capacity for toppling restive colleagues as deftly as she had toppled a few inconvenient state governments. Watching her in action to-day, surrounded by her courtier-ministers, all conscious that at any moment the axe may descend on their necks, one wonders whether a male liberation movement is not overdue in India or in Asia.[12]

Keeping the entourage uncertain and on its toes was not Mrs. Gandhi's invention. Shaka Zulu (founder of the Zulu nation and murdered by his half-brothers in 1828) would, when sitting in council, "by a movement of his finger, perceivable only by his attendants, point out one of the gathering sitting around him, upon which . . . the man would be carried off and killed. This was a daily occurrence."[13] Shaka in the end went out of his mind, but he was not entirely irrational, assuming that his goal was to hang on to power: "He killed chiefs and other important persons whose loyalty he suspected and replaced them with kinsmen and other favourites." This practice shaped the political strategies of the Zulu elite: "Throughout his reign, suspicion was enough to cause the violent removal of any lieutenant, and getting the despot's ear to plant suspicions was an important move to be made in the complex intrigues of the inner circle."[14]

Frank Moraes calls Mrs. Gandhi's entourage *courtiers*. "False is the cringing Courtier's plighted word," wrote the playwright John Gay. The term connotes flattery, deceit, ambition, intrigue, and above all danger and uncertainty. Courtiers intrigue against each other, and, if the opportunity offers, against the monarch. The monarch needs them; they are, as I said, his eyes and ears, and they are his hands, doing for him what would not be seemly if he did it for himself—anything from starting a rumor to arranging a murder. Monarchs too are caught in the same game of courtly intrigue and counterintrigue; they *dominate* their entourage (the word *lead* no longer fits) to the extent that they play the game more skillfully than the courtiers. The basic moves are obvious: Let no one courtier ever be without a rival of equal power; keep them uncertain about their future; in short, divide and rule. Indira Gandhi, Shaka Zulu, Hitler, Rafael Trujillo (the dictator of the Dominican Republic from 1930 until his assassination in 1961), Churchill manipulating and provoking his wartime advisers, Mrs. Thatcher, and virtually every other successful leader appear in the memoirs of their erstwhile courtiers as masters of intrigue. (The exception seems to have been Mahatma Gandhi, although, as you will see, not everyone believed him honest.) Roosevelt was a manipulative nonpareil. Among his courtiers were some ambitious politicians who themselves maintained a covert entourage of clients and advisers who kept them informed of the intrigues and maneuvers by their rivals. Roosevelt had "an intimate understanding" of these "complex matters," watching them "with tolerance and sometimes with amusement," himself quietly and unobtrusively intervening when any one of them seemed likely to threaten his own eminence.[15]

This was the same Roosevelt whose "fireside chats" on radio caused people to write "affectionate" letters to him, telling of their "hopes and worries and troubles."[16] That one-on-one intimacy shared simultaneously with thousands and thousands of listeners is, from one point of view, a magician's trick, even a confidence trick. But who is to say that the warm, compassionate person was not the real Roosevelt, and his Machiavellian scheming was no more than an unfortunate but unavoidable tactic required to deal with ambitious and unscrupulous subordinates? The question cannot be conclusively answered, and I ask it only to demonstrate its futility if one's concern is to understand how politics work rather than moralize about how they should work.

The People's Friend

In conformity with their ideology, left-wing leaders profess to have faith in the masses; some of them appear actually to have it. (Lenin did not. He dismissed the notion of leadership by the masses as "infantile.") This faith is quite distinct from the demotic idiom used to gain support, as when Lloyd George proclaims that he is "one of the children of the people" or Roosevelt begins his radio talks "My friends. . . ." Rather it is a profound belief, an article of faith, that wisdom locates itself in the common people: They know best. Nehru, India's prime minister from 1948 until his death in 1964, did not gather round him, as Gandhi had, a cadre of younger people from whom his successor might come. "After Nehru, what?" for some years was an Editorial and Op-Ed writer's cliché. Nehru is reported not to have been concerned because he firmly believed that the people would make the politicians choose the right person. The Cultural Revolution (to be discussed in Chapter 5) testifies to Mao's faith in the people's ability to bring the party bureaucrats back into line. The same conviction, that ordinary people are a repository of political virtue, appears in an interview with a former chief minister of the Indian state, Orissa. I recorded it in 1959.

> The years after 1947 were a great disappointment. People had been led to believe that freedom would be a millennium that would bring them a new and benevolent kind of ruler. But in fact the new system was beyond their understanding. Equally the [politicians] were out of their depth. They found that with the British gone, the system still survived, and they were powerless to bring about [changes]. Then they made a great mistake; they did not take people into their confidence and explain what

was going wrong and why it was going wrong and why they were help-less. They just went on making more promises. They humbugged the people.

I do not question that man's sincerity, nor the accuracy of his diag-nosis. Nor do I doubt that faith in the wisdom of the common people contributed to Nehru's failure to train a cadre of younger followers for the succession (it was not the only cause). Nevertheless, it is the case everywhere in politics that the enemy of my enemy is my friend, and when leaders step past their entourages and their bureaucrats to make direct contact with the people, whatever their motivation, whether or not they have faith in the people's wisdom, they are put-ting that adage into practice. That is what leaders do when they want to rein in the power of subordinates who stand between them and the people. Clinton and Reagan going on television to talk about their difficulties with the Congress were directly enlisting the common people's support against rivals who might diminish their legitimacy and lessen their authority. When leaders do that, they are saying, sometimes explicitly and sometimes leaving the listeners to draw their own conclusions, that their own enemies are also the people's ene-mies. Therefore the leader and the people are friends.

The message may be conveyed in more than one way, depending on how the leader sees the situation. Sometimes the leader may make a direct appeal for trust, without drawing attention to the intermedi-aries. I can recall two cases, briefly mentioned earlier, in which lead-ers, faced with an unambiguous and undeniable disaster, must have decided that it would be a mistake to blame incompetent subordi-nates; instead they themselves publicly accepted responsibility. The Egyptian leader Nasser resigned his presidency after a disastrous defeat in the six-day Arab–Israeli war in 1967. He was persuaded, almost immediately, to withdraw the resignation, and he continued in power until he died three years later. Castro gave a highly publicized pledge to raise Cuban sugar production up to 10 million tons by 1970. When that did not happen and the efforts to bring it about had caused some distress, he offered to resign. The offer provoked vehement popular expressions of support, as he may have intended. (He had long since made sure that there were no obvious replacements wait-ing in the wings.) Both of these incidents were, I think, what Nasser and Castro would have said they were—evidence of the trust their people had in them. They were successful appeals for demotic support. Clinton confessing on television to (some of) his personal failings had an element of this—throwing himself on the mercy of the people. Nixon's defiance—the reported "I am not a crook"—pointed the other way.

Nasser and Castro, in those single dramatic near-desperation gestures, were betting the farm: win or lose all. More often, when leaders feel their authority and legitimacy are at risk, they intensify measures that they believe will dramatize and strengthen their charismatic appeal. Nkrumah in Ghana and Sékou Touré in Guinea, as their policies produced more and more hardships for their countries and as their charisma declined, moved further and further into the unreality of grand public monuments, symbols that might leave for archeologists a record of splendor that contemporary miseries denied. (Saddam Hussein seems to be marching down the same road, if the reports about palace building are accurate.) Along with this very leaderlike defiance of rationality went the grim and practical device of the treason trial, in which intrigues were uncovered and traitors brought to justice. Show trials against alleged revisionist or counterrevolutionary elements in the political elite, sometimes in the leader's entourage itself, were a feature of Stalin's USSR. Since the traitors come from the elite, the trials demonstrate that the leader's enemies are the elite, who are also the people's enemies. Leader and common people, therefore, are one. That is how the tale is told.

Mass and entourage appear to be distinct domains that require different strategies for the exercise of leadership. In the next chapter I will complicate the picture by introducing a third entity. This is the bureaucracy.

5

Politicians and Bureaucrats

- When nothing much changes and everyone carries on doing what they have always done, and there are no ambiguities, there is little need for decisions, and therefore there is no call for leadership. This chapter will consider bureaucrats, whose job it is to promote exactly that kind of stability, and who, in that and other ways, tend to undermine political leadership.
- It will also review ways in which leaders may respond when their power to make decisions and set policy is threatened by bureaucratic expansion.

Civil Servants

The adjective *civil* separates nonmilitary from military employees of the state. When applied to behavior, the word has a different (but connected) cluster of meanings: polite, proper, not aggressive, obliging, cooperative, helpful, considerate, not rough, likely to do nothing disturbing or unexpected, following the conventions, and so on. That list of features more or less fits the idealized bureaucrat (a less respectful term for an employee of the state and its nonmilitary organizations). *Bureaucrat* also has a trail of other features that are not ideal, frequently deplored, but also considered inevitable. I will take the ideal features first.

Bureaucrats runs bureaux, offices that deal with a specific branch of government: judicial, trade and commerce, law enforcement, education, public health, foreign affairs, and the like. Their task is to implement decisions made by their masters, the politicians, working out how the general principles of a policy can be applied to specific situations. Therefore bureaucrats can, in theory, always be rational. They have been told what the goal is; their task is to find the most effective allocation of resources to reach it, and so they always have an agreed premise from which to reason. Rationality is the foundation on which all bureaucratic activity is supposed to rest. In principle there is perfect cooperation and no place for conflict.

Bureaucracies are built in layers, a feature which, although frequently deplored—"buried under layers of bureaucracy"—is necessary. Departments are divided into subdepartments and each of these into sub-subdepartments, which might again be divided into regional offices, and these into subregional offices, and so on, until one arrives at the familiar pyramid pattern of a chain of command. Reading the diagram vertically, from top to bottom, the perfectly rational end to means pattern can in theory exist, and with it the ideal of complete cooperation. Each decision at a higher level involves the allocation of responsibilities and scarce resources among units at the next lower level. The normal way to make allocations is through discussion among the lower-level heads in a committee chaired by the superior-level head. Ideally this discussion is rational, with every lower-level head putting the interests of his or her subunit second always to the interests of the higher-level unit. Properly speaking, no unit in this idealized portrayal has interests of its own; everyone has a shared interest in implementing, in the most effective possible way, the policy laid down by the politicians. There should be no private interests in a bureaucracy; only the public weal should count. In short, an ideal bureaucracy has no politics in it.

The goal of a bureaucracy is to anticipate every contingency and to have on hand a rule to deal with it. Given that goal, the uncomplimentary phrase "bureaucratic machine" is perfectly apt. Well-designed machines run smoothly. They can do so because they are machines and not human beings, who change their minds, act on a whim, take a rest when they feel tired, argue back when programmed to do something that they dislike, are affected by moral scruples, want to know what is the purpose of it all, and often put their own interests before that of the whole apparatus. Good bureaucrats are expected not to behave that way but to be wholly impersonal both toward themselves and toward the clients (as the people whose lives are regulated by the bureaucracy are called). Bureaucrats and their clients are that, and that alone; they are never brothers, or sisters, or lovers, or sharers of an ethnic identity (or ill-disposed toward the other's identity); they are just civil servant and client. They are, to use another complaining epithet, faceless, anonymous, having no name but only a title—Judge, First Secretary, Director of Education, Deputy Chief Constable, Vice-Chancellor—not people but the incumbents of offices.

Reflect on the difference between the image of a bureaucrat and the image of a politician. An *anonymous* or *faceless* politician is a contradiction in terms. Politicians live by name recognition, whatever the regime, whether dictatorial or democratic. Ends—the goals of policy—are not given to them, fixed and firm as premises from which to reason; they decide what the ends will be, and that is ultimately a matter of conviction, faith, intuition, divine guidance, or whatever else transcends or precedes reasoned argument. Politicians are expected to have what has been vulgarized as "the vision-thing": insight, foresight, political sagacity, dreams for the future, and various other qualities that, for their very lack of attention to practicality, would severely handicap a bureaucrat. Politicians live by uncertainty; indeed, insofar as they are leaders they must welcome it, for in its absence there is nothing for them to do.

Of course these two categories are ideal types, constructs of the imagination. As categories, they have neat, sharp edges, but the real world is fuzzy and there are no sharp edges. Real bureaucracies turn out to be political arenas, and bureaucrats are competitors both within their own organizations and in larger political arenas. Politicians, similarly, end up in disaster if their intuition does not tell them when it is wise to think like a bureaucrat and let bureaucratic norms prevail. Reality, in the case of both politicians and bureaucrats, is a continuum between the faceless official and the charismatic leader. Run through the list of American presidents or state governors or British or French or Italian prime ministers; some have nothing to be remembered by except the fact that they once held the office. Conversely—this takes more searching—there have been bureaucrats who are remembered as leaders. That apart, it is for sure the case that no bureaucrat ever

fulfilled his bureaucratic duty without departing from the bureaucratic ideals sketched out above. Real bureaucracies exist in contradiction
with themselves because there is not one of them that is not also a
political arena, a place where power is contested.

Logically that has to be so, because policy decisions do not in fact
end with politicians. The politician makes a decision and hands it on
to his chief secretary for implementation; the chief secretary con-
fronts the decision with what he believes to be reality (resources, personnel, timing, and the like), makes *his* decisions, and passes them on
to his subordinates, who in turn confront their more particular seg-
ments of reality, and make *their* decisions, and so on down the line
until the ships are built, or the banking system regulated, or the development programs initiated. Every time a decision is handed down, an
act of leadership has taken place. Rules are general and situations are
particular, and every movement down the chain requires a decision
that interprets a general rule to make it fit a particular situation.

The second reason why a bureaucracy must be a political arena is
that the parts of a bureaucratic "machine" are human beings, with
human failings (they get tired, they get cross, they can be bloody-
minded) and human concerns (they refuse to be faceless or to treat all
their clients as faceless) and human ambitions (they want power).
Every bureaucracy—certainly some more than others—is fueled not
only by bureaucratic principles of service to the common weal, but
also by the spirit of antibureaucracy, which is the service of particular
interests. This is called, disapprovingly, *goal displacement*: Every
branch puts its own expansion, or at least its own survival, ahead of
the job it is supposed to do. The decisions handed down from one
level to another are not only the outcome of a rational debate that
starts from commonly held principles at the higher level; usually there
has also been a contest between the units at the lower level, each one
striving if not for the lion's share, at least for what it considers its fair
share. Power is the prize and the spur to action.

Such goings-on, although undesirable from a purist definition of
bureaucracy, are generally considered inevitable. That is how bureaucracies, since they are run by human beings, work internally. They are
not, for that reason, to be considered corrupt. Corruption pertains
not to the internal workings of the apparatus but to its relationship
with clients; a corrupt bureaucracy does not treat them as faceless, nor
are the bureaucrats anonymous. The basic rule of impersonality is put

aside and favors (or disfavors) are done on the basis of ethnicity or religion, or class or gender, or kinship or whatever else. Or money is used to buy a decision. A variant of this form of corruption is *politicization*. Bureaucrats shelve the public interest in favor of a political group, sometimes out of conviction, often because they want the favor or fear the wrath of their political masters. Local school administrators discreetly bend before the embryonic politicians on the elected school board, or the nation's higher courts suit their verdicts to the desires of the nation's higher politicians. Those are instances of, so to speak, straightforward corruption.

Another form of goal displacement involves not units within the bureaucracy working to aggrandize themselves, but the entire apparatus. It might be considered an occupational hazard, in the way that black lung is a hazard for coal miners. Symptoms take the form of arrogance, a sense of natural superiority, a conviction that always they know best. Civil servants tend to forget that they are *servants*, and instead see themselves as masters. The bureaucratic activity becomes an end in itself and bureaucrats, if unchecked, invade and take control of all politics.

The ailment appears in various forms. One is red tape, which is excessive attention to routines, coupled with a rigid observance of regulations. The lower levels of bureaucracy that I encountered in India were notorious for this. Drawing money on a letter of credit from a branch in Orissa of the State Bank of India was an entire morning's affair, pleasantly and perfectly unbureaucratically spent drinking cups of tea with bank officials, while peons carried papers around from one department to another and from time to time brought them to me for signature. The peons were faceless but I was not and neither were the officials; by the end of the morning we knew a good deal about each other's positions and opinions. No harm was done; I had time enough and I was, anyway, in India to talk with people; there were, of course, costs to the bank in terms of efficiency. Also red tape may lead to corruption, because, even if the regulations are genuine and not invented for the occasion, clients know that every bureaucrat can speed the process, if motivated to do so. In the ideal bureaucracy rules have been multiplied until there is no conceivable situation for which there is not already a rule; red tape is the paradoxical consequence of trying to do just that. The outcome is the reverse of what a bureaucracy is supposed to do: It does not connect the politician's visionary world with reality, but replaces the vision with the bureau-cratic process itself. A first and easy reaction to this process is moral outrage—they should not be doing that. On reflection, however, it is more enlightening to model creeping bureaucracy as a natural system, an evolutionary process, an ailment that, one hopes, will eventually give rise to its own antigens before it destroys the body politic.

This tension between political vision and bureaucratic procedures shows itself in various contexts. In 1959 I spent most of a year in Orissa's capital, Bhubaneswar, asking politicians, civil servants, and other people about the transition from an authoritarian bureaucracy to a parliamentary democracy. The politicians mostly talked vision-things and when I asked, "How much of this has been done?" they would often say that implementation was difficult because it was hard to get past the bureaucracy and cut through the red tape. Civil ser-vants, they said, had been trained to think like the British and really did not like change—or at least did not know how to deal with it or make it happen. In that postindependence decade in India, however, no civil servant would dare say that he disapproved of change. Instead they would remark that visions are easy things to have, and talk about them is cheap and intended to win votes, but most visions were not practical propositions. Where would the resources come from, what else would have to be put aside, and what would be the as yet unfore-seen consequences? What the vision offered might be desirable, but either it could not be done at all, or, if done, the costs would likely exceed the benefits. It was their job, as civil servants, to make the con-sequences known and help the politicians bring their visionary schemes closer to reality.

Stirring Things Up

In the short run, politicians who cannot bend bureaucrats to accom-modate their political vision have failed as leaders because they have allowed another person to make a decision for them. On the other hand, by listening to expert advice instead of following their intuition, they may have saved themselves from a career-terminating disaster. To point this out is to put a different spin on the tension between politician and bureaucrat; it takes the focus away from the contest for power and sees their interaction as a form of cooperation, a dialogue that balances vision with practicality. Veteran politicians in Orissa, cabinet ministers with long experience of holding office, generally professed to have amicable and constructive relationships with their senior bureaucratic advisers, who, being senior, were also veterans. Less experienced officeholders and ordinary legislators, wanting some direct favor from a bureaucrat, were more likely to complain about obstruction.

Relationships between officeholders and bureaucrats in parliamentary democracies (and in some other kinds of regime) are complex and, in practice, eminently political—they are always, to some degree, a contest for power. Constitutionally their relative status is unambiguous: The politician is boss, the civil servant takes orders. But orders are nothing until they are implemented and that process can effectively negate the politician's intentions. Some ministers that I interviewed in Orissa were reputed to be under the thumb of the secretary (the department's chief bureaucrat). Others were powerful men, who, when provoked, would have the bureaucrat transferred to another—usually less desirable—post, thus encouraging the successor to be more compliant.

These encounters (wonderfully parodied in the BBC comedy series *Yes, Minister!*) no doubt add zest (or strain) to the lives of the individuals concerned, and sometimes significantly affect the careers of one or both of them, but the tension also has a larger significance. Tension, certainly inevitable, has some good effects: It makes the politicians more responsible, more likely to think twice about the consequences of what they propose to do. On the other hand, it also slows things down; it stifles enthusiasm; it devitalizes the political system. We have a most apposite cliché to describe that side of bureaucracy: It has a "dead hand." ("Dead hand" is a translation of the legal term *mortmain*, which is the ownership of property by *impersonal* entities, such as ecclesiastical or other corporations.)

India became independent in 1947 after more than fifty years of struggle by the Indian Congress Movement to oust the British, who had been India's rulers for almost two centuries. Orissa's politicians at that time spoke of the "Freedom Fight." 1959 was roughly a decade after the fight had been won and independence achieved. In Orissa, as in other states in the Indian Union, much had been accomplished in those ten years. Two general elections had been successfully held, despite difficulties in communication, more than half the voters in the state being illiterate and all but a small number of them newly enfranchised. There had been labor unrest and political violence from time to time, and there was a constant complaint about corruption and inefficiency. But it seemed to me, talking to people and reading the record of what had been accomplished in that decade, that the government and people of Orissa had reason to congratulate themselves. Politicians on the government benches in the Assembly did exactly that, loudly and frequently; the loyal opposition complained no less loudly and no less frequently about incompetence and failure to "implement the [Five Year] plan," but they remained a *loyal* opposition—they accepted the conventions of parliamentary democracy and were loyal to its principles. There had been a huge effort at economic and social development, including some spectacularly large capital investments in the Hirakud Dam (it produced electricity, provided irrigation, and put an end to the periodic and disastrous flooding of the Mahanadi River), in a steel plant at Rourkela and other manufacturing industries elsewhere, and in a new deepwater port at Paradip. In addition, and to some extent in competition with dams and steelworks and the like, resources had gone into improved agriculture and into expanded social services. All this, the politicians claimed (correctly), represented a sea change from the stagnant years when they were ruled by the British authoritarian bureaucracy. After ten years, I fancied, I should be hearing people quote Wordsworth (talking in 1809 about the French Revolution): "Bliss was it in that dawn to be alive."

But I never heard anything like that about the decade of the 1950s. Public pride in achievement confronted private disillusion and a complaining insistence that more should have been done. That was, of course, said in public by opposition politicians; it was their duty to offer constructive criticism of the party in power. Nor, I suspect, is there any democratic country in the world where it is not the custom to grumble constantly about the government. There was, however, something peculiar about this mood of disillusion, and it took some time for me to work out what it was. Complaints logically must be based on a comparison: The grass is greener on the river's other side. I had taken the complaint literally: more could have been done than had been done. But, I realized later, underneath there was another comparison that explained *why*, according to the complainers, more had not been done: They believed that the spirit of service in the 1950s was immeasurably inferior to what it had been during the

Freedom Fight. The blissful dawn was not self-government but the prior struggle to achieve it. Why should that be?

There are several answers. The cynical one—there was no less self-ishness in the old days, and people have selective memories and choose to remember the past as they would like it to have been—has some truth in it, but not the whole truth. A better explanation is that before 1947 there was a single clear goal, *swaraj* (independence), and a single clear enemy, the British (and their Indian supporters). After gaining independence, the Freedom Fighters had to decide what to do with it, how to divide up the positions of power that the British had vacated; then politics took over and those who had formerly stood side by side to fight the British now fought each other over the spoils of victory. Spoils apart, there was no longer the single unquestioned goal—freedom from British rule. In its place was a vague notion of prosperity and the good life for all, without any agreement on how to bring it about. I heard politicians say, "Our problem is too much politics." What they might have said was that they had too many politicians and too few statesmen who could be trusted to put the public interest before their own or their party's. But even if there had been more statesmen, the problem would not have gone away. What counts as the public interest at one level inevitably becomes private and sectarian when seen from the levels above it.

There is one further unfolding of the disillusion that I noticed in 1959. It reveals a nostalgia, especially among those who had themselves been Freedom Fighters (but not confined to them alone), for an attitude and a way of life that had been lost once freedom was achieved. There is no single name for it; it is the negation of Weber's disenchanted world; it combines enthusiasm, a sense of adventure, a readiness to take risks, a belief that faith will overcome all obstacles, a refusal to think about consequences, a readiness to act on impulse without planning ahead, to defy conventions, to ignore regulations and precedent, and so on. This fundamentally antirational, anticalculating feature went along with utter devotion to the cause (in some cases also to leaders, especially Gandhi) that totally overrode self-concern. They needed no Kennedy to tell them to ask what they could do for their country. Some would call that spirit "revolutionary." Alternatively it is what the practical and anti-imaginative George Bush senior, reluctant to be thought utopian, romantic, or visionary, but needing the concept, downgraded as the "vision-*thing*." Vision, the hallmark of a leader, is the denial of bureaucratic values; the good manager is not a visionary and has in him no romantic dreams.

India at that time had need not only of visionaries but still more of people who, besides having the vision, were sufficiently devoted to the cause to go as many extra miles as situations needed, without ever thinking about the cost to themselves. Vision-*talk* was there in plenty; dedicated *action*, self-sacrifice, and all of those other features that the Freedom Fighters remembered themselves as having were rare. Prosperity and the good life for the Indian people was iconized in the Five-Year Plan, but the Plan was not like *swaraj*, something easily defined. It was a complex bureaucratic operation that involved allocating scarce resources between different ends, which themselves were disputed, and between different beneficiaries, who were competitors.

Worse than that, the only people qualified to implement the Plan were civil servants, and at least in the lower ranks their philosophy was the very opposite of visionary. Nor were civil servants noted for their dedication and self-sacrifice. They tended to be cautious, practical, interested in their own careers, risk-shy, and concerned not to do things that might mark them in the eyes of their superiors as quirky and unreliable. The Indian Civil Service in the days of the British was primarily concerned with law and order. It did in fact also bring about many social and economic changes, some intended and some not. But the intended changes were accomplished mainly by fiat, not by enlisting popular enthusiasm and support. The magnitude of social, economic, and political changes envisaged in the Five-Year Plans called for a different kind of civil servant, one not so remote, who could inspire the common people and would themselves be inspired by the same spirit of adventure and dedication that had won the Freedom Fight.

After independence the politicians in India did some things to reform the bureaucracy, but nothing radical or dramatic. They changed the name of its elite formation from the Indian Civil Service to the Indian Administrative Service. Special cadres were recruited and trained for development work, but even those young administrators had the same career anxieties that made them reluctant risk-takers. From the beginning, as a matter both of principle and because it was economically necessary (and politically advantageous), the politicians tried to involve ordinary people in the process of development

and change, hoping to arouse their enthusiasm and enlist their cooperation. They tried to remove some of the majesty that had formerly
invested bureaucrats, Indian as well as British. Around the middle of
the 1950s an extensive system of democratic local government was
initiated and given a role in development. This measure certainly
diminished the power of local bureaucrats, but it did not end the
politicians' perception that bureaucrats were elitist, obstructive, and a
brake on change, development, and progress.

The connection between the mentality of the Freedom Fighter, the
disillusion of the 1950s in Orissa, and the tension there between
politicians and bureaucrats became clearer to me later when I read
about other revolutionary situations and encountered what at first
seemed the curious idea of a revolution that continues after the revolutionary war had been won. In July 1966, Chairman Mao, then 72
years old, plunged into the Yangtze River and swam downstream,
helped by a fast-moving current, for a distance, it is said, of just under
ten miles, completing the course in less than an hour. (The fastest
swimmer across the English Channel, which is twenty-one miles
wide, took a little under eight hours.) He was escorted by hundreds of
other people (most of them presumably young). It was a magical and
charismatic gesture that signified cleansing, youth and vigor, an
inevitable and irresistible force, and, not least, a continuing revolution
sweeping Mao along in its surge, alongside the young, among the
people, unescorted by any entourage. That swim, widely publicized
and preserved on film, inaugurated the Cultural Revolution, which
went on for three years. It was a revolution against Communist Party
bureaucrats, who were attacked because they had not only lost their
revolutionary fervor but also had abandoned the communist ideal,
which was to give power to the people; they had become "revision-
ists." Secondary-school and university student activists, mobilized as
Red Guards, were sent out to disrupt the bureaucracy and other institutions that bred revisionism, and in this way return power to the people. When the students got out of hand, soldiers and workers were
used to crush them. Universities were taken over and run by committees of workers; the educated elite was banished to work on farms and
relearn communist values from the peasants. After three years of
chaos, Mao declared the job done; the party bureaucracy had been
sufficiently shocked out of revisionism, and normality could be
restored, until it was time for the next administrative discombobula-

tion. Notice in all of this that the target was not particular bureaucrats who had fallen out of favor and who might have been quietly liquidated; the target was the bureaucracy itself. Also notice an entailment of that fact: Mao was not simply consolidating his personal power by removing rivals, as Stalin did in Russia. The party bureaucrats were not Mao's rivals; they were too small for that. The motive—he was explicit about it—was to revitalize the political process by removing, of necessity only temporarily, the dead hand of bureaucracy.

In this and the previous chapter I have modeled politics in the form of a three-layer pyramid: leaders, an intermediate element (bureaucrats and entourage), and ordinary people. Between leaders and bureaucrats there is an inevitable dissonance; their styles and their values are discordant. Politicians are visionaries; they are bold, ready to take risks, and eager to venture into the unknown. The bureaucrat's task is to reduce the unknown to the known, to make the political process nonpolitical by making it entirely predictable, so that it has a rule for every contingency and thus eliminates contingencies. The entourage, on the other hand, comprises politicians, potential leaders themselves, and therefore is also a source of peril (of a different kind) to the leader.

At the bottom of the pyramid are the people, the "faceless masses." So far I have looked at them as potential allies who can be mobilized by leaders against bureaucrats. In the next chapter I will begin to give them a face and present them as bearers of cultures that constitute both a resource for, and a constraint on, leaders and their strategies.

6

In Search of Trust

- Politicians talk about two kinds of guidance: One is intuition or the hand of God, which mandates, in an absolute way, the morally right action, whatever the cost; the other is a rational calculation of the likely payoff.
- The more culturally diverse the following, the harder it is for a leader to locate or construct a theme that will transcend cultural differences. Both kinds of guidance—moral and rational—rise above such differences.
- Gandhi selected moral absolutism and entirely subordinated cost–benefit calculations. He did so by presenting the political campaign for independence from the British as the lesser element in a struggle for moral and spiritual integrity. In other words, his transcendent appeal was to religion.
- This chapter will conclude with a nuanced interpretation of Louis McHenry Howe's "You can't adopt politics as a profession and remain honest."

"Intuition" and Calculation

Nehru was a modernist. (The word in his lifetime was not the insult that it sometimes is now.) He was a believer in science and progress, a rationalist who saw to it that, constitutionally at least, India came into independence as a secular state. Religion irritated him; superstition irritated him; he respected logic and cold reason. Recall the mixture of asperity and despair in his comments on the spiritual ambiance that surrounded Gandhi: It was "sheer revivalism," and "clear thinking had not the ghost of a chance against it." Also: "I felt angry with him at his religious and sentimental approach to a political question."

But he also wrote (when he himself got around to "clear thinking"): "What a magician . . . was this little man sitting in Yeravda prison, and how well he knew how to pull the strings that move people's hearts."[1] Elsewhere: "Gandhiji's phrases sometimes jarred on me—thus his frequent reference to Rama Raja as a golden age which was to return. But I was powerless to intervene and I consoled myself with the thought that Gandhiji used the words because they were well known and understood by the masses. He had an amazing knack of reaching the heart of the people."[2]

There could be a hint in those words that Gandhi himself was no more than a calculating politician. I do not think Nehru intended that, nor, I believe, was it the case. Gandhi was much given to writing and talking about his inner thoughts; there are hundreds upon hundreds of documented statements about God and Truth and Religion. They demonstrate to me (but not, as you will see, to everyone) that Gandhi was the truest of true believers: For him religion had an intrinsic, not merely an instrumental value. Nevertheless, what is intrinsically valued can also be instrumentally useful, and Gandhi, no doubt, was aware of the political effects of his sermonizing and his Hindu ascetic style of living. In the advice he gave to another Indian politician, Harekrushna Mahtab, there is a delicate indication that Gandhi knew what he was doing. He often spoke of God's guidance that came to him through "intuition." Mahtab confessed that he was not gifted with intuition. What should he do? Gandhi "smiled" and said that the word "judgment" would do as well. Perhaps it was the smile that prompted Mahtab to conclude that Gandhi's religiosity was a part of his "trying to make the masses move with faith and confidence to achieve the national objective."[3]

The word "judgment" takes the guiding hand of God sufficiently out of the picture to make room for calculation. Even if (as I argued earlier) all leaders have to be brash enough sometimes to go beyond logic when a decision is needed, they will generally think about their present situation, about what has been done on past occasions, about who will stand by them and who will not, and so on. Contexts of all

sorts—cultural, political, economic, social, historical, situational—
stand there both as a resource and as a constraint. Leaders generally
get some (or all) calculations wrong. (Gandhi's vision of postcolonial
India survived in the political arena as not much more than rhetoric;
even before he was murdered it was clear that the everyday reality
would not be *satyagraha*—the struggle for truth—but the *Realpolitik*
that he so much condemned. More on that later.) But even when leaders miscalculate resources and constraints, the missing or misinter-
preted parts of the context can still be used after the event to work out
why things went wrong. Similarly, when "intuition" gets the desired
result, if we want to understand why things turned out that way, we
have to reconstruct the intuition as if it had been a reasoned judgment
and a calculated decision.

To do so will sometimes misrepresent the processes that went on in
the mind of a leader, because it confuses two forms of calculation. The
first—Weber called it *the ethic of absolute ends*—is to make one simple
calculation: either *this is right* or *this is wrong*, without any thought
about consequences (other than the preservation of a moral imperative).[4] In 1920 Gandhi had launched a campaign of nonviolent noncooperation. Two years later (Nehru writes), "a mob of villagers had
retaliated on some policemen by setting fire to the police-station and
burning half-a-dozen or so policemen in it." (The tone set by "half-a-
dozen or so" is very un-Gandhian.) Gandhi immediately called the
campaign off. Nehru commented: "This sudden suspension of our
movement . . . was resented, I think, by almost all the Congress leaders—other than Gandhiji, of course." He added a pair of rhetorical
questions that perfectly exemplify judgment, calculation, and a strong
reluctance to be guided by an ethic of absolute ends: "Were a remote
village and a mob of excited peasants in an out-of-the-way place going
to put an end . . . to our national struggle for freedom? Must we train
the three hundred and odd million Indians in the theory and practice
of nonviolent action before we could go forward?"[5] The simple
answer—and Gandhi gave it over and over again—is that they must
do what was morally right, whatever the consequences. Nehru, by
contrast, factored in costs and consequences. That method of making
a decision Weber calls *the ethic of responsibility*.

Those who lean toward seeing the political arena in terms of
Realpolitik cannot afford to ignore people like Gandhi, for whom
absolute-end thinking was an imperative. What Gandhi did, as a

result of his "intuition," had consequences in the real world. Modernists (Nehru's "average modern") make their own estimate of its rationality. Nehru, despite the disparaging comments, had clearly calculated that Gandhi's value to the Congress Movement far exceeded the cost of his "revivalist" tendencies. (Recall the remark about Gandhi's "fads and peculiarities.") Moreover, since Nehru himself observed the rule of nonviolence and never supported the breakaway left-wing factions in Congress that did resort to violence, he must have decided that the payoff to nonviolence was positive.

The way leaders think is clearly part of our investigation, and their thoughts include whatever they hold as absolute ends. Gandhi had the luxury—if that is the right word to describe faith—of the instant decision that God made available to him and for which God would take the consequences. The labor of calculating those consequences or, after the event, drawing from them whatever knowledge would be of use another time was left to others. To say it again, if we are to make sense of leadership strategies, decisions guided by the ethic of absolute ends must be reexamined to see how far they were in fact consistent with an ethic of responsibility.

Strategies for Coping with Cultural Diversity

Any leader—Nehru, Gandhi, Clinton, the Bisoi, Churchill—working out a decision must take into account the followers, both entourage and mass, who have to implement or accept the decision. Followers are already preprogrammed; they have a culture, which is their own distinctive way of making sense of the world and their experiences in it. Culture puts a label on actions and policies and people, sorts out right from wrong, separates what might be possible from what is impossible, and so on; culture, therefore, tells followers whether or not the leader's decision is the right one.

If all the followers had identical values and beliefs, and never changed them, matching decisions with the followers' mind-set would not be a problem. But it always is a problem, because there is no single dominant culture; and the more diverse the following the greater the problem. In theory (and in his rhetoric), Gandhi's target following was the people of India, all of them (more than 300 million in 1931; a billion in 2000). They spoke thirteen different major languages and several hundred minor ones; about 80 percent were Hindu by religion, 10 percent were Muslim, and the rest were Sikh and other sectarian versions of Hinduism, Christian, Jewish, Buddhist, Parsi, and dozens of tribal religions (lumped together as Animist); there were royal families, big businessmen, rich landholders, peasant small-holders, landless laborers, and an urban proletariat; educated people at one end, illiterates at the other; and every one of these categories could be further subdivided, and every division and subdivision was, potentially at least, culturally distinct and able or willing to receive only messages that were tailored to its distinctiveness.

A theoretical answer to this problem is easy: simplify. Leaders must look past the diversity to find what common values followers have, and, if none can be found, they must create a value attractive enough to transcend differences. This search for a transcendent value was apparent in vote-getting strategies used in elections in Orissa in the 1950s. Recall the electoral environment (already briefly described): a high rate of illiteracy, very few radios, no television, most constituencies rural and large in area, and transportation rudimentary; voters in all but a few urban areas inexperienced in electoral procedures, not sophisticated about state or national issues, largely parochial in their sentiments, and party loyalties not a matter of habit; two main parties, the Congress, which was the successor of the Congress Movement that, under Gandhi, had led India into independence, and a party called Ganatantra Parishad, formed and headed by Orissa's dethroned royal families; Congress dominating the coastal half of Orissa (opposed only by a few Communist and Socialist legislators), Ganatantra holding most of the hill regions of western Orissa; a population of about 20 million (about 8 million voters), 140 legislators, 101 constituencies (some constituencies had two-members), and 646 candidates (in the 1957 election); a very marked division in culture between hill and coast, and to a lesser extent between different districts in each of these regions. All of these features meant that politicians had a problem with diversity and needed a strategy to overcome it.

One remedy was thought to be money. I heard many stories about voters in villages being offered four annas (about a quarter of the daily wage of a laborer) for their vote. I never met anyone who admitted taking the four annas, and there were many cheater/cheated tales of voters accepting money from both parties and voting their preference anyway, or about middlemen given money by party agents and keeping it for themselves. Money, of course, could win or lose an election (as it can in the United States—more on that in Chapter 10), but not if used directly to bribe individual voters. No candidate had the organization or the money to do that, and bribery on that scale would surely have been detected and penalized. Money was used, in Orissa as everywhere, to inform (or misinform) the voters. But the problem is still there: What kinds of information will transcend the diversity?

Less crude, but still essentially a strategy of buying support, were promises to steer money from development funds to satisfy local needs—to build a school or a dispensary, or to repair a bridge or build a road. Sometimes the politicians delivered on their promises and consolidated their support in that place. They paid a price, of course: They lost support in villages that got no benefits. The obvious tactical requirement is to dispense favors where they bring in more voters than they lose, so that favors tended to go to local big shots—they sometimes turned out to be only big mouths—who controlled what were called "vote-banks," which were collections of people who would vote (Tammany Hall style) the way the leader of the vote-bank told them, because they trusted him. (In that way the simple money/materialist equation—buying a voter or a follower—is complicated by a small intrusion of morality, in the form of trusting a leader. Such mixtures—at neither extreme but somewhere on the central part of a continuum—are what occurs when abstractions are brought nearer to reality.)

The next set of generalizing strategies do involve moral concerns. One is based on the apparently simple and worldwide notion of "one of us," already encountered in Lloyd George being "of the people" or in the rhetorical use of the vulgarism "Had to kick a little ass there!" Trust, it is assumed, comes easier between people who see themselves as similar in some fundamental way, as kinfolk perhaps, or speaking the same language, or in some other fashion having a common experience of life. It is harder, other things being equal, to put one's faith in someone who is alien in race or ethnicity, language, religion, class, or whatever else, including gender and generation. This is not, however, an absolute; "other things" can sometimes be manipulated. Indeed, successful leadership everywhere depends on being able to rise above in-group prejudices.

When the political parties in Orissa selected a candidate for a constituency, they compared the profile of the candidate with the profile of a modal voter in that constituency. Given "one-of-us" thinking it would seem logical to do so, because a positive profile match should provide an instant bonus of trust. The candidate with a negative match gets a negative payoff: Candidates from the hill region did not contest coastal constituencies; Protestants in Ulster do not run in Catholic areas (or vice versa) in those interludes when representative democracy functions there; and Blacks were not candidates for elective office in the southern United States until, in the 1960s, the federal government, aided by public outrage, took a hand. In India, however, matching candidates with electors was not a simple matter. It might seem common sense to select candidates who, since they could hardly be personally known to the majority of the voters, would at least be known by, for example, their caste; people from that caste might vote for them. But in Orissa that strategy could only have worked in the untypical constituencies (in tribal areas, which were about one-fifth of all constituencies) where a plurality of the voters belonged to one caste. Even then it did not work because all parties selected a candidate from the same caste, thus neutralizing the one-of-us factor. (In practice they often had no choice since many seats in those constituencies were reserved for tribal candidates, one of the many "headstart" measures that free India initiated.)

The next strategy goes beyond bribery and beyond primordial one-of-us notions and relies on making a connection between the candidate and some cause or institution that is both known to the voters and meets with their approval. Twenty-two out of 140 members of the Orissa Legislative Assembly in 1957 belonged to royal families (nineteen kings and three queens). Royalty, throughout India, was pensioned off in 1948, when India became independent. Rajas everywhere lost the political and administrative powers they formerly had. The Orissa rajas, the majority of them domiciled in the western hill areas of the state, formed a political party and contested the 1952 elections, most of them running in areas that had recently been part of their own kingdoms. They were elected (all except one). The charisma conferred by kingship clung to the person-as-legislator, perhaps because kings and MLAs (Member of the Legislative Assembly) are supposed to do a similar job—look to the welfare of their subjects/constituents. Seven ex-rajas also were elected on the Congress ticket. One of them boasted to me that if he had put up his elephant for the seat, it would have won.

The one ex-raja defeated on his own territory lost to a man who had distinguished himself in the same locality as a Freedom Fighter. Like the rajas, the leading erstwhile Freedom Fighters enjoyed name recognition. The seniors among them were men in their late fifties (in Orissa not many women had risen to prominence in the Congress Movement) and had been in politics since the 1920s, giving not just their services but also their whole lives to the Congress, from time to time going to jail, organizing nonviolent protests (with some violence in 1942 and after), arranging mass demonstrations, organizing boycotts of British goods, leading civil disobedience, and—some of them—elected to office in the coastal regions in the mid-1930s when the British allowed a legislature with limited powers to come into existence. These politicians, associates of Gandhi and of Nehru, had a clear start in the coastal regions, but not in the hill regions where the British and the rajas had, except in a few areas, kept the Freedom Fighters out.

By the middle to late 1950s, the significance of the Freedom Fight had begun to fade from Orissa politics. The heroes of that struggle were not forgotten, but the struggle itself no longer dominated the rhetoric of political justification. Both Orissa's chief ministers in that period and the majority of their cabinet ministers had distinguished records in the struggle for independence. But the disillusion that I described earlier had grown, bringing with it room for diverse interests and policies. One of the former chief ministers withdrew from politics to follow the Gandhian way of *sarvodaya* ("everyone's well-being," that is, social work performed as a calling rather than as a profession). There were increasingly sharp divisions between left and right in politics, between those who wanted the Gandhian version of free India and those who followed Nehru into modernism, between hill and coast, between those who advocated development at the grass roots and others who favored large capital projects, and so on. In the decade of the 1950s the former Freedom Fighters discovered that the homogeneity of purpose, which they believed they enjoyed during the struggle for independence, had been lost. There was no single shared vision of the future, neither among themselves nor among the larger group of actors on Orissa's political stage. In theory the common goal was to "implement the Plan." But the Plan itself, and the resources that it offered, provided a thousand bones to contend over, thus adding to, not mitigating, existing diversities.

The movement to and fro between unity and fragmentation of purpose seems to be a natural and inevitable feature of the political process. For a time, heterogeneity—divergent interests and purposes—is held in check, and then, when the goal is achieved and the transcending enemy removed, diversity reasserts itself. I turn now to the first part of that cycle and ask what Gandhi did to create the unity of purpose that, although far from complete, generally characterized the Freedom Fight. In particular I will ask how he was constrained by, overcame, and made use of culture.

What Gandhi Did with Culture

The unity of purpose that Gandhi did create was not complete. There were many Indians who supported the British and were content enough with the imperial rule. They included not only the royal houses but also some of those in the educated and influential upper classes from whom the increasingly large Indian contingent of senior administrative officials was recruited. There were others who would have settled for a greater measure of home rule that fell short of complete independence. Some Muslims joined the Congress Movement; others set up their own organization, the Muslim League, wanting independence but not as part of what they thought would be a Hindu state. (Out of that came Pakistan.) Others, mainly Hindu, differed with Gandhi about tactics, and would have preferred to continue an older style of nationalism that made use of violence and terrorism. The Congress Movement itself from time to time split into factions over the issue of nonviolence, over political differences between socialists and right-center sympathizers, and over regional nationalisms (some Congress leaders in Orissa had difficulty reconciling their loyalty to Orissa with their loyalty to India, both before and especially after independence was won). This catalogue of diversity could be extended, but that is enough to show that the cards were not stacked in Gandhi's favor when, at the end of the First World War, he became the de facto leader of the Congress Movement.

At that time, the Movement was elitist in composition and to some degree in outlook. Beyond the activists there lay, inert, the unmobilized mass of peasants, workers, and petty bourgeois, who worried less about independence for India than about the problems of everyday life. The Movement was founded in 1885 and had been in existence for almost forty years before Gandhi reshaped it. Until that time it had been an association of middle-class, well-educated, professional people of influence and standing. In the early 1920s, when Gandhi took control, the leadership continued to come from that category. Gandhi was a lawyer with professional qualifications gained in London. Nehru, the son of a prominent lawyer-politician, was educated in England at Harrow School and the University of Cambridge. The generation of Congress leaders whom I knew in Orissa in the 1950s were from less exalted backgrounds, but few came from poor families or from low castes; most were born into landowning and/or professional families. They themselves, however, rarely qualified for a profession because they joined the Congress before they had completed their education, enlisting at the time when Gandhi was radically changing the class profile of the Movement.

Devising a strategy (or understanding another person's strategy) is akin to making sense of the world: The only way is to cut through the complexity and assume that things are much simpler than you know them to be. Reduced in that way, Gandhi's task was to win the support of just two categories: the Indian bourgeoisie and the masses. I should make clear at once that Gandhi never talked that way. He insisted—I quoted this earlier—that "all men are brothers" because in all of them was a capacity to recognize the "truth" that God had placed in their hearts; and if one stayed long enough at the task, truth would eventually be found. Everyone, he believed, was open to that epiphany—factions in the Congress that leaned toward violence, British administrators from the viceroy down to the district officer, policemen, petty officials, business tycoons, landlords, moneylenders, high castes, low castes, Untouchables, Muslims, Christians—everyone. He preached, to everyone alike, the sermon of human dignity and human equality to be achieved by *swaraj* (self-rule), *satyagraha* (the nonviolent struggle to find truth), and *sarvodaya* (working for the welfare of all). Those were the themes used in his daily prayer meetings, in his abundant writings, and in his public addresses. Diversity was, in this simple way, refused recognition, its reality implicitly denied; one message would reach all. Nor did he use weaker interpretations as "all men *could* be brothers" or "all men *should* be brothers." *Satyagraha* affirms that the truth *is* there, waiting to be discovered; the mood of truth is indicative, not subjunctive. (From another point of view, Gandhi lived with the propagandist's illusion: Say it often enough and firmly enough and it will be true.)

So much for the talk. What did Gandhi *do* to present himself and his message to the Indian masses? (Once again I stress that we are looking at what his actions mean to an outsider. Whether or not Gandhi would have recognized himself in this interpretation, I do not know.) Earlier photographs of Gandhi—for example, when he practiced law in South Africa—show him dressed like a lawyer, wearing a suit, and a collar and tie, and shoes. But the world knows him in the very different uniform that he adopted from the 1920s onward: shirtless, a dhoti, sandals on his feet, and sometimes a shawl around his shoulders. Those clothes carried a message. In February 1931 Gandhi met with Lord Irwin, the viceroy of India. (At that time the British were making a second attempt to negotiate an end to Gandhi's civil disobedience campaigns.) The meeting provoked an imperial outburst from Churchill, who was revolted by "the nauseating and humiliating spectacle of a one-time Inner Temple lawyer, now seditious fakir, striding half-naked up the steps of the Viceroy's palace, there to negotiate and parley on equal terms with the representative of the King-Emperor."[6]

In the Hobson-Jobson *Anglo-Indian Dictionary* a fakir is "Properly an indigent person, but specially one 'poor in the sight of God,' applied to a Mahommedan religious mendicant, and then, loosely and inaccurately, to Hindu devotees and naked ascetics." Some features of that definition no doubt presented themselves to the mind of any Indian, educated or not, who encountered Gandhi in dhoti and shawl, striding, a staff in hand, bare-headed, often, like any villager, with an umbrella opened against the sun. For us the word "mendicant" stands out—a person who begs and does not work. But in Hindu or Muslim culture the emphasis is on the ascetic style of life and on religion. For a Hindu to live that way is to be a *sannyasin*, a person in the fourth and final stage of life, close to God. The word bundles a cluster of religious connotations, two of which have political significance. First, the *sannyasin* stands outside normal society, rises above its diversity, and therefore is identified with no particular group or interest. Second, to be sufficiently holy is to have mystical powers that are generated by control over the emotions. Mastery of the passions, or *tapas*, can influence events in the world. From "experiments in the spiritual field," Gandhi wrote, he had "gained such power as I possess to work in the political field." He did not mean that he had learned how to keep his head, or his temper, or his confidence when situations were difficult; he meant something much more literal—he could make things happen in the real world, natural or social. In our idiom, he could work miracles. (It is a small irony that when Gandhi spoke of *swaraj*—control over the self or self-rule—he meant control over the passions, and only secondarily political independence.) A nonbeliever finds *tapas* a strange notion. From Churchill (if he knew about it) it would have provoked derision. Neither did Nehru subscribe to that world of enchantment. But others, educated people too, were believers, including the man who asked Gandhi what he could do to make up for his lack of intuition. It surely also was a useful foundation on which to build the popular adoration that made Gandhi the most charismatic of the Congress leaders and enabled him to reshape Congress as a mass movement.

Gandhi's ascetic style has in it a subtext that was addressed less to the peasants than to middle-class, educated Indians. That enraged and scornful comment from Churchill reveals the sense of effortless superiority that most (not all) whites ("pinko-grey" as E. M. Forster calls them) had over their brown-skinned subjects. (E. M. Forster's *A Passage to India* well conveys the complexities of that relationship and the anger and frustration it aroused in Indians.) Churchill packed several resentments into that one sentence. Gandhi had been given the chance to be like an Englishman ("a one-time Inner Temple lawyer") and had rejected it. Worse, he had claimed equality ("negotiate on equal terms") with the highest official in India, the King-Emperor's representative. Worse still, he did so "half-naked" in the garb of a "fakir," a gesture that was disrespectful because it asserted equality between whatever attire the viceroy wore for the occasion and Gandhi's dhoti, equality between the two cultures and the two peoples. India, Gandhi's message was, is a nation, not a dependency.

That subtext was threaded through Gandhi's philosophy and through his presentation of himself. The British—again I stress that this is a stereotype—admired those Indian peoples whom they called the "martial races," such as Sikhs, Pathans, or—cream of the crop— Gurkhas. They were manly, straightforward, soldierly (and therefore *not* nonviolent). The obverse was a creature the British called the Bengali Babu, a low-level clerk, devious, fawning on his superiors, bullying those beneath him, corrupt, lazy, cunning, hopelessly passive when initiative was needed, given to a self-regarding form of religiosity, cowardly and effeminate. On the Bengali Babu the British based a more general colonialist stereotype of the Indian character: passive, self-centeredly religious, overly given to spiritual matters, indifferent to the public weal, unfitted for government and responsibility. Gandhi inverted these characteristics, positing them as Hindu virtues not found in the colonial character, which was obsessed with material things, being greedy, acquisitive, and aggressive. *Satyagraha* and *sarvodaya* together manifested true virtue, which is the courage to abstain from violence, the desire to find truth, and the wish to serve others.

From the early 1920s onward, an impressive number of young middle-class Indians sacrificed their careers (outside politics) to the cause of Indian independence. Why did they do it? They did it for the cause, which was *swaraj*, independence and the end of British rule. Gandhi's larger message that concerned *swaraj* in its other sense (control over the passions) and a form of society (village-based, anti-industrial, antibureaucratic, wholly decentered, and wholly unrealistic in the mid-twentieth century—the "fads" that Nehru said were "not to be encouraged") was mostly set to one side by the practical men who took control of the new India. Some features of the Gandhian style of politics did survive. One was the technique of nonviolent protest. Another was the Gandhian rhetoric—and sometimes the action—of service to others. A third was the idiom that allowed Indians to respect themselves and their culture and to reject the image that their former colonial masters had of them.

A Kind of Dishonesty?

"You can't adopt politics as a profession and remain honest." Did Gandhi "adopt politics" and yet "remain honest"? Bad things have been said about him, and not only by Churchill and the imperialists. I heard Dr. Ambedkar, the leader of the Untouchables, respond in two sentences (on a recorded BBC radio program in the 1950s) to someone who had called Gandhi a saint: "He was no saint. He was a rascal." He did not elaborate. It will be instructive to work out what he might have had in mind.

In 1932, responding to the demands of Ambedkar and perhaps thinking that Gandhi, who abhorred untouchability, would approve, the British government proposed reserved seats in the legislature for

Untouchables (then called "Depressed Classes") to be elected only by Untouchable voters. Gandhi, however, was strongly opposed, believing that separate electorates would only serve to perpetuate divisions (as happened when in 1909 separate electorates were established for Hindus and Muslims). Untouchability would only be ended if all Hindus had a change of heart, and he announced, from the Yeravda prison where he was being held, that unless the proposal was withdrawn he would "fast unto death." This form of suicide has, in Hinduism, an inverted *tapas*-like quality; it visits harm not only on those whose conduct has provoked the fast but on everyone, indiscriminately. Gandhi fasted for six days, each day coming (it was announced) ever nearer to death. Three-part negotiations went on, Ambedkar and the British assuming separate electorates, and talking about how such elections would be conducted, how the candidates would be chosen, and how long separate electorates would remain in existence, and Gandhi holding out against them. Then Ambedkar visited Gandhi in jail and together they reached a compromise very much in Gandhi's favor—no separate electorates and a vague promise that more representation would be given to Untouchables. The "Yeravda Pact" was signed and subsequently approved by the British government, and Gandhi ended six days of the "Epic Fast" by drinking a celebratory glass of orange juice.

In fact the negotiation with Ambedkar and with the British government was no more than a sideshow, almost a feint, an occasion for something much larger and more fundamental. Entering the fast Gandhi had said, "If the Hindu mass mind is not yet ready to banish untouchability root and branch it must sacrifice me without the slightest hesitation."[7] Hindus, it became clear, were not ready to sacrifice him. Here is Nehru's description of the response (he had been complaining about the "religious and sentimental approach to a political question"): "Then came the news of the tremendous upheaval all over the country, a magic wave of enthusiasm running through Hindu society, and untouchability appeared to be doomed."[8] He added the sentence quoted earlier: "What a magician, I thought, was this little man sitting in Yeravda prison, and how well he knew how to pull the strings that move people's hearts."

Ambedkar thought him a "rascal" and rascals are by definition dishonest. In the Yeravda episode where is the dishonesty? The *Oxford English Dictionary* suggests that the honest person is "sincere, truthful,

candid" and does not "lie, cheat, or steal," and is "a law-abiding man."
I would guess that Howe, who said that politics and honesty could not
go together, had in mind insincerity and probably also lying, cheating,
stealing, and other criminal activities. Those sleazy features, however,
were certainly not, in any direct and unambiguous way, part of
Gandhi's political repertoire. What, then, had Ambedkar seen in
Gandhi's politics?

I think he saw the fundamental dishonesty that rational minds suspect in the mysticism of an educated and otherwise intelligent person.
Ambedkar, born an Untouchable, against all the odds and with luck,
determination, and some patronage, was educated at Columbia
University in New York and at the London School of Economics, and
was, like Gandhi, called to the bar in London. He despised what
Nehru had called "revivalism," probably with even more feeling than
Nehru, since he was himself, as an Untouchable, victimized by Hindu
beliefs. He valued rational argument and used it to the full when he
became one of the main architects of the Indian Constitution that was
written immediately after independence. To the extent that he could,
he wrote Gandhian ideals out of the Constitution, saying, of Gandhi's
desire for a village-based nation, "I hold that these village republics
have been the ruination of India. What is the village but a sink of
localism, a den of ignorance, narrow-mindedness and communal-
ism?"[9] Such firmly rational minds have only two ways to interpret
mysticism. If the proponent of mysticism is also a true believer, then
he is a fool. But fools are not rascals, which leads to the other conclusion. Those who talk mysticism, to the extent they are intelligent,
must know that what they are saying is false; they do not believe in it,
and are therefore hypocrites who misuse other people's superstitions
for their own advantage. Since Ambedkar believed that fasting had
not a hope of ending untouchability (and that Gandhi knew it),
Gandhi's motive must have been his own aggrandizement; the
Untouchables were merely being used. (An analogous instrumentality is implied, but not condemned, in Nehru's comment about the
strings of people's hearts.)

Howe's apothegm, amended by Ambedkar, would read: "You can't
adopt politics as a profession and see yourself as honest, unless you are
naïve." Gandhi's own devotee, Sarojini Naidu, referring ironically to
his life-style, said, "If only Bapu knew the cost of setting him up in
poverty!" That comment, coming from her, surely pointed to

Gandhi's otherworldliness, his naïveté. The same words, if said by Ambedkar, would have been a charge of hypocrisy—that the ascetic life was a public-relations gimmick.

That, of course, is not the end of the story. What is considered honest changes from culture to culture, from situation to situation, and, of course, from person to person; it depends on who gets to define the situation. We will come to those complexities, still in the context of Gandhi and India's struggle against the British, later.

Part *THREE*

How to Win: Leaders and Opponents

*It must be considered that there is nothing
more difficult to carry out, nor more doubtful
of success, nor more dangerous to handle, than
to initiate a new order of things. For the
reformer has enemies in all those who profit by
the old order, and only lukewarm defenders in
those who would profit by the new order, this
lukewarmness arising partly from fear of their
adversaries, who have the laws in their favour;
and partly from the incredulity of mankind,
who do not truly believe in anything new until
they have had actual experience of it.*

—Machiavelli, *The Prince*

- This third part of the book is about the strategies that leaders use to defeat their adversaries and shape political structures to their own design. It also is about the unintended and unanticipated patterns that emerge in this competitive process.
- Strategies are partly shaped by the existing order, which I interpret more fundamentally than Machiavelli to mean the presuppositions, which everyone carries with them into a political arena, about how things are and how they should be.
  - One set of presuppositions concerns the adversarial nature of politics: Why do people fight? Chapter 7 describes some alternative answers to that question, derived from different views of human nature.

- Another set concerns the political process, analyzed as a function of three kinds of rules:
- normative, which prescribe proper conduct;
- strategic, which advise on effective moves;
- and pragmatic, which describe strategies that are effective but violate normative rules.
- This framework is set out in Chapter 8. The neat distinctions that it makes are blurred in reality by the coexistence in any situation of more than one normative framework and by the consequent ambiguous status of particular actions. This ambiguity makes it possible for leaders to deploy strategies intended to alter (or maintain) a particular "order of things."
- Chapters 9–12 are organized around three persons—two historical and one fictional—who in their different ways defied an existing "order of things" in order to change it, to escape its control, or, paradoxically, to protect it.
- Lyndon Baines Johnson anchors Chapters 9 and 10, in the first (mainly his presidential years) as a superb strategist, in the second (campaigning earlier for a seat in the Senate) as an uninhibited pragmatist.
- Chapter 11 provides, first, a view from below where recalcitrant rank-and-file people make their own political space and covertly defy regnant structures; second, it briefly discusses factionalism, in which defiance of any kind of structure is open, uninhibited, and likely to produce chaos.
- Chapter 12, taking off from a discussion of factions in the previous chapter, is about revolutions, which are overt attempts to displace a regnant structure and put another in its place. The revolutionary process, I will argue, in a renewed discussion of Gandhi's campaign to end British rule in India, can be understood by the same basic model that makes all political processes comprehensible. In that model the competing designs that people present are clear and unambiguous; the reality is all confusion and compromise.

7

Can't We All Get Along?

- This chapter describes the notions that people have about why contests occur. There are three basic models.
  - People fight because they do not like one another; the winner's prize is to witness the loser's pain.
  - A fight is over something that is in short supply; liking or disliking is irrelevant, because the contestants are modeled as being entirely rational. When both sides realize that the cost of fighting exceeds any possible benefits, they will not fight.
  - In the third model, people fight because they have not yet understood that fighting is evil and togetherness is good.
- Each model suggests a strategy for dealing with opponents: They can be terrorized; they can be bought; or they can be persuaded. The choice of strategy affects the nature and course of the encounter, producing patterns that will be examined in later chapters.

Evaluating Struggle

I begin with an incident that happened some years back. The account is taken from the World Wide Web and, although written in the style of an objective report, it is distinctly partisan. (I have corrected a few misspellings; some misinformation that the document contains will come to light as we go along.)

Rodney King is a black man who is known by the police. He has been arrested by the police twice for violent crimes. He was a drunken paroled robber and briefly out of prison, he was also known for drunk driving and assaulting his wife.

On the night of March 3, 1991 there was a car chase between the police and Rodney King, he was driving about a 100 miles per hour. When they finally stopped him, he was (according to the police) acting in a way that frightened the police. Then they started to beat him up.

A couple in the neighborhood woke up because of the noise, and taped the episode. They only taped from when the beatings began, not the car chase. Nothing that preceded the beatings on the tape had been recorded. They sent the tape to a news station, and the tape was shown all over the world the same day.

It took almost a year before the trial of the four officers accused of beating Rodney King began. The media followed the case in every detail. The jury couldn't find criminal fault and the officers were found not guilty of all charges.

Then the riots in Los Angeles exploded. Black people ravaged the city, they were attacking innocent white people. The riots caused the death of 53 people, nearly 2,000 arrests and property damages for 1 billion dollars.

King's in-laws persuaded him to switch to a black lawyer and limit his interviews to black reporters. In 1994 the strategy paid off to the tune of a 3.8 million dollars jury award in a civil suit against the city of Los Angeles.

I will have more to say later about this document and the attitudes it reveals, and about the incident itself. Here I want to note something that Rodney King himself, reacting to the riots, is reported to have said: "Can't we all get along?" Whether or not those are his exact words, I do not know, but the implication is clear enough: Conflict is not inevitable; it can be avoided. It is like a sickness that in practice can be controlled and, at least in principle, perhaps could be eliminated. King's plaintive words were repeated again and again on television and radio and in the newspapers; clearly they expressed a sentiment that caught the public's (or at least the media's) imagination.

Not every motorist pulled over for speeding, not even those who attempt to get away, are brutally beaten by the police, and even those who are beaten or shot for resisting arrest are not inevitably the occasion for civil disturbances on the scale of the 1992 riots in Los Angeles. (In fact the immediate reason for the rioting was the acquittal of the policemen who did the beating. Later they were charged with violating King's civil rights and two of them were convicted and imprisoned, a fact left out of the account given above.) Some speeding motorists—not many in this part of the world—get off with a warning. Most get a ticket, are fined, have an entry made in their driving record, and may have their insurance premiums raised. In those cases the contest between the offender and the policeman does not get beyond an embryonic stage. Other cases are disputed and settled later by a court hearing. A few erupt directly into extreme violence when a motorist—occasionally a policeman—is shot. Rarely does the incident provoke public disorder, as it did in the case of Rodney King. Thus encounters vary from the virtually orderly, where actions and reactions stay within the expected bounds of rules and regulations, to those that give rise to chaos. How far an encounter moves in the direction of conflict and chaos is clearly a variable that prompts one to ask what else varies along with the nature and severity of the encounter?

In the Rodney King affair the immediate answers that dominated public discussion began with the fact that he was a black man and the officers who assaulted him and who were acquitted at the first trial were white. (That trial was held in an area, Simi Valley, where the majority population was white, and consequently so also were all twelve members of the jury.) A commission of inquiry, chaired by Warren Christopher, was appointed and released a report one hundred days after the beating. It made public many instances of the use of excessive force by the police and included a large number of recorded police messages in which racially offensive terms were used to describe minorities, in particular blacks.

But racial issues constitute only the beginning of an explanation for the chaos that followed Rodney King's beating. Racism apart, one can also ask about the style of the Los Angeles Police Department. Police forces vary from, at one extreme, the caricatured English "Bobby," everybody's friend, whose main function is to tell people who don't have a watch what the time is (now, in the United States, dubbed "community policing"), to, at the other extreme, a conspicuously armed paramilitary force that rides around in automobiles and talks to no one unless they are giving (or in) trouble. Obviously the second type is more likely to be involved in contests than the first, and those contests are likely to turn into violent encounters. Institutional features of that kind will explain (in part) why the Rodney King affair escalated so dramatically.

These explanations segue into more generalized ideologies about the form of the good society and the nature of the people who live in it. Then—last in the line—there are general notions about human nature and the value or disvalue put on conflict itself. All of these explanatory variables, arranged, so to speak, in a series of concentric circles from the specific to the general around the incident of Rodney King's beating, contribute to the way people make sense of what happens and construct for themselves whatever strategies they feel they might need.

I should make clear exactly what is to be investigated. My focus is on politics and primarily on strategies. I will not try to construct, *directly*, profiles of human nature. Instead, my interest is at one remove, pointed to the models that people use when *they* construct profiles of what is going on in the mind of another person. Out of these profiles (and other data) they build strategies.

Strategies and Human Nature

Rodney King's phrase "get along" has two referents that may be connected in practice but often are not, and certainly are analytically distinct. One is hard-headed and the other is sentimental. The team of woodsmen who pruned my Torrey pine tree (Chapter 3) did so with perfect coordination and efficiency, getting on with the job in a faultlessly coordinated manner. Whether they liked one another or not, I have no idea. Nor, in logic, is liking a necessary or a sufficient condition for good teamwork. The idealized bureaucracy functions harmoniously just because idealized bureaucrats lack the capacity to like or dislike. Perhaps there was an element of that essentially bureaucratic notion in what Rodney King said: If the institutions had been in good order, if the police force had satisfactorily policed itself according to its own rules, if justice had been regularly done in the courts, then, notwithstanding racial antipathies, there would have been no beating and no riots. That interpretation, however, is less plausible than the common one that takes emotions into account: In that phrase "get along" Rodney King had in mind the virulent racial anger that often informs dealing between different ethnicities in Los Angeles (and elsewhere). In other words, sentiments of harmony come before institutional arrangements; if the attitudes are right, the institutions will adjust themselves accordingly. (That was Gandhi's view of the world; I will come to it shortly.) Probably, also, that philosophy caused Rodney King's words to resonate with the public, most of whom see "getting along" as a function less of institutions than of emotions and human nature.

In this philosophy, it seems, mutual respect and mutual love, harmony, and cooperation are good, and making them part of human nature will, ipso facto, build them into the institutional reality. But that point of view is not universally accepted. In fact the public—those who speak for it—when they think about the part conflict plays or should play in social life, look in two directions. War gets mixed reviews. The Beatles sang "Give peace a chance." We pray for "peace in our time." Shakespeare spells out what its absence means: "Tumultuous wars/Shall kin with kin and kind with kind confound;/Disorder, horror, fear, and mutiny/Shall here inhabit" (*Richard II*, act IV, scene i). On the other hand, "Let me have war, say I; it exceeds peace as far as day does night. . . . Peace is very apoplexy, lethargy: mulled, deaf, sleepy, insensible" (*Coriolanus*, act IV, scene v). In Bertolt Brecht's *Mother Courage* we read: "They have gone too long without a war here. What is the moral, I ask. Peace is nothing but slovenliness, only war creates order." Rarely, when you listen to those who have fought in a war, will you fail to hear praise for the good and desirable qualities that war fosters and enhances, not bravery and the martial virtues alone but also endurance, self-sacrifice, and, above all, comradeship. That message resonates in novels and poems, particularly those of the First World War, even when it is conjoined with a detestation of war itself and an utter contempt for military institutions and military values.

Nor is the sentiment that good qualities emerge from strife confined to such apocalyptic settings. There is an opinion that (to improve on Socrates) the uncontested life is not worth living. We need the stimulus; it is part of our nature to strive against others and to want to win, and those not given the chance to prove themselves in combat are unfulfilled. Aggression—an eagerness for combat—comes with the species; it is a part of human nature and cannot be denied. Nor should it be denied, because without it we remain inert, accom-

plishing nothing, attempting nothing, worth nothing. Such sentiments appear also on small stages, as in the comment of a feisty university dean whom I interviewed a year after he had retired from
office. He had come up the hard way: a worker, a foreman, and then
a manager in a factory, later a degree and a doctorate in political science. The story of his life (as he told it), both before and in the university, was an epic of (usually victorious) encounters, ostensibly and
ultimately with situations and problems, but primarily with people
who got in the way of what he wanted done because they were too stupid to see what was best, or (an irony) too concerned with winning
battles. Retirement from the deanship was a let-down: "Just some
teaching and some writing. Life is dull. No more fights! You need
fights to stay alive."

That remark, however, is not a good clue to the way he ran his
office. He did not base his strategies on the assumption that other
people were programmed for aggression, fighting because they liked
to fight. What he called "fights" turned out to be encounters that had
more in common with a poker game than with the clash between
Rodney King and the LAPD. His colleagues, some of whom I interviewed, thought he was tough, generally effective, usually fair, certainly useful, although by no means lovable. He was in fact a very
unsentimental person and the strategies he used, despite the virtues
that he claimed to find in strife and despite his aggressive manner,
were based on the assumption that victory in combat was not an
important element in his colleagues' mind-set. The aggression directed at Rodney King—and his provoking of it—starts with a presump-
tion (revealed both in actions and in the words recorded on police
tapes) that the other person will certainly fight. The dean, on the
other hand, knew that his colleagues could be made to listen to reason; in other words, they could be controlled by demonstrating to
them that they would benefit from doing what he wanted them to do,
and they would pay a material price if they did not do it. Every man,
so to speak, had his price and the dean knew what it was.

As I listened to him, and now as I read over my record of the interview, he seemed not to have much respect for those who were in his
charge or for those above him in the hierarchy, with the exception of
one man whom he described (in what seems to me a contradiction) as
"very smart, very cunning, totally honest, straight as a die." The disdain in which he held the members of his faculty was not expressed in

words of direct denigration but in stories of how simple it was to manipulate them into doing what he wanted done. They needed him to show them what was in their own best interest; he served them by protecting them from their own foolishness, making sure that their instinct to put their own particular interests ahead of everyone else's and their disregard for the general interest did not end in everyone's undoing. He surely would not have been pleased to hear me make the comparison, but I can see a distant similarity between his patronizing attitude and the way Los Angeles policemen looked down on inner-city blacks. The motto painted on police cars, however, might not have offended him: *Protect and Serve.*

Of course there are differences. The dean did not fear his faculty; he did not see them as dangerous to himself; quite the reverse—they were like children, a danger to *themselves.* Fear, however, is written all over the encounter between Rodney King and the policemen (on both sides). Fear excludes the idea that the opponent might be rationally persuaded to behave rationally. The dean, far from being afraid, was protected by a sense of effortless superiority that recalls Rudyard Kipling's colonial administrator who took on "the White Man's burden" and ruled over his "sullen peoples,/Half-devil and half-child." (Besides fear, there are also some obvious institutional-contextual differences between the dean's case and that of the LAPD. I will come to them later.)

What the dean and the policemen do share, I suggest, is the belief that to ask "Can't we all get along?" is pointless, because that is not the way things are. It is a plain fact that we do not get along and, given that fact, the proper task can only be to so manage the situation that the least harm is done. Both the dean and the Los Angeles policemen (perhaps not all, but certainly those who confronted Rodney King) start with a presupposition that human nature (Shakespeare's "affections") is fixed and simple and a determinant of strategy. The dean and the police of course make different assumptions about human nature, and use different strategies: control by reward versus control by punishment. But neither the dean nor the police contemplate going deeper and seeking to change their opponents' mind-set to make it possible for everyone to "get along." The dean in fact had a hard-nosed contempt for those who thought they could manage institutions successfully on the basis of "moral platitudes." One didn't try to change human nature; one adapted to it, and exploited it.

I should have talked to the dean about Gandhi, but I did not think of it at the time. I suspect that he would have said that Dr. Ambedkar got it right: Gandhi was a cunning tactician and the morality he preached about the need to "get along" was only what one said on public occasions, not what one did to keep things in good order. Alternatively, he might have decided that Gandhi was naïve and simply mistaken; leadership must start with the assumption that everyone is self-interested; and the debacle of Partition in India and the violence in which half a million people were slaughtered clearly demonstrated the need to base policies on the assumption that morality is not enough and there can be no "getting along" without institutional constraints. If that is the case, I might have asked the dean, how is it that Gandhi, more than anyone else, was the leader who succeeded in driving the British out of India. How much credit for that goes to Gandhi's strategy, and whether the strategy he publicly advocated was in fact the one that brought freedom to India, are questions that I have already briefly discussed. The strategy, however, deserves a more detailed examination, because, unlike the LAPD and the dean, Gandhi did assume that human nature is not rock-like, not a given, but is a *potentiality*, something unformed that can be shaped in such a way that we will all be able to get along.

In Gandhi's case there is a formidable wealth of detailed evidence on which to draw. In contrast, my portrait of the LAPD philosophy is stark and unsubtle, deduced from media accounts of policemen's behavior and from statements by the police themselves and various other people (also reported by the media, most of it in the *Los Angeles Times*) about the way the police view both themselves and the people they deal with. Thus my analysis is made at several removes, it is a portrait of a portrait of a portrait: my take on the media's take on the policemen's take on what goes on in the minds of people like Rodney King, each remove being a simplification abstracted from its predecessor, and all the portrayers (including myself) with an ax to grind. This process produces clarity of a sort but also comes near to caricature, to what is now condemned as "essentialism." The portrait is un-nuanced. In the case of the dean there is only my interpretation of what he said about himself and his colleagues in the course of a two-hour interview, and my interpretation of what his colleagues said about him. Here too the representation that emerges is relatively uncomplex. That, however, is not the case with Gandhi: His philosophy is described, interpreted, and reinterpreted in hundreds upon hundreds of publications. There is a publishing house in Ahmedabad devoted entirely to his writings and writings about him, and on the cover of one of the many anthologies of his sayings and writings (*All Men Are Brothers*, compiled by Krishna Kripalani) are listed twenty-two books by Gandhi himself.

It is quite difficult for (as Nehru put it) "an average modern" to follow Gandhi's reasoning, and it is still more difficult to work out how his philosophy of nonviolent resistance to injustice, when translated into strategy and put into practice, could have been effective in driving the British out of India. Yet, up to a point, it was; and the British certainly failed to find an effective counterstrategy. Gandhi, on the other hand, had more or less correctly anticipated how the British would react to nonviolent forms of protest and resistance. To a surprising extent (although certainly not on all occasions) they colluded by responding to nonviolent protest with measures that, for sure by Rodney King standards, were also nonviolent.

The center of Gandhi's philosophy is the not uncommon idea that truth exists and it is single; one can meaningfully speak of *the* truth. Gandhi's idea of truth is revealed in an illuminating exchange in 1920 between him and an English lawyer before the Hunter Commission, which had been appointed to inquire into the deaths of four hundred civilians and the wounding of a thousand others when soldiers, under the command of General Dyer, opened fire on an antigovernment rally in Amritsar in April 1919. In March of that year Gandhi had launched a nonviolent protest against the continuation of certain wartime laws that curtailed civil liberties. These protests turned violent; shops were looted, buildings set on fire, and several English civilians, including a woman, were murdered. Gandhi immediately called off the campaign, announcing that he had made a "Himalayan blunder." He called on his followers to fast for twenty-four hours, and himself fasted for three days. But the protests and the violence continued, culminating in the massacre in the Jallianwalla Gardens.

The Hunter Commission's counsel, probably wondering, as I am doing now, in what contexts nonviolence could be effective, asked about truth.

COUNSEL: However honestly a man may strive in his search for truth, his notions of truth may be different from the notions of others. Who then is to determine the truth?

GANDHI: The individual himself would determine that.
COUNSEL: Different individuals would have different views as to truth. Would that not lead to confusion?
GANDHI: I do not think so.[1]

The lawyer emerges from this exchange as another "average modern," puzzled because for him truth was a "notion," whereas for Gandhi it was a metaphysical absolute that was the foundation of society and the potential instrument of our ability to "all get along." *Satyagraha*, "the struggle for truth," is not a struggle between individuals, one against the other, but rather a cooperative endeavor to find truth through an exchange of opinions. Truth is attained when all concerned *voluntarily* agree on what is truth; truth can never be imposed by violence; it can only be accepted.

This procedure seems not unfamiliar to us: a kind of give-and-take that sounds like negotiation. But negotiation was *not* what Gandhi had in mind; in *satyagraha* there is no element of bargaining, no idea of making compromises, of giving up a part of what one wants in return for concessions from the other side. Gandhi's "negotiation" is wholly cooperative, not a bargaining session or even a debate but rather a discussion that will uncover the one and only truth. Neither party bargains, yielding up a portion of its "truth" in the process. There is only one truth and it is not theirs to be bargained away; it is something absolute, which belongs to no one other than God. Given this concept of truth, the domain of politics has been subsumed into religion. In Kripalani's anthology this passage occurs: "There is an indefinable and mysterious Power that pervades everything. I feel it, though I do not see it. It is this unseen power which makes itself felt and yet defies all proof, because it is so unlike all that I perceive through my senses."[2] Elsewhere: "I believe that we can all become messengers of God, if we cease to fear man and seek only God's Truth. I do believe I am seeking only God's Truth and have lost all fear of man."[3] And: "*Ahimsa* [nonviolence] is soul-force . . . when soul-force is fully awakened in us, it becomes irresistible."[4]

How do such truth-seeking encounters—efforts to uncover innate human goodness—turn out in practice? Gandhi would probably not have liked the word "encounter," which hints at hostility. Yet I think that in reality Gandhian truth-seeking exchanges can only be encounters, not with a problem in the course of searching for its solution, but between individuals, victory going to the contestants who most obstinately hold on to their own notion of truth. One can read such encounters—look again at Gandhi's answers to the Hunter Committee's counsel—as a game of chicken, the first to yield being the loser. Gandhi said it himself, "Strength does not come from physical capacity. It comes from an indomitable will."[5] He himself had that stubborn quality. Recall Nehru's comment: "One has the impression that one is addressing a closed door." Where that strength came from is revealed in the sentences quoted above (being one of the "messengers of God," the "unseen power" that stands with him, having "lost all fear of man," and the "irresistible soul-force"). The practical entailments of those metaphysical phrases are a strategy for struggle that, Gandhi's belief notwithstanding, is less a matter of finding truth than of imposing one's will on reluctant others. If one drops the notion of a single truth, the struggle is to make one version of truth prevail over other versions (as counsel in the Hunter inquiry was trying respectfully to suggest). The real situation, in other words, is a "negotiation" to define the situation, with one party (Gandhi) unwilling to make concessions—therefore, it is a contest.

The dean operated through negotiation, often pitching his initial demands (or threats) high enough to make room for concessions later, to convince his colleagues that his version of what should be done was superior to theirs and was truly in their interests. Gandhi's "negotiations" are different and are aimed at psychological transformation. He entirely rejected appeals to material self-interest in favor of a moral imperative, *sarvodaya*, which is to serve others. Nevertheless, *sarvodaya* had a payoff, not material but spiritual, in the form of self-respect. Nonviolence also promoted self-respect and was intended, in addition, to win the respect of others, even an opponent's. Nonviolence was not cowardice: "The people of a village near Bettia told me they had run away whilst the police were looting their houses and molesting their womenfolk. When they said they had run away because I had told them to be nonviolent, I hung my head in shame. . . . Such was not the meaning of my nonviolence. . . . It was manly enough to defend one's property, honour, or religion at the point of the sword. It was manlier and nobler still to defend them without seeking to injure the wrongdoer."[6] Nonviolence ennobled the resister and shamed the attacker. The *satyagrahi* gained self-respect; his opponent lost it.

The villagers, I am sure, understood what Gandhi meant when he talked of the "point of the sword" and in doing so they probably contemplated the risks of striking back at rampaging policemen. I am also sure that they were no more clear than I am about what Gandhi meant them to do when he talked of the nobler and manlier course of nonviolence, apart perhaps from engaging the police in a dialogue with a view to having them agree that their conduct was unethical—which is hard to imagine. The sticking point is that nonviolent protest rests on the very large assumption that the attackers are, at the very time their adrenaline is in full flow, capable of feeling guilt. Sometimes, perhaps, they might look back on what they have done and feel remorse. General Dyer did not; he was convinced that he did the right thing by shooting all those people in the Jallianwalla Gardens, believing that by making an example of them he prevented violence that might have broken out elsewhere; thus he saved lives. That is the fallback excuse for police violence everywhere.

There is another dubious assumption in Gandhi's philosophy of nonviolence—that the attackers will not see passivity as weakness or cowardice, but will respect the victim's courage. But that higher kind of courage, which is manifested in a refusal to strike back in self-defense, is certainly not practiced by policemen anywhere, even in the most disciplined forces, nor do many of them respect it. There is also a third assumption, which in many cases does not obtain, that the attackers have some residual respect for their victims as a class or category. It came out in the Hunter inquiry that General Dyer, born and educated in India, had a huge and perfectly racist contempt for Indians. He gave out an order (which his superiors swiftly canceled) requiring all Indians passing a place in an Amritsar street where a woman missionary had been attacked to crawl on their hands and knees. In Los Angeles the Christopher inquiry brought to light a similar gross racial intolerance. When the victims are already completely dehumanized, no amount of courageous nonviolent endurance will make the attackers feel guilty.

For Gandhi this was not a problem: *Satyagraha*, the struggle for truth, was an end in itself, not a strategy to be judged by its results. The victims could respect themselves, and that was enough. There are, however, other and less soul-concerned ways to see such situations. If the strategy is judged by results, there is an obvious payoff if attackers who are themselves immune to feelings of *guilt* can be struck by *shame*, which is awakened by the opinion of other people about them, especially when that opinion brings on material penalties. General Dyer's military career came to an end; two of Rodney King's attackers went to prison. If there is a strongly disapproving third party, such as public opinion or higher authorities who can be made to feel disgust or, better still, vicarious guilt, then the refusal to fight back may be an effective strategy. Had there been no man with a video camera recording what happened to Rodney King, and had he not sent it to a news station, or had the station refused to air it, then given his record King would have been convicted of dangerous driving, of driving when drunk, and of resisting arrest. He would have gone to prison and no more would have been heard of the matter; there would have been no riots. Instead he became a martyr in the cause of oppressed minorities. The presence of a scandalized third party— public opinion—made the difference. Nonviolence worked in the southern United States not because the police and the political authorities there felt guilty about the violence they used on blacks and on white protesters, but because the nation at large was outraged, just as it was in the case of Rodney King. There is always the risk, of course, that not enough people, or not enough significant people, will be ashamed; the Simi Valley jurors evidently were not. There was a vigorous agitation, both in India and in England, in support of General Dyer as the "Saviour of India."

No doubt there are other people besides Gandhi who see nonviolence as a moral absolute, an end in itself. No doubt also they derive from that belief qualities of tenacity and courage that make them politically significant. But from a less spiritual perspective the significance of nonviolence is not what it does for the individual's soul but the way it is read by the bystanders, third parties in the encounter, and the capacity it has to move them to action. This can result in curious inversions—travesties—of Gandhi's strategy. I talked with a young man in India who, long after Gandhi was dead and India was free, led protest movements against the government. The protests were always announced as nonviolent and involved assembling large crowds, blockading government buildings (post offices and police stations were favorite targets), preventing the passage of trains, and so forth. Many of them ended in disorder. I recall him giving me a perfectly cynical lesson in the strategy of nonviolent protest. The key to success, he said, was to confront the police or the soldiers robustly enough to make them open fire, but not too much or too often. More than a few casualties put an end to a protest; people went home. But a stray bullet in the early stages of the encounter, when the police generally fired over the heads of the crowd, that killed just one person was the ideal. That single person, whoever he or she was, an activist or just a passerby, became a martyr for the cause and of great use to the protest organizers. Once again I should have asked the young man what Gandhi would have thought of this strategy, which is surely a very *Realpolitik* version of *satyagraha*.

In this chapter I have looked at three radically different definitions of human nature that contribute to three different strategies for making the other person do what you want him to do. General Dyer and the Los Angeles Police Department (insofar as it is adequately represented by what was done to Rodney King) dehumanize the opponent, who at best is seen as a Pavlovian half-wit to be domesticated and kept in order by the threat—and the experience—of pain. Respect for one another does not feature in this situation, neither for the controllers nor the controlled, unless one reduces the idea of respect to plain fear. (The word sometimes has that meaning. I once heard a tenant in a slum apartment house complain about cockroaches: "They don't give you no respect.") The dean's strategy for dealing with his colleagues likewise implies a disrespectful definition of them, but mildly so: They are greedy, short-sighted, and unable to see that the general interest (as he defines it) can also be their own best interest. No violence is involved: The institutional setting does not provide for it. Nor is it necessary so long as the dean can efficiently manipulate rewards and threaten deprivations. (I did visit one campus where the system had broken down to the extent that a meeting between the dean and the collectivity of his colleagues, which I was allowed to observe, consisted only of complaint and countercomplaint delivered in words that were the verbal equivalent of brawling.)

Gandhi's world was different from both of these. For him there are no opponents because, as he said, "all men are brothers," and therefore they share a common humanity and are able to cooperate with one another. Neither fear nor material rewards are needed, and to enforce cooperation by the use or threat of force is to make cooperation impossible. Education, in a very literal sense of "drawing out" the good qualities that are inherent in us all (Gandhi's "truth" or "soul-force"), is the right strategy. The difficulty, as I have suggested, is that "truth" of that kind can be found only in a few contexts and is by no means the default situation. If it existed at all in General Dyer or in the policemen who beat up Rodney King, it was buried deep enough to be inaccessible.

These three definitions of human nature—savage, calculating, or educable—are analytic. They are linked to strategies, and although the strategies are logically distinct from one another and in various ways mutually contradictory, they can be deployed serially or even simultaneously in any one contest. Politicians are likely to be poor strategists if they remain always consistent with themselves. The political art, as I said, is to win an encounter by doing what the opponent has not anticipated. Strategies change, and along with them the definitions of human nature change. Gandhi, as Nehru said, could intimidate people; he also knew how to make a deal, as he did in many of his encounters with representatives of the British government. In addition to the strong-arm style of law and order there is also community policing, and there are many occasions, especially in emergencies, when the police are seen as protectors and servers. In other words, the three leadership styles—force, rewards, moral persuasion—are ingredients that go into a strategic mix in different proportions for different situations.

In that mix there are other ingredients, which have to do with differences in institutions and in culture. They are more complicated than those involved in judgments about human nature alone. I will approach them in the next chapter by describing some basic concepts that are needed to construct a grammar of strategies.

8

Three Types of Rule

- Ideas about human nature that shape strategies are relatively simple, offering only a few alternatives. Ideas about institutions are much more complex and present a huge variety of alternatives, which must be reduced to a few general categories in order to select a suitable strategy or to understand a political process. One way to do this is to rewrite institutions in the form of rules.
- There are three kinds of rule: normative, strategic, and pragmatic. All three serve as both constraints and resources for contestants, and, along with goals, shape their strategies.
  - normative rules prescribe the proper forms of interaction, both cooperative and combative;
  - strategic rules tell a competitor how to win; and
  - pragmatic rules, a subset of strategic rules, evade (but do not openly challenge) normative restrictions.
- The neat analytic distinction between the three types is blurred in practice because allocating any particular action to one or another category is a matter of opinion and the allocation can serve as a weapon. In that case rules are not guides for action but rhetorical tools to justify or condemn actions.
- The situation is further complicated by the presence, in a single situation, of contradictory normative frameworks. Beyond them lies an implacable reality that, often later rather than sooner, decides which normative frames are fit to survive.

- The chapter closes with an outline of the model of politics and social change that will shape the rest of the book.

Institutional Frameworks and Rule-types

The difference between leader–*follower* and leader–*opponent* interactions is at first sight quite uncomplicated: cooperation in the first case and, in the second, an adversarial encounter out of which comes a winner and a loser. But in fact the world of politics cannot be realistically represented in that simple way. Roosevelt's relationship with his followers ran the range from a simulacrum of trust and intimacy, which caused people to respond to his radio talks with confessions of their personal hopes and worries, to the cynical and sometimes cruel manipulation that he used to play off members of his entourage against one another. Another American president, Lyndon Johnson, was powerful and effective (until he took a fall over the Vietnam War) just because he knew how to make deals that turned opponents into allies, ready to cooperate with him, at least for the occasion. (More about him later.) Gandhi—a third example of how the real world confounds neat analytical distinctions—insisted that the political process could be entirely one of cooperation, and need never be adversarial. In short, the clear binary division between followers and opponents, between cooperation and contest, which abstract thinking makes possible, is blurred when confronted with reality. Reality is the continuum that earlier I called *competition*. Therefore we need a model that conjoins cooperation and conflict as a variable and attends to the forces that push toward one or the other end of the continuum.

The variable that locates an encounter or a strategy on that continuum is the extent to which antagonists allow themselves to be directed by the rules of fair play, in other words, by the degree to which their confrontation is kept orderly by an institutional framework. The word "institution" is used in two connected ways. A university is an institution; so is a hospital, a nunnery, the military, the U.S. Senate, the Supreme Court, the British Parliament, and so on. These are relatively concrete things; you can be educated in them, treated in them, retreat into them, enlist in them, be appointed to them, or be elected to them. But marriage also is an institution; so is democracy, the family, and inheritance or succession to office; so is criminal law and civil law and every other kind of law; so is the housing market or the job market or the stock exchange; so is boxing or football or any other organized sport; and also capitalism, literary criticism, and many other isms. Any interaction that is bound by rules can be read as an institution.

Institutions of this second kind are sets of values or conventions or rules that define appropriate and inappropriate behavior and so permit relatively orderly interaction between persons. Soldiers, professors, healthcare workers, legislators, and judges each have their own distinctive values—bravery, scholarship, compassion for the sick, concern for the public weal, justice, and so on—that can be translated into a code of conduct, both cooperative and adversarial. Seen in this way the two meanings of the word come together: universities, hospitals, the military, and so forth also can be written out as sets of rules.

These rules may be formal, codified as laws and regulations, or they may be matters of etiquette or convention. We sometimes talk of "mere" conventions, implying that they are trivial because they are not formally sanctioned by the law; but in fact conventions have political consequences. They constitute a default mechanism that distributes power and maintains order, leaving a relatively small arena in which formal legal mechanisms intervene. An acquaintance in Minneapolis offered me an "ethnographic vignette" of American male working-class culture. We went to what he said was "like a pub"; but it was unlike any pub I had seen in England, being only one long, narrow, windowless room, dimly lit, a row of stools against the bar, a mirrored wall behind the bar, and no tables. There were no women. There was very little talk and my escort cautioned me not to play the anthropologist and try to engage other people in conversation, not even to look at them, because eye-catching might lead to unpleasantness. He assured me that fights did break out from time to time for just that reason. Drinking and conviviality did not go together, and from that informal rule one can deduce the appropriate strategy for avoiding a fight (or provoking one—I can't think what else would make people choose to drink in such an unpleasant place, if not to enjoy the vicarious or direct thrill of a fight). In their own peculiar way the drinkers in that bar had a code of proper conduct, including, I suppose, a set of conventions about what should be done when a fight did break out, what constituted a fair fight, who had the right to join in the fight or intervene to end it, and so forth. None of these rules, so far as I know, was written down; they were informal and yet, for the patrons of that bar, authoritative. These are *normative* rules: They define proper conduct.

There are also normative rules that are not informal, that are written down and promulgated, publicly known, agreed upon, and enforced. The rules that govern sporting contests—football, cricket, wrestling, boxing, and the like—are an example. The Eighth Marquis of Queensberry was a keen patron of prizefighting, and in 1867 he published a set of normative rules for the sport. Before that time fighters fought bare-knuckle and the fight went on until one of them was incapacitated. The Queensberry rules require that padded gloves be worn; that the opponents should be within a specified weight bracket; that the fight should be divided into three-minute rounds with a minute's rest between each; that there should be a fixed number of rounds; that the winner should be decided by a knockout or by points or by a disqualification; and that the encounter should be supervised by a referee who not only ensures fair play but also decides who is the winner if both contestants are still on their feet at the end. The rules also lay down what can and cannot be legitimately done to win, in particular which areas of the body are off-limits. What before 1867 had been virtually plain *fights*, limited only by the rule that fists must be used (no kicking, head-butting, or wrestling), were transformed by the Queensberry Rules into boxing matches, or closely regulated sporting *competitions*.

The Queensberry rules are normative: They tell a boxer how to fight fairly. They do not tell him how to win. There are such rules, which summarize conventional knowledge about ringcraft and therefore guide behavior: How to avoid being hit; how to feint an attack from one direction and make the opponent leave his other side unprotected; whether to aim for a points-win or go for a knockout; how to pace oneself through the fight; how to trick the opponent into being overconfident; when to cover up and when to counterattack; and so on. These are *strategic* rules and, just as the rules of chess are relatively simple in comparison with the huge array of moves open to a chess player, so also are the strategic rules of boxing infinitely more numerous, more complex, and more rapidly changing than are the Queensberry rules, which, being normative, are relatively fixed. Strategic rules colonize the huge free space that normative rules leave open and unregulated.

There is a third set of rules in boxing (strictly a subset of strategic "how-to-win" rules) consisting of moves or strategies that offend normative standards. These rules tell a boxer how, when hurt, to get into a clinch so that the opponent has no room to use his fists; how to goad the opponent into losing his temper and along with it his caution; how to feign agony so that the referee will declare a low blow and penalize the opponent; how to use a head-butt and make it appear an accident; how to maneuver onto the blind side of the referee and deliver a painful and momentarily incapacitating kidney punch; and how, in many many other ways, to break a normative rule without being penalized for it. These are *pragmatic* rules: They tell you how to cheat.

Pragmatic rules are part of the practical wisdom that politicians tap into when they want to avoid the shackles that normative rules put on them and cannot think of any straightforwardly strategic way to do so. The rules exist mostly as folk wisdom, an art to be acquired through hearsay and practice, and generally are not formalized as a science or systematically described in handbooks. Machiavelli's *The Prince* is an exception. So also is the *Arthasastra*. Kautilya, unashamedly pragmatic, goes into detail. He describes (Book V, Chapter 1) several ways to deal with "a seditious minister," who presumably is too powerful or too cunning to be removed in a normative or strategic manner. "A spy, under the guise of a physician, may make a seditious minister believe that he is suffering from a fatal or incurable disease and contrive to poison him while prescribing medicine and diet to him." Pragmatic (and strategic) political wisdom may also be found in a small corpus of humorous books, two golden examples from the first decade of the twentieth century being F. M. Cornford's fastidiously ironic *Microcosmographia Academica: Being a Guide for the Young Academic Politician* and William L. Riordon's robust *Plunkitt of Tammany Hall: A Series of Very Plain Tales on Very Practical Politics*. Anyone, also, willing to take the trouble can abstract pragmatic rules from the biographies and autobiographies of politicians and statesmen. Robert Caro's narrative dissections of Robert Moses (*The Power Broker*) and of Lyndon Johnson (*The Path to Power* and *Means of Ascent*) are rich sources. There are many such books about men and women who have achieved fame or notoriety, and even hagiographies can be useful, once you learn to read into tales of resourcefulness and courage the underhandedness that every effective politician from time to time must use.

Rule-types as Weapons

Like most academics I have served time in university councils and committees, both in Britain and in the United States. The normative intent of committees or councils is cooperative, but since they use an adversarial procedure (a debate) to come to a decision, they also are arenas; one may read the record of a meeting as a series of encounters in which there are winners and losers. There is, therefore, given that *Homo* is not only *sapiens* but also *pugnax*, always the possibility of disorder.

In the United States, particularly in large assemblies like a university senate, conduct is explicitly and formally regulated (in the manner of the Queensberry rules) by *Robert's Rules of Order*, a small handbook written by General Henry A. Robert and first published in 1907. The book describes itself as a manual of parliamentary procedure based on the premise that "it is necessary to restrain the individual somewhat, as the right of an individual, in any community, to do what he pleases, is incompatible with the interests of the whole." The *Rules* are explicitly designed to ensure that "though the minority shall be heard and absentees protected, the majority will decide." Most of the rules that General Robert provides are normative, logically derived from the premise of majority rule. They deal, in considerable detail, with such matters as "Motions and Their Order of Precedence," "Debate and Decorum," "Voting," and other procedural matters. They are enforceable and the chairperson or speaker has the right to discipline offenders.

> It is the duty of the presiding officer to enforce the rules and orders of the assembly, without debate or delay. It is also the right of every member, who notices a breach of a rule, to insist upon its enforcement. In such case he shall rise from his seat, and say, "Mr. Chairman, I rise to a point of order."

Robert's Rules are marvelously meticulous. Here is an example taken at random from a section that specifies the rights and duties of a chairman:

> The chairman shall rise to put a question to the vote, but may state it sitting; he shall also rise from his seat (without calling anyone to the

chair) when speaking to a question of order, which he can in preference to other members. In referring to himself he should always use his official title, thus: "The chair decides so and so," not "I decide, etc."

General Robert had noticed, however, that debaters do not always play by the rules or sometimes do not know them. He also understood that chairmen are likely to get into contests with the members of the committee or the assembly, and he gives advice on strategy. The advice in effect consists of strategic rules for preserving normative intent against the inroads of debaters inclined to make pragmatic use of normative rules. He implies, in a section headed "Hints to Inexperienced Chairmen" (#50), that rules can serve as weapons:

> While in the chair, have beside you your Constitution, By-Laws, and Rules of Order, which should be studied until you are perfectly familiar with them.

He counsels a strategy of impersonal courtesy and restraint in dealing with potential opponents:

> Never interrupt members while speaking, simply because you know more about the matter than they do; never get excited; never be unjust to the most troublesome member, nor take advantage of his ignorance of parliamentary law, even though a temporary good is accomplished thereby.

But he also gives some sage advice (#19) on how to take strategic advantage of those who, through ignorance or thoughtlessness or malice, offend against parliamentary procedures. In certain conditions motions to "lay on the table" are open to pragmatic abuse. A motion to lay on the table (i.e., not discuss the question further for the time being, something more urgent having come up) requires only a majority vote. It can be used, unfairly, to suppress questions that the majority prefer not to have discussed. General Robert suggests several countermaneuvers. One involves the quick and dexterous use of a "point of order":

> Persons are commonly in such a hurry to make this motion [to lay a question on the table] that they neglect to address the chair and obtain

the floor. In such case one of the minority should address the chair quickly . . . making the point of order that . . . the other member not having the floor was not entitled to make a motion.

Failing this (Robert concedes that the "evil" is only "slightly diminished" by this tactic) he goes on to advise the minority that they should hang around in the hope that enough members of the majority leave before the end of the meeting to allow the minority, now become a majority, to pass a motion to "take the question from the table." Evidently the rules themselves can serve not only as guides for conduct but also as weapons.

Tricks of that kind are possible because the status of any particular action may be ambiguous and therefore is arguable. Consider the line between what is strategic (morally neutral) and what is pragmatic (a normative violation); it is not always clear. The trickster may claim that he did nothing worse than take advantage of the opponent's incompetence. I saw that game played one day in the Orissa legislature. It is a convention of parliamentary procedure that a government must resign if defeated on certain kinds of motion that are considered an index of confidence in its ability to govern. Question Time on that day was attended by about thirty members from each side of the House (it had 140 members). When Question Time ended, more members of the opposition quietly filed into the chamber until they very much outnumbered those seated on the government benches. The minister of revenue and excise rose to introduce a bill. It was midafternoon and when the Speaker asked for those in favor of the motion he received a rather sleepy "Aye." That happened again. When the minister rose for a third time, and the Speaker put the question, there was a stentorian collective shout of "No!" from the opposition benches, followed by some self-congratulatory chuckling and handshaking. The Speaker, surprised, first tried to finesse the situation by announcing that the ayes had it, but the outcry was such that he had to call a division. Government members were rounded up from the library and the tearoom, but in the event there were not enough of them on the premises and the government was defeated. It was a neat strategic trick, perhaps verging on the pragmatic because it offended the normative intent of parliamentary procedure, although no identifiable normative rule was broken. The government, however, refused to resign, arguing that this was a "snap" vote and could not be considered a motion of confidence. The courts, acting with untypical dispatch, gave normative sanction to that decision.

The category of normative can be made ambiguous in other ways. It is easy to confuse the *is* and the *ought* and make the line between a claim and a statement of fact uncertain. For example, the politician who states that there *is* everywhere an inalienable right to hold private property is making a normative claim (an *ought* statement), not a statement of fact that is open to empirical testing. The statement is a moral premise presented as if it were an unquestionable *fact*; it is a *presupposition* that begs the question. The statement of a normative ideal does not describe anything in the world of experience, except what someone has in mind as the right and proper state of affairs; it is an assertion of what they think ought to be the case, not an account of what is the case. Yet when politicians attempt to define a situation they often present a normative framework (the one they like) as if it were a literal and complete reality.

This strategy—the *normative façade* deployed to conceal a reality—can be used not only to launder a soiled past but also, with more subtlety, to anticipate a future so as to reap, pragmatically, a present advantage. In the aftermath of the Second World War there was what now seems to be an astoundingly naïve belief in the efficacy of social engineering and planned economic development, and an equally inexplicable failure to even glance at, let alone clear, the political minefields that lay in the path. I can recall from the 1950s glowing accounts of the marvelous progress toward democratic freedom and prosperity (summarized as "modernity") that was taking place in some Third World countries, presented as fact, replete with institutional details and hyped personality profiles of inspirational, dedicated, and tireless leaders (less poetic versions of those miracle stories about Mao). The reality, which began to surface even before the decade ended, proved that these stories were nothing more than projections put together by planners and politicians, a mixture of blueprints and normative aspirations that served to encourage the leaders, justify the power they wielded, conceal corruption and mismanagement, and keep development subsidies, grants, and loans flowing in. The purported reality was a clear fabrication. In fact all normative frameworks are fabrications, not realities but definitions of what someone would like reality to be. The fact that they all are imaginative constructs is tacitly downplayed because it pays us, politicians and nonpoliticians alike, to pretend that certain values and beliefs—those that we approve—are the permanent and irreplaceable foundations of our social existence. The logic of the *Realpolitik* point of view—that whatever people do, they do it because it is to their advantage—holds that any normative frame is a fabrication, at best a partial and distorted reflection of the social reality, and is not a guide for action but a propaganda weapon used to condemn an opponent's actions and justify one's own. Certainly when anyone makes a claim to be guided by conscience and a sense of duty, the sensible skeptic will follow Cicero's advice (in the *Pro Milone*, when he defended Milo, a political thug, who had murdered another like himself, Clodius) and ask *Cui bono?*—Who benefited? That entirely pragmatic question is always at hand for the asking, even in the case of politicians like Gandhi who acquired a virtually unassailable reputation for probity.

Pragmatic rules appear in many guises and not all of them fall into the crudely unambiguous category of the kidney-punch or the head-butt in the boxing ring. Robert's rule (#36) that begins "In debate a member must confine himself to the question before the assembly, and avoid personalities" and his dictum that "It is not the man but the measure that is the subject of debate" also apply in the British Parliament, but the rule did not stop Disraeli from describing the leader of the Liberal Party, Gladstone, as "a sophisticated rhetorician inebriated with the exuberance of his own verbosity." Recall (from Chapter 3) Churchill's attack on the Baldwin clique: "resolved to be irresolute, adamant for drift, solid for fluidity, all-powerful to be impotent." In the strict sense that speech addressed a policy (when and how fast to rearm the nation); but it was couched unequivocally in terms of character. The applicable pragmatic rule that seems to negate the normative rule of decorum would be: "Personal attacks will not be penalized if done wittily," and indeed it is the case that the art of delivering the sharpest of personal insults wrapped in one or another variety of doublespeak is much admired and carefully cultivated in deliberative bodies, especially academic ones, which pride themselves on their sophistication. Style seems able to purify the pragmatic device and turn it into a legitimate strategy. Style apart, the rule against personal attacks may also be waived in times of crisis: "You have sat here too long for any good you have been doing. Depart, I say, and let us have done with you. In the name of God, go!" That was Leo Amery, a Conservative, addressing his prime minister, Neville

Chamberlain, also a Conservative, in Parliament in May 1940. (Amery, wishing perhaps to justify his breach of parliamentary good manners, acknowledged borrowing the words from Oliver Cromwell's admonition to the Rump Parliament in 1653.) Five years earlier, James Maxton, addressing Ramsey MacDonald, who was making his last speech in Parliament (1935), was less polished: "Sit down, man! You're a bloody tragedy."

Contradictory Normative Frameworks

In parliaments and other legislative bodies that consist of a government and an opposition, there is a custom of "pairing off." Two members from opposed parties, who want to be elsewhere on the occasion, agree not to vote on a particular scheduled motion. So far as I know the normative rules of parliamentary procedure have nothing to say about this device. The parties themselves, however, do have normative rules that require members to vote the party line "when the whip is on" and penalize any member who does not. Pairing is a way to avoid those penalties (except when there is a "three-line whip"), but whether the device is strategic or mildly pragmatic is hard to say.

Notice in this last example that there are two separable arenas, each with its own normative rules: the parties and the legislature. An unequivocal ambiguity between normative and pragmatic arises from the presence of two or more incompatible rule-structures in a single situation; an action that is normatively respectable in one may be pragmatic in another. Pragmatic rules are part of *Realpolitik*, which, paradoxically, requires close attention to normative codes, not in order to be guided by them but to use them as tools that will serve another (and sometimes contradictory) purpose. When they are so used they may lose their moral standing; that was Ambedkar's point when he called Gandhi unprincipled and dishonest (a "rascal") for using normative forms of religion to gain political ends. Nehru too felt uncomfortable with Gandhi's religiosity, seeing in it a hint of pragmatism, but nevertheless applauded it as politically effective. Later, in newly independent India, he worked with Ambedkar to frame a constitution that made India a secular state and put a normative barrier between religion and politics. Yet the barrier turned out to be quite porous: From the moment independence was achieved, the same religious idiom that Gandhi used to exert political pressure on the British (and sometimes on his colleagues) has been employed by Indian politicians to coerce their governments. It was in regular use by Orissa's politicians in the year I spent among them. Individual politicians, unable to get what they wanted through constitutional procedures, went on hunger strike or practiced other forms of nonviolent protest.

All such maneuvers can be rhetorically justified on the grounds of a higher morality, which is in effect to invoke an alternative set of normative rules and claim that they take precedence. Leo Amery's woundingly personal attack on the prime minister—"Depart, I say, and let us have done with you"—can be defended as right and proper because the welfare of the nation comes before the conventions of parliamentary procedure. Hunger-striking politicians can likewise defend their actions on the grounds that their cause is too important to be put aside merely on procedural grounds. "God's law" is always available to justify breaking secular law. Even what seems to be unambiguously criminal may be upheld in this way, although it is hard to imagine that poisoning a minister could be considered a normatively proper way to reshuffle a cabinet or change advisers, even if they are seditious. Kautilya also suggests that the brother of a seditious minister may be offered the job, on condition that he first murders his brother; then, the murder having been committed, the murderer "shall be put to death in the same spot" under the charge that he has committed fratricide. Kautilya considered such tricks morally justified because they are done in the public interest—"to suppress treason against the king and his kingdom," as he put it.

Over the remaining chapters I intend to show how the three types of rule, and the ambiguity that arises when using them to categorize particular actions, provide a model for understanding situations that involve Machiavelli's "new order of things." Here is a preview of the basic propositions.

We could not survive without the fiction of a stable and unchanging normative framework. It is part of human nature to look for and need to find meaning in what happens, and endless movement is not different from meaninglessness. Rules and regularity go together, along with predictability and order, and it seems entirely to be expected that such notions as order, truth, and God cluster around one end of the continuum, leaving the other pole to Satan. Order is anchored in religion, in faith, in a normative framework regarded as an eternal verity.

That framework, however, is under attack from three directions. First, part of the myth that makes normative frameworks acceptable is that they are guides for conduct. They make life both orderly and they give it meaning. But in reality behavior is not entirely directed by conscience and a sense of duty; it also is the product of self-interest, ambition, and fear. People do not always do what they are normatively supposed to do. Second, what they are supposed to do is often far from clear because contradictory advice comes from alternative normative frames. Third, beyond the institutional framework there exists a natural world that changes of its own accord, and then the guidance that a normative framework gives might become outdated and dangerous, and when that happens the result is an absence of order and meaning; that is, the result is chaos. In this way, normative frameworks are faced with a perpetual contradiction: How to adapt to a changing environment and at the same time present the appearance of being an eternal verity.

The world of contradiction and movement is what Heraclitus saw. The social order is not a fixed thing, and culture is not a collection of eternal verities, but a never-ending make-and-mend job, and, from time to time, a seemingly radical discarding of an outdated model and the installation of a new one. The following chapter is about the make-and-mend part of the political process and it will demonstrate that underlying the seemingly ad hoc unpredictability of political improvisation there is a perceptible pattern. That restores Plato's view of the world.

We will come to revolutions later.

9

Manipulation

- Lyndon Baines Johnson, who was a superb strategist, anchors this chapter. He also dominates the following chapter, in which he appears as an unhesitating pragmatist.
- This chapter is about acquiring and controlling information, operating as a broker across the space between different arenas, and constructing a consensus.
- It also briefly considers the conditions, mainly institutional but also psychological, that make these strategies possible and effective.
- In both this and the following chapter the underlying theme is incremental (as opposed to radical) change. Chapter 12, returning to Gandhi, for whom normative rules (his own version of them) were imperative and absolute, will examine and render problematic the concept of revolutionary change.

Information, Brokers, and Consensus

General Robert assumed that the chairman likely "knows more about the matter" than the ordinary members do. A chairman has the advantage of standing beyond and above the contesting speakers. To have more information, whether about procedure or about matters of substance, is to have power.

One of the Distillers in Bisipara—not the man identified as keeping a *devata*—owned a house and paddy fields in the village, but spent most of his time eight miles away in the district capital, Phulbani, where he had a shop in the marketplace. It was one of three or four general stores, all owned by Distillers, and selling rice, lentils, canned goods, cigarettes, sugar, tea, coffee, flour, molasses, cloth, opium, kerosene, patent medicines, and various other necessities of daily life. His name was Basu. By the time I knew him he seldom presided in his shop; he had branched out into other businesses. He had a contract to feed the prisoners in Phulbani's jail. He won other contracts to carry out various small construction projects. In late June and early July, when paddy seedlings are planted, and again in January when the main harvest is gathered, he came back to Bisipara to supervise his field laborers. He also owned land in other villages, which he let out to sharecroppers. He was among the wealthier proprietors in Bisipara, and no one would even have considered accusing him of harboring a *devata* and killing the girl. Besides, his contacts with officials in Phulbani and his familiarity with the working of the administration would have made him a formidable adversary.

Basu was a man of influence. When I drove the dying girl to the government hospital in Phulbani, we stopped in the marketplace to pick him up and take him along. His function was to make sure that whatever the civil surgeon ordered done would in fact be done by the hospital orderlies. He bribed them directly or else they did what he asked because of past or promised favors or simply because they knew what kind of man he was. People in Bisipara who had dealings with government officials—that is, with the clerks in the offices—would sometimes first enlist Basu's help. At that time very few ordinary villagers had the skill and connections to make the government work for them, and they believed that he could do things in that domain that they could not. They knew that bribes were normally required, but they did not know how and where to place them most effectively. Basu had that information and, as time passed, he had acquired a clientele of people who were obligated to him.

It was, therefore, no surprise that when local government councils were set up, Basu was elected the first *sarpanch* (chairman) of Bisipara's statutory *panchayat* (the adjective distinguishes between the new institution and the villagers' own traditional *panchayat* over which the Bisoi presided). He was elected not because he had done favors for the majority of voters in the village but because there was a general belief that the function of the new local government institutions (*panchayati raj*) was to funnel development money down to the villages, and that Basu was the person who had the resources to do this most effectively; he had the contacts with officials and clerks. The villagers knew that their Bisoi, whom they would have preferred to be *sarpanch*, had some contacts in the administration, but in fact would not be much use, because his options were limited in ways that Basu's were not. Congress politicians had labeled the hereditary office that the Bisoi held (his title was *Sirdar*, or headman) a "relic of feudalism" and they intended to abolish it. In any case, being technically a government servant, the Bisoi was not allowed to stand for elective office. So they chose Basu. (The old *panchayat* continued to function and it was the venue in which Tuta's fate was decided.)

Before Basu had been very long in office the villagers began to regret their choice. They said that next time, "if the government would let them," they would elect the Bisoi. If Basu had held meetings, they complained, no one had ever been invited. Some funds had come to the village to build a fish-breeding pond; but it was so badly constructed that the water drained away and all the fish died. There was also money to erect a cattle-pound to keep straying animals off the crops. But the village already employed its own herdsman. The first they heard of the pound, they said, was when an inspector arrived and Basu hastily pointed to his own cattle shed. Basu, they insinuated, must have applied for the money and then pocketed it. They were not surprised; from the beginning they had little trust in him but elected him anyway because he seemed otherwise the best qualified. So Basu blew away his chance of becoming dominant in Bisipara's politics. (He was aiming higher. He stood as an Independent for election to the State Assembly—and forfeited his deposit.) If he had aspired to dominate village politics, as *sarpanch* he was in a good position to do so; interpreting the consensus of village opinion to the government, and the government's wishes to the villagers, was normatively the task of the statutory *panchayat* and its chairman. The philosophy underlying *panchayati raj* was wholly democratic and in spirit quite Gandhian: There must be a consensus between government and the people about what should be done.

The villagers knew about consensus. No votes were ever taken in their own *panchayat*. They talked things over until they were in agreement about what to do, and if they did not reach agreement, then nothing was done, which often happened. Sometimes what appeared to be a consensus was consensual only in appearance; agreement was reached only because one or the other side had run out of stamina. The Bisoi presided over these meetings, apparently with a light hand, letting everyone have their say (only adult males belonging to clean castes—no Untouchables—were allowed to attend and speak because they met in a sacred building, called the *mandap*). Then, when he judged the moment right, he would announce briefly what he considered to be the consensus. If he had judged the exhaustion factor rightly, the dissenters held their peace and the issue was settled. Sometimes there was caucusing outside the meeting, men of influence getting together to make deals that they did not want bandied about before the larger gathering. Bisipara's Warrior caste was divided into two factions (called *dola*, or sometimes they used the English word "party") and the arguments in the *panchayat* often took place along factional lines. If the Bisoi thought a matter to be of sufficient importance (as when Tuta's *devata* ran amok and killed the girl and another child) he met privately with the leader of the opposite faction before the meeting and together they decided on a common strategy. In general, people were disturbed (as Gandhi was) by the notion of terminating adversarial procedures through a vote; everyone set a high value on consensus in the spirit of *vox dei*—a consensual agreement was a sanctified agreement, the voice of God. (Anything less than unanimity was called in Gandhian circles "51 percent democracy.")

The word "consensus" ("being of like mind") can be used in different ways, but it always has a referent of some kind. It does not describe a general state of mind like euphoria or gloom; nor is it just solidarity; it requires a target—"There is a broad consensus that XYZ is the case." When focused further and contrasted with majority-vote decisions or with the coercion of unwilling people, it requires a statement of an action contemplated or taken—"The decision to adopt XYZ . . . was consensual."

There are two ways in which consensus, whether in the broad or the narrowly focused sense, comes about. One is the way of unanimity; the other is the way of pluralism. The first occurs when everyone has a common goal that they expect to achieve through cooperation. In other words, everyone gives their consent because they believe it is the right thing to do. This kind of consensus goes with charismatic leadership or with true belief in a cause. It also is associated with diseducation, in that the consent, once given, is not supposed to be subjected to continuous critical reevaluation. I will call this *direct* consensus; it is of the kind envisaged in those eulogies to Chairman Mao and others in an earlier chapter. A team put together with direct consensus is likely to have the unthinking solidarity that makes for confrontation and lessens the chance of compromise. It would also, by definition, incline toward defining situations in terms of issues rather than interests, being the product of enthusiasm (or, if you disapprove, of fanaticism) rather than calculation.

The pluralistic form of consensus is different. It occurs among people who have different goals, but who need each other's help to achieve them. Those who give their consent do so because it is to their advantage; it is the smart thing to do. This second kind, which is *brokered* consensus, requires a leader who knows how to put deals together and make a sufficient number of people obligated enough to cooperate in doing what he wants done. That he has an agenda of this kind distinguishes a leader from a mere broker, who takes his profit in a material rather than a political form.

A brokered consensus is achieved by the method of payoff, but it is not the same as straightforward hiring. Mercenaries are not followers but employees, and an employer is not, in the strict sense, a leader. Those who do what the leader wants in return for getting his help to do what they individually want are not hirelings, even though their support is, in a broad sense of the word, bought. A purely mercenary force is homogeneous. In that respect it resembles one produced by direct consensus: An identical relationship (in the one case moral and in the other material) exists between the leader and every one of his hirelings. In both cases the method of assembly is, so to speak, that of mass production. In contrast, a brokered consensus is crafted, each link being individually constructed. This difference in team-building goes along with institutional, historical, and personality differences, and the teams that result have different strategic capabilities. Those differences will be considered later.

Lyndon Baines Johnson and his dealings with the U.S. Senate in the early years of his presidency will provide the example of manipulative strategies used to achieve leadership through a brokered consensus. The strategies he chose were a function of his goals, the resources that he had, and the constraints under which he operated. I will begin with a brief account of what he accomplished.

Johnson and the Congress

President Kennedy was assassinated in November 1963. Johnson, the vice president, served out Kennedy's term and in 1964 was himself elected president in a landslide victory over Barry Goldwater, the Republican candidate. His four years in office had a bright half, which was his Great Society program, and a dark half, which was the war in Vietnam. At the end of his term, facing diminished authority and vanished popularity, he declined to run again and withdrew from politics. The transitional year and the first years of his presidency were brilliantly successful. Programs concerning civil rights and social welfare, which in Kennedy's tenure had been stalled in the legislature or not yet presented to it, were successfully implemented and, if the war in Vietnam had not brought him down, Johnson would have been mainly—and justifiably—remembered as the most effective reforming president since Franklin Roosevelt. How did he do it?

Johnson's weakness, according to the biographer from whom I have drawn most of this account (Doris Kearns Goodwin), was a total inability to empathize with—to make sense of—true belief. An ethic of absolute ends, a refusal to think about consequences, the all-or-nothing quality of ideological thinking, and the readiness to push politics to the point of open conflict both frightened and disgusted him, and he did his best not to arouse feelings of that kind among people who might oppose him. The game was played through persuasion and manipulation, not by the open use or direct threat of force.

In any case, he did not command that kind of force. He did not command it constitutionally, since he was a president, not a dictator; he required the advice and consent of the Congress before any bill that he wanted could become law. Nor, initially, did he command it by the force of his political reputation or by popular acclaim. The people knew him as Kennedy's vice president and vice presidents are, under the American system, not much more than nonentities in a high seat, unless, as happened, the president dies in office. Johnson, furthermore, inherited cabinet officers who had been selected by Kennedy, and who, by and large, considered Johnson a culturally and socially inferior person. He did, however, have one institutional resource. Before he became vice president, he had been for eleven years a member of the Senate and its leader for the last five (before that, between 1937 and 1948, he had represented the Texas 10th District in the House). In that time he had acquired an intimate knowledge of legislative procedures and conventions and—no less important—he knew a great deal about, and of course was known to, many individual legislators.

Kennedy, during his (almost) three years as president, had set a sociopolitical agenda (the "New Frontier") that included civil rights, federal aid to education, medical care for the aged, and the alleviation of poverty in the cities. At the time he was assassinated these programs had not passed into law. Civil rights reforms were opposed by many legislators from southern states; so were some of the education provisions; and so—not only in the South—was the entire program, to the extent that it followed in the tracks of Roosevelt's New Deal and increased federal authority over the states. Johnson, inheriting this agenda, proclaimed that he would implement it, both because it was right in itself and because it was his obligation to complete a program hallowed by Kennedy's martyrdom. The nation—people, officials, legislators—in the weeks and months following the assassination was in a state of deep psychological shock and there was a general feeling that the time had come for radical change. That feeling, together with Johnson's dignified and compassionate public demeanor (helped out by the ostentatiously "tough guy" performance of his Republican opponent, Goldwater), returned him to the presidency in 1964 with a margin in the electoral college of 486 to Goldwater's 52.

That result, together with elected majorities for the Democratic Party in the Congress, appeared to be a mandate from the electorate to continue the New Frontier programs, to introduce the necessary bills to the Congress, and to see them passed. To do so would require the construction of a sufficient consensus among the legislators to vote for the bills that the president sent before them, including some that, in their Kennedy version, had failed to move forward. The campaign that Johnson conducted to push these bills through the Congress, in which the large "Dixiecrat" section of his own party (Democrats representing southern states) disapproved of the reform agenda, stands as an exemplary blueprint for the consensus-building style of leadership in the face of considerable constraints.

He took care, first, to involve key individual legislators in the preparation and drafting of bills in order to find out what they would accept and what they were likely to oppose. More is involved in this than simply removing what legislators find objectionable. Such "cooperation" is also a form of psychological manipulation—I have heard it called "stroking"—a way of making a person feel important, part of a team, a way of suggesting that the bill is not just the president's but theirs too. The consultations (on the telephone or through presidential aides) were discreetly done, if not in secret at least not in the public eye, because publicity at this stage might also have given the impression that legislators were being manipulated by Johnson, or vice versa. The benefit of behind-the-scenes negotiation for the legislators would be that if things went wrong, they would not be publicly associated with any debacle; and if things went well they could brag about the part they had played. The benefit for Johnson was that discreet consultation allowed him to keep confidential what he had in mind and so lessen the chances that opponents could launch an anticipatory strike. A third risk, of which Johnson was very sharply aware, was that open consultations might lead to grandstanding over matters of principle that in private could be tacitly sidelined in the interests of making a deal.

In addition to co-opting selected legislators to help him draft bills, Johnson endeavored to manipulate the legislative process. That too had to be done discreetly, not only because direct presidential interference in the business of the legislature is constitutionally unacceptable (it violates the doctrine of the separation of powers), but also because it is the reverse of stroking, as it diminishes the role of legislators and, if done crudely, is likely to put their backs up. Nonetheless, it was done. Johnson kept a chart showing the progress of every bill through its different stages. His liaison officers talked with legislators and every day reported back to him the legislators' opinions and what they said about the opinions of others. In that way Johnson could find out who at the committee stage was likely to vote which way, and whose mind might be changed and what would be needed to change it. Later, if a close vote on the floor was anticipated, similar investigations would be made about possible swing voters, especially those whose opinion carried weight with their fellows. He invited influential legislators to sponsor bills in which they had some kind of stake. He had a very comprehensive knowledge of the resource-and-constraint profile of individuals, where they stood on this or that issue, what sticking points they might have, what their own problems were, and what assistance they might need from him. One assumes he also factored into his calculations their personal vulnerabilities. In his own words:

> If it's really going to work, the relationship between the president and the Congress has got to be almost incestuous. He's got to know them even better than they know themselves. And then, on the basis of this knowledge, he's got to build a system that stretches from the cradle to the grave, from the moment a bill is introduced to the moment it is officially enrolled as the law of the land.[1]

The first two sentences recall Tammany Hall and Senator Plunkitt:

> I know every man, woman, and child in the Fifteenth District. . . . I know what they like, and what they don't like, and what they are strong at and what they are weak in, and I reach them by approachin' at the right side.[2]

The technique was not Johnson's invention; in fact it is the essence of—to use Plunkitt's word—*practical* politics, or the politics of reward and punishment, which can be applied anywhere at any time.

All of this suggests a possible crudeness in his approach—"Do this, or else!" or "What do you want in return?"—but, by Goodwin's account, the manipulation was not that crass, not usually a matter of "slapping backs, twisting arms, trading dams." A straight quid pro quo is a dangerous tactic, because, if it becomes known, it tempts others to do the same—Israeli governments seem to have that problem perpetually—and makes the leader dependent on the supposed follower. Instead there was a kind of tally sheet, favors generally not immediately linked to the present instance, but given to regular supporters when they were in need. In other words, these were mostly not straight transactions between faceless dealers in a political marketplace, but rather the kind of exchange that involves credit and trust, and that marks status, in this case the status of a leader and his subordinate allies.

In addition to this vast and complicated networking, in which every link might be different from every other one, Johnson kept an eye on the larger context within which the manipulation of individuals and interests was taking place. Public opinion was both a resource and a constraint (what the public thought about the Vietnam War toppled him). The larger context is epitomized in the question "How do the people feel about this?" The answer requires a kind of intuitive boldness that is not needed in the rather precise calculations made possible by the dossiers that Johnson accumulated about the fears, ambitions, and prejudices of individual politicians. For example, he was well aware that the profound shock of Kennedy's assassination gave him an opportunity to push radical reforms past people who in normal times would hasten to block them. He also knew that time tends to close such windows; for that reason he maintained an unrelenting pressure to keep the legislative process continuously and rapidly on the move. But neither was he reckless. With each bill there was a calculation to be made about what could be yielded without destroying its essence. He was also astute about timing and the need not only, like a surfer, to catch the wave, but also to so structure the program that it would develop its own momentum. Bills that would more easily go through came before difficult ones, on the principle that nothing succeeds like success, and that a bruising fight, even if it ends in victory, diminishes enthusiasm to get back into the ring.

He also knew both when to stay his hand and when to seize an opportunity. In the first months after Kennedy's assassination he made clear his opposition to what was seen as the inevitable watering down of a civil rights bill in order to avoid a filibuster by southern senators, who were of course, like the president, Democrats. There would be no "deal," he announced, and he won the two-thirds vote needed to close down a Senate filibuster by negotiating support from the Republican leader, Everett Dirksen. He argued that it was in the interest of the Republican Party not to be seen in alliance with Dixiecrats and he strengthened the argument by offering Dirksen a generous packet of favors. The Civil Rights Act became law in July 1964.

The struggle to get the bill passed left sufficient acrimony that Johnson decided to let some time pass both to give his officials a chance to implement the bill and to let the wounds heal among the politicians before he went further and introduced a bill on voting rights. He planned to do that in the spring of 1966.

In March 1965, Martin Luther King led a march from Selma to Montgomery in Alabama. The governor of the state, George

Wallace, sent police to break up the demonstration. Television screens across the nation showed blacks beaten with clubs and savaged by police dogs. Protest demonstrations were organized and there was a massive campaign to pressure Johnson into mobilizing the National Guard and immediately enforce civil rights for blacks in Alabama. Johnson waited two days, believing that precipitous action would be seen as federal intervention in states' affairs and might make Governor Wallace a martyr to the cause of states' rights. Two more days of police violence, shown on television, made that interpretation impossible and legitimized the use of federal forces to restore order. Johnson sent in the National Guard and instantly became the nation's hero. He seized the opportunity to advance the Voting Rights Act, introducing it himself to a joint session of the Congress, and making a highly emotional speech, "We Shall Overcome," which was televised. He became, as Goodwin says, a "moral leader," adding to the brokered consensus that he was achieving among the legislators the weight of the direct consensus of public opinion.

Consensus-making Strategies

Johnson in that speech made reference to God, and it is clear from what he said, and still more from what he did, that he did not believe, as leaders sometimes say they do, in leaving everything to God: "God will not favor everything we do. It is rather our duty to divine His will. But I cannot help believing that He truly understands and that He really favors the undertaking that we begin tonight."[3]

God helps those who help themselves. Johnson seems to have worked out his strategies in an impressively rational manner, calculating with great care and in infinite detail both the resources at his command and the constraints within which he had to work, and making the corresponding calculations about his opponents. The story of Johnson's successes in putting through the Congress the measures that constituted his Great Society program is, like any historical narrative, unique, the product of historical accident and of Johnson's own personality and capabilities. But out of it can be extracted both a pattern of strategies for any leader who proposes to lead by brokering consensus and an inventory of the conditions in which brokering is likely to be effective.

The basic strategy is to minimize hostile confrontations. Thinking back to the continuum of political encounters that run from cooperation on the left to plain fighting on the right, the essence of consensual politics is to put a brake on the natural tendency of political encounters to move toward the right. Admittedly the basic encounter has to be adversarial—there would be no need to broker a consensus if a direct consensus already existed and everyone was willing to cooperate—but, taking that into account, it pays to keep the exchanges unheated and to avoid a showdown that might make the other party dig in its heels and refuse further negotiation.

It follows that anyone normatively opposed to the measure should not be invited to join in the negotiation, because they are likely, as a matter of principle, to turn the offer of a deal into a fight. There can be no brokered consensus with those who consider whatever is at issue a moral imperative that in no circumstances can be compromised. Those senators from the South who were unable to contemplate anything less than total white supremacy were not invited to make deals. Johnson did not bargain with them; he maneuvered so as to defeat them. To tempt them with deals would have been a waste of time.

From this can be deduced a corresponding rule, which Johnson followed: Find out who is the least committed to the opposition point of view and work on them to change their minds. A low commitment implies commitments to other principles or interests. A Republican senator mildly disapproving of civil rights and voting rights because the newly enfranchised Black vote was likely to be preponderantly Democratic might nevertheless be willing to support those bills in return for federal projects in his own state (for the obvious reason that they bettered his chances at the next election). That kind of deal swung Dirksen, and behind him a sufficient number of other Republicans, to block a Dixiecrat filibuster against the civil rights legislation in 1964.

Behind this lies a general principle: Frame any substantive discussion, so far as this is possible, in terms of interests and not in terms of issues, because issues by their very nature are likely to excite true beliefs, and true beliefs are not negotiable. On the other hand, make offers in such a way that acceptance of them can *appear* to be a matter of principle. Exactly what is said will depend on the persons involved, their roles, and their personalities. There are some politicians who appear to be wholly undisturbed by their own hypocrisy, but others, probably the majority, take pains to have the normative side of the argument made more visible than the handout. Dirksen's deal was, I suppose, presented to his fellow Republicans as good for the party's image with northern voters, not as a package of goods for the state of Illinois. Nevertheless, the reality of the negotiation between Dirksen and Johnson was not the *issue* of civil rights, nor the well-being of the Republican Party at large, perhaps not even federal funds spent in Illinois, but Dirksen's *interest* in strengthening his hold over the Illinois electorate.

Acquiring information and controlling its flow is a key part of a consensus-making strategy. Johnson was effective as a consensus-maker to the extent that he had, through his own knowledge and through the work of his staff, an intimate knowledge of the goals, resources, and constraints of key individuals in the Senate and the House. On any particular issue he generally knew beforehand not only *who* would be his allies and who would be opposed, but also *how* supportive or *how* negative they were likely to be. Second, the outward flow of information of all kinds was controlled. Congressmen were quietly sounded out so as not to let likely opponents know what was in the wind. Deals done with them also were kept quiet, because everyone involved in the deal, both Johnson and the congressmen, like politicians everywhere, wanted it generally believed that what they did was done because it was right, not because it carried a payoff on the side. Consensus in its direct form is normatively respectable; the particular deals that make up a brokered consensus are generally less respectable, or sometimes not respectable at all.

Information also has to be shared. A controlling consideration is that withholding information where it is needed may diminish the chances of reaching a consensus. Once in the negotiating arena, allies and prospective allies should not be subjected to surprises that might inhibit their capacity to anticipate what offer is likely to be made next and so move smoothly toward striking a bargain. Johnson remembered, from his time as an aide in the House, how upset House Speaker Sam Rayburn became when President Roosevelt made some move without first warning him and giving him a chance to prepare the ground to deal with possible opposition.[4] Surprised allies are handicapped allies and, if surprised often enough, are likely to feel that they no longer are trusted.

Finally, a strategy for consensus-making generally does not rest exclusively on cold rationality; it also requires an element of trust. This trust is in part a rational expectation that the other party will play by the rules and stand by the bargain, despite the fact that none of these bargains is formally and publicly ratified. It would not be rational for a negotiator to acquire a reputation for being unreliable. That is, perhaps, the bottom line: The consensus-builder who regularly fails to deliver on his or her promises will soon cease to be one. But there seems also to be in the negotiations a trace of the nonrational kind of trust that comes from continued cooperative interaction, a mutual respect, a kind of amity. At least a simulacrum of something less than hatred and pure enmity must be present, and where those sentiments do not exist, consensus-building is unlikely to succeed. The exchanges between Johnson and Dirksen (the "banter" reported by Goodwin) have a little of that quality.[5] Johnson was indeed a uniquely persuasive person when dealing one-on-one. In the middle of the Alabama crisis, Governor Wallace requested a meeting with the president. He emerged from Johnson's office, after three hours, saying, "If I hadn't left when I did, he'd have had me coming out *for* civil rights."[6]

That Johnson had other less amiable qualities will become apparent in the next chapter.

Conditions for Consensus-making

These thoroughly rational and energetically implemented strategies enabled Johnson to accomplish in a relatively short time what Kennedy would have found difficult, had he lived. But the strategies did not give Johnson complete control over events; no leader can have that. Nor were the strategies alone responsible for the successes that he had. He was gifted with a variety of talents that allowed him to deploy the strategies effectively. He possessed, as I said, a singular capacity to persuade other people when meeting them face to face. (He was less persuasive as an orator; only on rare occasions, as when he presented the Voting Rights measure to the Congress in the aftermath of the Selma troubles, could he convey this magnetism to a large audience and so command a direct consensus for his policies.) He also was determined, single-minded when it suited him, phenomenally hard-working, and able to extract hard work—sometimes devotion—from his staff. He had good tactical judgment, as demonstrated in his timing of the Selma intervention. (That was patently not the case in his direction of the Vietnam War.)

The Johnson package of strategies for consensus-making is employable only in certain conditions, most of them already mentioned. First, they are not needed in conditions where direct consensus is strong, as in wartime (some wars) or in India's Freedom Fight. Nor do they work across a gulf of fanatical enthusiasms, as I noted earlier. Johnson had an unfruitful exchange of letters with Ho Chi Minh, who dismissed Johnson's overtures with the statement that the Vietnamese cause was "absolutely just." Where one form of consensus prevails, the other has a thin existence.

Second, the Johnson package works best when there exists a well-established convention for civilized encounters, as in bureaucracies or representative government or (usually) in the corporate business world. Such institutions operate with an as yet unwritten normative guidebook—*Robert's Rules for Wheeler-Dealers* or *The Back-Scratcher's Vade Mecum*.

Third, there is an obvious limit to the scale of operations. Brokered consensus-making requires the personal touch; it has to be done face-to-face between people who more or less know each other in the round, as individual personalities. The classificatory convenience of bureaucratic categories—the one-size-fits-all world—is only minimally applicable. For that reason, Johnson's techniques worked more smoothly when he was leader of the Senate and dealing with the other ninety-nine senators than it did when, as president, his field of action comprised the entire government, the entire bureaucracy, the entire nation, and ultimately the entire world.

Fourth, the infrastructure that is needed, since it is composed of individually built links, cannot be instantly put together. Therefore it is not well adapted to crisis. When urgent decisions have to be made, they are made either by force (without consensus) or through one or another form of *direct* consensus (which is the moral equivalent of force), or else they are not made at all. The passing of Johnson's Great Society legislation, to some degree a response to the crisis of Kennedy's assassination, was made possible not by that alone but by the years of experience—and the contacts—that Johnson had acquired as a congressman and as a senator.

The Johnson manipulatory package exists somewhere in the no-man's-land between normative and pragmatic politics. Some negotiations are kept quiet because it would be tactically foolish to let the opposition know what is planned. There is no shame in that and no necessary cause for embarrassment if the facts come out later. Likewise there are deals that carry a faint whiff of impropriety, such as trading a vote for the president's agreement to nominate X for an ambassadorship, but are in fact not so embarrassing if they happen to come out, because they can be normatively justified by insisting that X was in fact the best available person for the job. Indeed, all of those quiet agreements to allocate military bases or other federal projects to a state are, from the point of view of *that* state, entirely right and proper. Many consensus-making deals, although struck behind closed doors, if they do leak out can be fudged as "really" normative. The entire Johnson package could be presented in that way: The means may seem dubious, but whether they are or not, the Great Society goal warrants them. I will return to the end-justifies-means arguments later.

The next chapter will consider actions that are less easily justified by normative special pleading. The central figure is again Lyndon Johnson, this time in the years before he rose to prominence in the Senate.

10

Pragmatism

- In the previous chapter, LBJ was a hero, of sorts; in this he is a villain, but with some ambiguity. The tale is about a period in his life before he became a senator and it concerns the pragmatic strategies that he used to advance himself. He did not openly defy the normative structure; he subverted it, surreptitiously, to gain his ends.
- What he did, however, has a larger evolutionary significance: pragmatism is an unadvertised and sometimes unintended instrument that controls political change.

"A Remarkable Man"

I need to make some preliminary remarks about LBJ and about the two-volume biography that has been my main source for this chapter. The author is Robert Caro. His book covers the period from Johnson's birth in 1908 to his becoming a senator in 1948, and it reads like a demonography, giving an impression of the man that is very far from the tragically heroic figure, felled by his own limitations, who emerges in Doris Kearns Goodwin's earlier portrayal. Johnson comes unambiguously off Caro's pages as everything that Gandhi was not: a deliberate and accomplished pragmatist, who failed, at least in these early years of his career, even the test of doing bad things for a higher purpose. Johnson's main—perhaps not quite his only—purpose, as presented in Caro's two volumes, was his own aggrandizement, made visible in the attainment of office and in deference from people around him.

He grew up in rural poverty, the son of a man who was as honest as Johnson was not, who had made a small name in public life and then failed, in part because he was an honorable man, becoming the object of his neighbors' pity and, to an extent, of their ridicule. Johnson attended the Southwest Texas State Teachers' College at San Marcos, where, Caro writes, he "invented politics," deploying various strategies, many of them pragmatic, to become a person of influence. I will describe some of the strategies later, for he continued to use them throughout his rise to power. He then went to Washington as an aide and secretary to a Texas congressman; there too he created a political domain for himself where none had before existed. He became a congressman in 1937, at the age of twenty-nine. In 1942, after the attack on Pearl Harbor, he enlisted in the navy and flew, as a passenger and an inspecting dignitary, on one combat mission over New Guinea, for which he received a medal. Caro's account of this episode and of Johnson's six months of service in the navy make both the service and the combat mission as derisible as Johnson's own public statements made them glorious. When Roosevelt recalled the eight members of Congress who were on active service, four chose to resign their seats and stay in uniform, and four went back to politics. Johnson returned to his seat in the House of Representatives, where he served for a further six years until he was elected to the Senate in 1948.

Johnson was a man of abundant energy and impressive determination, capable of exerting himself to the point of physical breakdown. Yet in those eleven years in the House he introduced only five bills that had reference to more than his own district, spoke in defense of only one of them, and had none passed. He had a knack of avoiding commitment on issues, while appearing to agree with whatever position pleased the person whose support he wanted. "Convincing liberals he was a liberal, conservatives that he was a conservative, that was his leadership, that was his knack," one of his financial backers (George Brown) said of him. His style is neatly caught in a phrase that came into use in the 1960s and could have been invented for him: He was a prototypical "wheeler-dealer," taking whatever stance on policy at the time best suited his requirements. His requirements were power first and second money. In 1943, shortly after his return to civilian life, he used his political clout to purchase and expand a radio station (held in his wife's name), and in a short time he turned himself into a million-aire. But that was almost a detour; mostly he raised and disbursed money for political purposes, to finance campaigns for himself and for his party. The money did not come from door-to-door soliciting; it was given by large corporations, principal among them Brown and Root, an enterprise that rose to power through government contracts (hydroelectric dams, military bases, and other public ventures) secured by Lyndon Johnson's assiduous cultivation of politicians and officials who had the authority to make the necessary decisions.

From the beginning he showed a capacity to find and charm patrons. He won the confidence of the president of San Marcos College to the extent that he was given a say in handing out jobs that the college made available for its students, most of whom were poor. (The jobs went to those who showed Johnson obsequious respect, and showed it in public.) When still a congressman-elect, in 1937, he met President Roosevelt, and before long he had become "our man in Texas," on occasions able to solicit successfully Roosevelt's interven-tion in administrative decisions. The Speaker of the House at that time, Sam Rayburn, was a Texan too, and a man of great influence, who had come to know Johnson when he was still an aide. Rayburn welcomed him as a congressman, sponsored him, and brought him into the informal circles of power that centered on the Speaker. "He was like a father to me," Johnson said. (Later there was a falling out, Rayburn believing that Johnson had deliberately misrepresented his views on the New Deal to Roosevelt.)

He charmed his colleagues and associates too. He was enthusiastic, tireless ("That guy's got extra glands!"), prodigiously well informed on the gossip level, and a great raconteur with a fund of stories about politicians and about Texas. "He never bored me. He never bored anyone. He was a magnetic man physically, and you never knew what was going to happen next. He was a remarkable man." Some of this personal charisma must have entered also into the relationships he had with the corporate magnates who provided money when he need-ed it and with the network of lawyers who operated as brokers between these bosses and the politicians. They rallied around Johnson when his unscrupulous electioneering got him into deep trouble in 1948. It is true that their ox too would have been gored, along with Johnson's, if they had not saved him. Nevertheless, there is a slight

whiff in Caro's description of the kind of solidarity that is represented by *omertà*: They were committed to protecting "their man." But
perhaps not; they too were professional manipulators, accustomed to
handling people as instruments and managing their relationships, as
Johnson mostly did, on a cost–benefit basis.

Johnson was not always charming. Caro maintains that he selected
his immediate entourage—those who ran his office—for their inability to stand up to him and refuse his incessant and often unreasonable
demands. He was rude, habitually foul-mouthed, and generally incon-
siderate of the needs and feelings of those who did relatively menial
work for him and who depended on him. When he was not being rude
to them, he called them "son" and had them call him "chief." Those
who could not stand the pace—or the abuse—were eased out. Those
who "made the team" had learned how to put up with the cursing,
and—just as frequent—with the hugs and compliments that could be
as extravagant as the curses. For sure that was Johnson's personality,
but, whether calculated or not, the total absence of reserve (together
with the selection process) made those who continued to work for him
devoted to him.

In addition to the little band of bullied and charmed lackeys at the
bottom and a few patrons at the top, such as Rayburn and for a time
Roosevelt (their numbers diminished as Johnson himself rose to
power), and as well as the wider network of lawyers and businessmen
and politicians like himself, wheelers and dealers connected by ties of
mutual instrumentality or party membership (and in some cases perhaps genuine friendship), Johnson had a fourth political clientele that
required his attention to make them value him, or at least to give him
what he wanted. This clientele was, in the years between 1937 and
1948, the voters in the Texas 10th District, which he represented in
the House, and, in his final year as a congressman when he campaigned for the Senate, all the voters of Texas.

To reach a mass of voters there are three rhetorical themes that have
normative respectability: first, talk about issues (what people care
about); second, talk about record (what has or has not been done) and
programs (what is planned or offered); and third, talk about character.
The third item, character, is somewhat risky, and if it is to remain normatively respectable it must stay with at least the spirit of General
Robert's rule that "It is not the man but the measure that is the subject of debate." This can be done by demonstrating that there is a link

between character and issues, failures or accomplishments, and the likely fulfillment of a promised program. In practice there is a huge gap in that particular normative barrier and through it passes many different kinds of self-puffery or, conversely, character assassination. The competitor who stays rigidly with the rule of "no personalities" is greatly handicapped. I will come to that shortly; Johnson's opponent in 1948, Governor Coke Stevenson, for a long time remained within the bounds of propriety, running on his own record and a reputation for probity, and choosing, until close to the end of his campaign, to say nothing about his opponent's lack of both. (This was a primary election to select a candidate for the entirely safe Democratic seat. Both Stevenson and Johnson were Democrats.)

In fact Johnson did have some achievements. In the 1937 House campaign he presented himself as the person who could bring the benefits of the New Deal to the 10th District. He spent much of his energies steering federal loans and grants to local communities and their leaders. The most conspicuous of these efforts occurred during his early years in the House and concerned rural electrification. Since about 1935 Roosevelt had been putting pressure on privately owned utilities to make electricity available in rural areas, which the companies believed would be unprofitable. Roosevelt then established the Rural Electrification Administration (REA), which, among other functions, provided financing to encourage small farmers to band together in cooperatives that would deal with private utilities and create the infrastructure needed to connect the widely scattered farms and small communities. The district that Johnson represented contained areas so impoverished that the utilities were reluctant to take part even in a government-guaranteed scheme. Johnson put his energies into getting it off the ground, on one occasion persuading Roosevelt to override an administrative decision that would have blocked further progress in the part of his district where Johnson himself grew up. He made himself a reputation for effectiveness both with Roosevelt, who offered him the directorship of the REA, and with ordinary people. He was a man who could turn on the spigot of federal money (or turn it off). In this way, the reputation that he had earned himself with big business was extended to those voters who had benefited from, or at least knew about, his manipulations.

No campaigner, however, relies on that strategy alone; inevitably, for everyone who benefits there are others who do not. Moreover, ordinary voters have not absorbed the spirit of *Robert's Rules* and do not concern themselves exclusively and dispassionately with policy; they look at the candidates not only as past or potential providers of benefits, but also as persons *intrinsically* valued for what they are. Recall Nehru, speaking of Gandhi: "Whether his audience consisted of one person or a thousand, the charm and magnetism of the man passed on to it, and each one had a feeling of communion with the speaker." Candidates understand the "feeling of communion" in voters, and they try to create it by making personal face-to-face contact (or at least its simulacrum) with as many of their constituents as they can reach.

In the years between 1937 and 1948, Johnson conducted three campaigns (all primaries) in Texas: The first got him into the House; the second (in 1941) failed to get him into the Senate; and the third made him a senator. In all three he canvassed with great energy and determination. The aim, in Texas as everywhere, was to contact as many voters as possible by shaking hands and making stump speeches, but Texas is large, more than 265,000 square miles. Even the neatly rectangular 10th District, where he campaigned for a seat in the House, is approximately 200 by 150 miles. In 1937 such direct access to voters was difficult; two-thirds of them were rural; many lived in small towns or on isolated farms; roads were poor; and many communities were still without electricity and therefore beyond the reach of the electronic media. Johnson's 1948 campaign (although he still exhausted himself) was altogether different. Texans had radios and televisions and Johnson had money in plenty to buy time on the air; and he stumped around the state in a helicopter, the first candidate in Texas ever to do so. The *technique* is perfectly rational: The helicopter goes faster and therefore to more places than a car. At the same time it stands alongside hand-shaking and baby-kissing (Johnson kissed everyone, even sometimes men) as a perfectly nonrational form of communication with voters, because its message bypasses questions about record and program. At that time the helicopter, symbolizing power and modernity, was also an entertainment (what in India they called a *tamasha*, a spectacle) that promoted political diseducation—for sure a legitimate strategy, not literally dishonest, but definitely in the smoke-and-mirrors category. It helped give Johnson the "larger than life," impossible-not-to-notice-and-admire (or fear) image that, from his college days onward, he had never ceased to cultivate.

His opponent in 1948, former Governor Stevenson, did none of those things. There was no need, because in Texas he already had "communion." He was a public figure, widely known and widely respected; people called him, with affection, "Mr. Texas." He campaigned the old-fashioned way, motoring from one community to another, and asking for votes because "You know me. You know what I have done. You know what kind of administration I run." He asked for—and in the first part of the campaign got—financial support from wealthy individuals who approved of his conservative philosophy and admired his integrity. (Later this support, suborned by Johnson's lies, faded.)

This brief description of the use of character and record of service as campaign devices for getting in touch with the mass of voters touches no more than the surface of what went on in those three elections in Texas. Most of what I have so far described are honest strategies. To say "This is what I have done and this is what I will do" and "This is what my opponent has failed to do and will fail to do if you elect him" is well within the rules of the game (assuming, of course, that the claims have some truth in them). So also is maneuvering to get things done for one's constituents or for one's political allies or for the general good. Even back-scratching—exchanging favors with other powerful people—is not normatively offensive if done in the public interest. All political systems—all nonmechanical systems—can work only if the rules are constantly reinterpreted to fit present circumstances. Unfortunately, rule interpretation and rule breaking are difficult to keep apart, and in politics, as I said at the outset, rule-breakers, if they can get away with it, are likely to win.

That brings me to how Johnson and those who worked for him broke the rules and won two out of his three primary elections. (He lost his 1941 Senate primary campaign to "Pappy" O'Daniel, who campaigned with no more of a conscience than Johnson himself.) I will focus on the 1948 election for the Senate primary, when Johnson defeated Governor Stevenson.

Lies, Graft, and Money

The difference in goals, constraints, and resources between the two candidates will explain why Johnson made a headlong descent into the baser kind of pragmatic strategies, and why Stevenson, refusing to do so, did not win the election.

The immediate goal of both candidates, obviously, was to be elected. But the notion of *goal* is more comprehensive than that; packed into it are beliefs about what should be properly done with the power that a Senate seat confers, and, beyond that, basic ideas about what would be a good world to live in and for whom it should be good. Speculations of this kind paint very different portraits of the two men.

Stevenson's reputation was, in every sense of the phrase, that of a public servant, a person concerned for the general good (not his own or that of particular cronies), who had, moreover, an almost obsessive concern for legal propriety. A self-taught lawyer, he had been a district attorney, a county judge, a member and later (for an unprecedented two terms) Speaker of the Texas House of Representatives, lieutenant governor, and then governor of Texas. Despite this record, he does not come off Caro's pages as a man hungry for office because it gave him power, but rather one who accepted office out of a sense of duty. Caro portrays him as a man who would not break either the law or the normative standards of fair conduct simply to win an election. Johnson, as Caro tells the story, was quite the opposite, motivated less by an ethic of *public* service than by the power derived from making the government work for the benefit of those who would support his ambitions (not his policies—at that time he appears to have had none). There were many things that Stevenson would not do to win the election; Johnson was ready to win in any way he could, just or unjust.

That difference in outlook connects with a difference in access to political resources. Stevenson, to put himself across to the voters, needed to do no more than let the record and his existing reputation speak for him. Johnson, on the other hand, had a major image-fabrication task. It was not so much that the ordinary voter knew him as a wheeler and dealer with a king-sized ego and a minuscule conscience; he was a politician and many politicians were like that. Rather, the problem was that they did not know him in the way that they knew Stevenson. Johnson was not (except for a time in Roosevelt's mind) "Mr. Texas."

Stevenson had other advantages. In those years, Texas was a Democratic state, but the majority of Texans who had money and influence were not "Roosevelt Democrats." In the 1930s few of them were New Dealers, and they resented what they saw as federal interference. They thought of themselves as conservatives, and in the years after the war they worried about socialist tendencies, about threats to the Taft-Hartley Act (which curtailed the power of labor unions), about anything that would affect the ability of businesses to make money and the propertied classes to hold on to their wealth, and about the "fiscal irresponsibility" of New Deal economics. In 1948 Stevenson stood solid with such people; they trusted him; as governor he had transformed a deficit when he took office to a surplus when he left. Johnson, on the other hand, moved in circles that made him suspect; he had at one time—and at the time he was not slow to make it known—the ear of Roosevelt. On this score too he had a problem of image management with most of the influential conservative-minded voters in Texas.

Of course he did not have that problem with big business, in particular with Herman and George Brown, the brothers who ran the vast Brown and Root enterprise. They and Johnson had worked together from the time he was first elected to the House. They had backed him in his 1941 Senate campaign, when he lost. (On that occasion an Internal Revenue Service inquiry into illicit donations by Brown and Root was stopped only when Johnson was able in private to persuade Roosevelt that the inquiry was not in the interest of the Democratic Party.) Nor were the Browns his only "clients." For the select few who controlled large sums of money, Johnson had an attraction that the straightforward Stevenson, who had no reputation as a wheeler-dealer, entirely lacked.

In brief, Johnson's strategic situation was this: He started with a reputation among many voters that did not come within a mile of Stevenson's; he had access to seemingly unlimited amounts of money; and third, his opponent, being the man he was, could probably be relied on to play the game more or less according to the normative rules. The solution for Johnson was obvious: use the money to make over his own image and to damage his opponent's; second, use it to get votes.

Not everything he did was extravagantly dishonest or unfair. Some of his tricks hover between the strategic and pragmatic. Most politicians exaggerate, and at least in some cases the exaggeration becomes a lie that is hardly considered a lie because it makes a good story; and Johnson was an enthusiastic raconteur. In 1942, as I recounted, he had volunteered for service and become a lieutenant commander in the navy. At first he arranged not to be sent to a war zone and spent sev-

eral months inspecting naval installations on the West Coast, by
Caro's account enjoying himself, partying, and not doing much work.
Then, Caro implies, he realized that this was not good for his politi-
cal image, and he had himself sent to a war zone, New Guinea. There
he flew, as a passenger, on a bombing mission, and came under attack.
He behaved, Caro says, with exemplary coolness, showing no signs of
fear. General MacArthur gave him a medal and he came back to the
United States a hero. Not long afterward he returned to civilian life.

Johnson's award was clearly political; no other member of the crew
got a medal on that occasion. The episode was certainly not inglori-
ous, but that single flight and the Silver Star were used on the campaign trail to manufacture the image of a war hero with a distinguished record of service. Whenever possible he had himself introduced from the platform by a war veteran who had lost a leg or an
arm. He instructed his aide to make sure that the Silver Star was in
the lapel of whatever jacket he wore, so that he could point to it when
he talked of his gallantry and of his service to his country.

Other lies went beyond the mildly distasteful, in particular the fabrications in the systematic campaign that he ran to discredit
Stevenson. Johnson said the governor was campaigning for the Senate
only because he wanted the $15,000 salary. The governor, at sixty, was
too old to do the job, and Johnson, a clever mimic, took to mocking
his accent and his demeanor. Those tricks are, perhaps, no more than
in bad taste, certainly far short of the bald lies that he told about
Stevenson's policies, all the more brazen because the allegations he
made about Stevenson better fitted himself. He insinuated in print,
over the radio, and in his speeches that Stevenson was not a conservative at all, but in league with the bosses of the American Federation
of Labor (and their Russian masters) in a plot to rescind the Taft-
Hartley Act. He hinted at Communist sympathies, inviting the governor to formally deny the charges on one day, and on the next day
asserting they must be true, since the governor had not responded.
The funds that his backers provided made it possible to repeat these
messages. "Repeat the same thing over and over again," one of
Johnson's aides recalled, speaking to Caro. "You knew it was a damned
lie." But repetition made the lie stick and by degrees those grassroots
conservatives who supported Stevenson and financed his campaign
began to withhold their money. Johnson's lies had subverted them.

He also had other ways of spreading the message. "Missionaries" would be given $50 a day to visit bars, stand a few drinks, and spread stories about Stevenson's left-wing sympathies. These tactics were all the more successful because Stevenson refused to answer back and defend himself, relying, I suppose, on his reputation, and perhaps believing that such tactics, because they were so blatantly dishonest, could not prevail. Only very late in his campaign did his aides persuade him not only to defend himself but to go on the attack by talking about Johnson's dismal record as a legislator and his dubious contacts with trade unions, New Dealers, and other leftist sympathizers. But by then it was too late; the funds that he needed to mount such a campaign effectively had already been closed off by Johnson falsehoods.

That is half the story of Johnson's pragmatic strategy. The other half is not about buying publicity and winning the voters' minds by filling them with lies, but about winning elections by stuffing ballot boxes. By 1948 the larger urban areas in Texas had automated voting systems that were more or less tamperproof. But old-fashioned graft (the Eatanswill style immortalized in *The Pickwick Papers*) was still possible. There is a vivid description in Caro's *The Path to Power* of Johnson in his 1937 primary for the 10th District sitting at a table with a fistful of $5 notes that his assistants would distribute, trusting that the voters would not, having taken the money, vote the other way.

Where the vote was not automated, more cost-effective stratagems were available. "There was common knowledge," Caro writes, "in the upper levels of Texas politics of the precincts that were for sale." Influential individuals were bought not for their own vote but for the control they could exercise over voters or over the voting process; there were places where they managed to return majorities for Johnson with percentile scores in the high nineties. In one county, for every one Stevenson voter (38 of them) there were 110 Johnson votes. No less useful were people who controlled not the voters but the voting procedure itself: tellers who counted votes cast for Stevenson in Johnson's favor, the poll watchers being either bought or intimidated; political bosses who obtained tax receipts (evidence of a right to vote) and cast the votes in bulk for Johnson; and officials who simply altered the polling station returns, without reference to what was in the ballot boxes, sometimes stalling sending in their returns until Johnson's people had phoned to tell them how many votes were needed.

The most notorious incident that came officially to light occurred in the town of Alice in Precinct 13 in Jim Wells County. After being declared the loser, Stevenson had gone to law, and his lawyers had discovered evidence that the number of votes in that precinct had been doctored in Johnson's favor. People whom Caro interviewed years later, including those on Johnson's team, said that this was the case. But the skill of Johnson's lawyers and their political connections in Washington—they had the case moved to the federal courts—gave Johnson a victory on a legal technicality.

Governor Stevenson did not again seek high office. He lived until he was 87, contentedly according to Caro, on the ranch that he had bought and to which he had retired in the intervals between holding office. He refused an invitation to seek the second Texas seat in the Senate when it became vacant (if elected, he would have been Johnson's junior), and said in 1964, when asked about the presidential election, that he would vote for Goldwater, the Republican candidate.

The Significance of Pragmatism

A coroner's jury, giving their verdict on a man drowned in a canal, wrote that the death was "an act of God, helped out by the scandalous neglect of the waywardens." The man was drunk; God had made him a drunkard; that was his nature. On the other hand, if the setting had been different and the towpath had been properly maintained, then, even drunk, he might not have fallen into the water.

Likewise, there are two general explanations for why Lyndon Johnson was such a rascal (at least as he emerges from Caro's account of the 1948 election). The first points to the man: that was his nature; God made him that way. The second points to the setting: no one could operate effectively in Texas politics without being a rascal. But Governor Stevenson was a successful politician for many years in Texas, and he was (again according to Caro) an honest man. The conclusion seems to be that Johnson was a rascal by nature; but he might not have been able to indulge his rascality so freely if the political setting had been different. But what exactly was that setting and what significance does pragmatism have in it?

Let us run with both themes—person and setting—and see where they take us, in the process lofting another Hail Mary comparison (to

go with Tuta/Dukakis or *mafiosi*/Swat Pathans), this time a three-way
between Gandhi, Governor Stevenson, and Lyndon Johnson.

Stevenson and Gandhi shared a common morality, at least when
contrasted with Johnson. They both were lawyers of a kind that is not
much talked about at the present time. Lawyers are by calling adversarial; but there is a difference between those who enter a contest
solely to win, and others who see it as the most effective way to arrive
at the truth. Stevenson, Caro writes, had a reverence for the law as an
institution, and his loathing for Johnson came not only from losing to
him, but also from seeing him violate the law and get away with it.
Gandhi likewise respected the law, not British-Indian law but the law
of God, which he called *satya* or truth.

In at least one respect they also shared an image of the good society,
believing that every individual deserves respect. It is at first sight odd
to associate Stevenson's frontier individualism with Gandhi's mystical
humanism, but they do have a common feature. Stevenson epitomized
the pioneer, self-reliant, self-respecting, and hard-working; he dis-
trusted federal agencies and their increasing control over states' rights;
he disliked big unions because, like big business, they concentrated
power into the hands of the few and took away an individual's control
over his or her own life. Gandhi was in the same camp: Government is
bad, because individuals should decide things for themselves, and the
bigger the government, the more undesirable it is.

The contrast between both of them and Johnson is obvious: They
were statesmen concerned with what they considered the public weal
and they were guided by an ethic of absolute ends, whereas Johnson
was a politician in the least complimentary sense of the word, moved
by an ethic of responsibility (for his own advancement). The strategies of Stevenson and Gandhi were normatively directed; Johnson's
strategies were mostly, or verged on, the pragmatic.

But that verdict, although true, oversimplifies reality; there is more
to be said. Stevenson and Gandhi were moral men; Johnson, if meas-
ured by their standards, was not. But why use their standards? As Caro
remarked, it was "common knowledge" that precincts were for sale.
Johnson's defenders could point out that his kind of campaigning was
statistically the norm. What weight should be given to a normative
rule that almost everyone breaks? In what sense can such a rule be said
to exist? If the rule does not exist, how could Johnson have broken it?

Of course in the eyes of the law that is pure sophistry. There were laws against stuffing ballot boxes, intimidating poll watchers, voting the dead and other absentees, and altering returns (the voters who gave Johnson a majority in Precinct 13 appear to have come all together in a group to the booth, arriving after everyone else, and to have voted in alphabetical order, their votes also being recorded in a different shade of ink). The law had clearly been broken. But Gandhi broke the law too: He urged people not to pay taxes; he proclaimed that the government was not legitimate. He was, as Churchill said, "seditious." Where is the difference between what he did and what Johnson did?

One obvious difference is that Johnson won his primaries because he had no conscience; Gandhi, who also was victorious (not in his own eyes but in the eyes of the world), had a surfeit of it. Gandhi made all his moves in the open; Johnson was secretive. Gandhi, when on trial or before a commission of inquiry, defended himself not by legalisms, and not by denying what he had done, but openly, on normative grounds, asserting that he had acted in accordance with a higher morality. Why Johnson could not have done this is easily understood. The politicians in Texas were engaged in an election, which is a competition regulated by a comprehensive set of normative rules, both legal and conventional, which apply to all the competitors and which they all have promised, implicitly or explicitly, to observe. The Freedom Fight in India was not a competition but a revolution, an attempt to alter a basic rule about eligibility to enter the political arena. An election is not an attack on a structure, an attempt to change the rules of the game; a revolution is exactly that. Johnson was contesting an opponent, not *openly* impugning the validity of the electoral system. But he was impugning something. What was it?

At this point it is necessary to shift from judgments of right and wrong toward thinking about process. From this perspective Johnson's pragmatism is understood not as a form of moral turpitude but clinically, so to speak, as part of a natural or evolutionary process in which one structure of power gives way to another. Johnson's pragmatism was an instrument of fate, by means of which the political system in Texas evolved from one structure of power to another.

Normative rules everywhere benefit someone. Gandhi and Governor Stevenson and everyone else who supports a particular set of normative rules would surely assert that their rules have an absolute value and have nothing to do with partisan advantage. But the reality remains that those who control the rules are better placed to win the game. In the 1948 stolen election in Texas, Stevenson clearly would have benefited from an honest election and Johnson would have been disadvantaged. British laws and conventions in India obviously worked to British advantage, until Gandhi was smart enough to use the same laws and conventions against them. I will come to that later.

Who would have lost in Texas if the electoral rules were enforced? Johnson, obviously, but not him alone; his backers too were at risk. Governor Stevenson, in his life-style and values, represented an older elite in Texas politics that did not include the new entrepreneurs whose profits depended in part on having reliable contacts in the federal government. Johnson and people like him provided that contact. No one ever voted in Texas who was not an individual. But individuals are not represented in democratic assemblies; classes or interests are. Johnson's pragmatism (of course not his alone) was the device that enabled Brown and Root, Humble Oil, and other corporations to gain a say in the political arena at the expense of the smaller capitalists whose icon Stevenson had been. In this process, the legal structure that governs elections is left in place, but is circumvented. A variety of pragmatic conventions permitted those who were acquiring power to exercise it without having to first make revolutionary changes in the normative rules.

A similar process might, perhaps, have happened in India. Beginning in the last quarter of the nineteenth century, Indians were recruited into the higher levels of the administration in increasing numbers and there was also a slow and grudging British acquiescence to the formation of representative institutions. There might have been a relatively nonconfrontational, gradual process of change toward freedom, as there was in some of the so-called white dominions, for example Canada and Australia, perhaps leaving intact the monarchy as a symbolic vestige of British rule. Gandhi did not wait for that to happen, and in any case he would surely have been distressed by the pragmatic subterfuges and compromises that accompany such evolutionary and incremental processes of change.

Gandhi's strategies will be further considered in Chapter 12. In the meantime we will look at a different kind of pragmatism, exercised not to dominate others but to avoid being dominated by them.

11

Recalcitrance and Factions

- This chapter describes three manifestations of agency that, in varying degrees, threaten a regnant structure's dominance.
- Two involve rank-and-file pragmatism, which is practiced by those who are normatively excluded from competing for power. It takes two forms.
  - One is goldbricking: People do not challenge the normative system that excludes them, but exploit it for their own individual advantage. They do not advertise what they are doing.
  - The second—"rough music" or charivari—is said to be a kind of "do-it-yourself" politics; it occurs in spaces that the regnant normative framework leaves unoccupied. Whether or not rough music challenges regnant normative patterns is an open question.
- The third manifestation—factionalism—is related to the other two as evidence of inadequacy in the normative political structure, but it differs in a significant way: By openly pitting normative orders against one another, and at the same time discarding normative restraints, it moves the political process closer to chaos.

Švejkism

Švejk is the hero—or antihero—of the picaresque novel *The Good Soldier Švejk*, written by Jaroslav Hašek, a Czech journalist, an eccentric anarchist, an irregular Marxist, a bigamist, and a drunkard, who died in 1923 at the age of forty, leaving the novel unfinished. Švejk, a Czech, enlists in the Austro-Hungarian army in the First World War and fights against the Russians. As I recall, in more than 700 pages of adventures, only once did Švejk encounter a Russian soldier, an escaped prisoner of war bathing in a lake, who ran away leaving his uniform behind. Švejk tried it on and was himself promptly arrested, despite his protests, by a patrol of Austrian military police and held for a time as a prisoner of war. The novel in fact is not about fighting; it is about the incomparable stupidity of the Austro-Hungarian army's officers, commissioned and noncommissioned, and about Švejk, the apparent accident-prone bumbler, who contrives at every step to outwit them and insult them and get away with it. The book, presented as knockabout comedy, is a ferocious satire on authority.

Not everyone is fond of *The Good Soldier Švejk*. Hašek, as his translator puts it, lived a bohemian life: He was an adventurer and a person of irregular habits. In other words, neither Švejk nor his creator had much respect for the public good as represented by persons in authority, who, with a few exceptions, appear in the novel as drunken, lecherous, gluttonous, brutal, obtuse, and untrustworthy. Hašek offers a ringing celebration not so much of disorder itself, but of every person's natural right to resist domination by the state and its servants. *Švejk* is an epic in praise of rank-and-file pragmatism; it glories in the virtues of disrespect. From another point of view, *Švejk* is a grossly irresponsible encomium of an evil way of life that entirely lacks the ethic of public service and which, if followed by everyone, would swiftly reduce the social order to consummate chaos.

Moral posturing, whether in favor of Švejk or against him, is hard to avoid. My own view is that the Švejks around us are, paradoxically, a necessary and effective antigen for a morbid condition that overtakes any institution that is not constantly challenged. Also, life would be very dull if there were no tricksters. More on that later. In the meantime I will describe the settings in which Švejkism occurs and the methods that a Švejk typically uses.

I wrote earlier, in Chapter 5, that the goal of bureaucrats is to find a rule for every conceivable situation so that no one need ever be in doubt about what is the right thing to do. Such a goal, obviously, is unreachable, and I noted that if it ever were to be reached, political leaders would have nothing to do because it is their task to confront the unexpected and tame it. Obviously they are likely to find bureaucrats irksome. They are not alone; everyone finds an overabundance of rules frustrating and dehumanizing. Bureaucratic rules, moreover, can be out of line with the ethics of everyday life, for example, when they prevent favors being done for kinsfolk or friends. More generally, a wholly ordered social universe would be a joyless place, lacking wonder and spontaneity, lacking—in a word—freedom. It is therefore comforting that the goal of perfect bureaucratic order is beyond reach.

Nevertheless, the goal exists, and we work toward it willingly both because it pays us to do so (experience soon shows that chaos is not pleasant) and because we have all been socialized into an ethic of service. Institutions—schools, churches, armies, communities, nations—drum into us a sense of duty and a corresponding unease when we catch ourselves shirking. But there are problems about where the lines are to be drawn. No one's social life is so perfectly organized that there is never a clash of obligations between, say, family and vocation. Should time be spent with one's children or in getting ahead with one's career? How much in each? The problem is compounded because those in charge of institutions, in particular of formal organizations, want everyone to "go the extra mile."

Moral exhortations of that kind are well and good where the setting unambiguously and exclusively fronts ideas of duty and service, as in religious organizations or any organization that is built around a cause. They do not sound so apposite when profits and payments are involved, although manufacturing and business enterprises do make free use of "loyalty" rhetoric. In general, however, they rely on another kind of persuasion: the straight mercenary appeal of "It will pay you to do as we say."

Joined with that rhetoric since the opening of the twentieth century is a particular form of production and a technique of management that have a strong tendency to alienate workers. The technique, called "scientific management," rests on two assumptions: First, the need for craft skills should be reduced to a minimum; second, a worker can be turned into a virtual extension of a machine. From the management point of view that would be good because machines do not have family obligations, do not daydream when they should be working, do not steal from the firm, do not look after themselves at the company's expense, are not militant, have no pride, and do not complain about working conditions; in short, machines are not human. The procedure begins by taking scientific measurements of a worker's actions at a machine (the science is called Taylorism, after Frederick Taylor, the man who invented it; he died in 1915), a reasonable product-per-hour-quota is ascertained, and then the worker is paid more (on top of his basic wage) if he exceeds the quota. This is known as "piecework," a product of Taylorism. A related set of ideas emerged as Fordism, which is the use of a production line, as in the car-assembly lines in Henry Ford's factories.

The captains of industry—and many other people too—saw nothing wrong and everything right in scientific management. It vastly increased the amount of consumer goods produced. It broke the hold that skilled workers formerly had over production, by virtually removing the need for any skill at all. Those who worked at repetitive machine tasks were euphemistically called "semiskilled." It provided employment to huge numbers of immigrants and gave them money enough to buy the cheap mass-produced products they created. By this reasoning everyone—owner, shareholder, manager, worker—should have been a winner. Everyone should have been happy.

In fact, there was much unhappiness. Scientific management constantly pushes competition along the political continuum toward conflict. Workers and management become enemies. In a piecework setting the managers have an interest in raising the quota as high as they can, because the higher it is, the less each piece costs them. Correspondingly, it pays the worker at the machine to keep the quota low. The ingenuity that goes into organizing Taylorism then is matched by the ingenuity of workers intent on beating Taylor's system. A plethora of verbs appeared in the early years of the twentieth century to describe the actions of the low-level employee or servant of an organization who cheated or swindled it out of what the organization considered its due. The terms usually reflect the normative position of the speaker. Managers and owners and officials talk of stealing or swindling or cheating or shirking. The word used by their subordinates is "fiddling," for sure not a term of outright approval, but also not forthrightly marking the action as unethical, and often indicating a mild admiration for the ingenuity involved. The British military slang word for stealing army property was "winning" or "liberating." Shirking (evading duty) was "skiving" or "ducking." Flattering superiors to make them overlook shirking or to make fun of them (a Švejk specialty) was "flanneling." In the United States a generic term for cheating and swindling and slacking is "goldbricking."

Why, in a book about politics, should actions that are generally written off as deplorable, certainly, but also, from the point of view of serious politics scarcely worth attention, be considered at all? Goldbricking is a minor irritation in the body politic and has nothing to do with public policy. The Švejks are, quite literally, beyond the pale that surrounds the legitimate arena of public politics.

There are two answers. First, recalcitrance is part, and sometimes a large part, of the political process. The individual Švejk himself has little impact, but Švejks in aggregate may not only diminish control by a central authority but also, in certain conditions, cause the normative rules that govern political encounters to be changed. Even without such a change, the effect of fiddling may be surprisingly large and may, paradoxically, be the reason why an unrealistic and potentially oppressive normative structure goes unchallenged. James Scott calculated that evasions by Malaysian peasants reduced the income accruing from Islamic tithes to the clerical authorities by 80–90 percent.[1]

The second answer is more nuanced. Švejk is a laminated figure. The surface presentation of self reveals an honest patriot, a loyal citizen whose only desire is to serve "His Imperial Majesty the Emperor Franz Joseph." To his superiors he uses the most respectful forms of address—"Beg to report, Sir. . . "—and he insists time and again on his unflagging desire to do his duty. He speaks from the high moral ground that belongs to honest citizens and good patriots. There is never a word of sedition, never a hint that he imagines there could be any other regime than that of "His Imperial Majesty." There is no direct word of protest against the brutality and the stupidity and the dishonesty of doctors and colonels and generals and chaplains (they too are fiddlers par excellence). Švejk is presented—to use a modern term that severely begs a question—as wholly prepolitical.

Beneath the outer layer, however, another Švejk is revealed in his endless wacky tales about life in general and the military life in particular, and in the overwhelming irony that gives meaning to the entire novel. This Švejk is a direct contradiction of the sentiments that he continually mouths. This—Švejk's inner voice—is the voice of Hašek. It carries two messages that are wholly political: First, power in the Austro-Hungarian empire was in the wrong hands, at the top and all the way down to the pettiest functionary; second, power, masquerading as authority, is anywhere and at all times an evil. Authority is evil; anarchy is good.

That is not, however, the lesson that I want to take here from *The Good Soldier Švejk*; I am not in the business of making recommendations. The novel speaks first to institutional excesses, and second to the relativism of political claims about what is and is not normative. Certainly institutions could not function without having some authority or without there being some sense of public duty; that sense provides them with the power needed to determine ends and to organize collaboration in the public interest. But, inevitably, they grasp for greater and greater control over their constituent members, whether these are individuals or subordinate organizations. (This tendency is sanctified in the—surely ironic—claim that sometimes is made for religious organizations or totalitarian political parties: The only true freedom lies in surrendering one's self wholly and entirely to the requirements of the institution.) Excessive demands erode the sense of duty and begin to give normative status to its opposite, which is the rights of an individual.

I said that the term "prepolitical" begged a question. Hašek himself did have a somewhat intermittent professional experience of working within a normative political frame. He spent part of his life as an *apparatchik* in Soviet Russia, ending up, before returning to Czechoslovakia, as head of the International Section of the Political Department of the 5th Army. But the creed that he preaches through Švejk suggests no normative structure as God's chosen design for the world, unless one counts the well-being of the individual (the particular self, not individuals in general). The point is arguable. On the one hand, Švejk and those like him certainly feature on any map that shows the distribution of power in a population; therefore they are politically significant. On the other hand, it can be readily argued that since the Švejks have no positive program to put forward, have no ideology beyond their own comfort, and are not working to install any alternative political structure, but only enjoy making things difficult for the existing structure, they must be prepolitical. Certainly there can be a Švejkist ideology, but there could never (without contradiction) be a party with a Švejkist program, any more than there could be a party of Independents or a government of Anarchists.

The point is arguable, but in fact is easily settled. It only comes up because, a generation back—E. J. Hobsbawm's *Primitive Rebels*, published in 1959, is an eloquent example—it was the fashion to write about bandits in peasant societies as if they were protorevolutionaries whose dominant concern was to overthrow the ruling class. For sure such people did exist, but no less surely it would be a mistake to assume that every manifestation of fiddling and skiving and insolence and disrespect is a revolution in embryonic form, or that every bandit wanted to be a Castro or a Mao. That the Švejks do not have such ambitions does not, of course, make them irrelevant in political arenas: A 90 percent evasion of a normative rule that helps support a political elite certainly is politically significant.

Rough Music

Rough music is a way of showing contempt, not in Švejk's ironic posturings of subservience, but directly. There is no need for irony's protection (irony leaves room for disavowal) because the makers of rough music not only think themselves to be on high moral ground, but also are powerful enough not to fear retaliation. Rough music is a weapon used by the weak on the weaker. It is played by banging together pots, pans, kettles, spades, shovels, milk cans—anything that can be used to produce a cacophony. The performance may also be without percussion, using only catcalls and insulting songs, or it may be done, with or without noise, by piling cowmuck against the door of the offender's dwelling.

The victims were people who had contravened the community's expectations of what was right and proper. An old man who took a young wife or—worse—a liaison or a marriage between a woman and a younger man, a man cuckolded, a henpecked husband, a young woman jilted, the village priest if there were no marriages during Carnival (the season preceding Lent), or anyone else who, deliberately or not, featured in some event or condition that was considered undesirable—all could be assailed with rough music or other acts of unpleasantness. The list is interesting because it contains not only misdeeds (as locally defined) but also misfortunes beyond the offender's control, such as the jilted girl or the priest who conducted no marriages during Carnival because no one came forward to be married. The priest would be put into a barrow, wheeled through the streets, and then tipped onto a manure heap. It is hard to grasp the logic behind punishing a man for something he did not control, until one learns that the priest could buy himself off if he made an appropriate gift to his tormentors. There is a glimmer of an extortion racket in that and in many other instances. If a village girl married a man from outside, the party that came to fetch the bride would be refused entry until they paid a fee. On most occasions there is evidence of a trick-or-treat mentality; the timely payment of a fine or a ransom could avert or put a stop to the mock-judicial torment.

The institution seems to have been present in most European peasant populations from about the seventeenth century down to the 1970s and perhaps beyond. The tormentors were young males, past puberty but as yet unmarried. In the Alpine regions of southern France they were called Companies of Fools, *Les Fous*; in northern Italy, *I Stolti* (The Crazies) or *Gli Asini* (The Donkeys) or *I Pazzi* (The Madmen). Those appellations suggest, as "silly" does in English, an unreadiness for responsibility. That period in the male life—between puberty and taking on the burden of a household and family—seems everywhere to be more or less one of licensed horseplay. People in my youth spoke as if every young man had in him a fund of immaturity that had to be dissipated; they needed opportunities to "get the silly out of them." They got drunk, they were rowdy, they made fools of themselves, they played pranks, and sometimes they destroyed property. It was supposed to be done without malice, all in fun, healthy and to be expected, a kind of inverse training for the responsibilities of adulthood by spending several years in licensed unruliness, just as excesses in the weeks of Carnival are a preparation for the mortification to come in the Lenten fastings and abstentions. Carnival is a time of excess and indulgence, of masked irresponsibility, of duties put aside, of innocent, childlike enjoyment. In a similar way, the Companies of Fools enjoyed year-round the privileged irresponsibility of Carnival.

Les Fous were makers of petty mischief, certainly vexatious for the authorities but stopping short of the point where a trick becomes a crime. They are like the students of my Oxford college who climbed the steep chapel roof to hang a chamber pot on the spire (the rector disposed of it with a shotgun), or those who sowed the immaculate and velvety college lawn with radish seeds, which grew fast and revealed a vulgar five-letter word. The young men (*les jeunes*) in a French village in the 1970s used to drive their small Citroën autos onto the ice-rink and play Dodgem cars. They went in gangs to fêtes in neighboring villages and enjoyed themselves by getting drunk, playing the fool, and causing chaos; the lads from neighboring villages did the same to their fêtes.[2]

Mischief was by no means random and spur-of-the-moment. In past times the young men in each community were organized as "companies." They appointed their own officers and gave them titles borrowed from the nobility (Lord of Misrule) or the clergy (Abbot of Unreason). They sometimes dressed the part, creating uniforms that, Švejk-like, mocked the aristocracy and the dignitaries of the church. They were the ones who organized the fun part of religious festivities. The same young men who wrecked the village ice-rink (the village by the 1970s had gone in for winter tourism) also arranged the dance and fête for Mardi Gras, the last day of Carnival; they also organized the annual ski competition.

This list of what the young men did, and in some places still do, swings between the poles of order and disorder, between actions done for the public benefit and other actions that, Carnival-like, defy the proprieties of convention-bound everyday life. There have been, understandably, several different interpretations of what is going on, some of them directly political (concerned with power) and some not.

Euclide Milano, writing about the Piedmont region that now spans the French–Italian border, focused on a quasi-political aspect.

These [Companies of Fools] were genuine expressions of the spirit of association that belonged to the middle ages, a relic of pagan traditions, and an instrument of rebellion on the part of the bourgeois against the feudal classes and an expression of liberty against theocratic and reactionary principles. More than anything else they were satires and parodies of feudal and ecclesiastical organizations. . . . They demanded official recognition as the holders of special privileges and rights, such as, for example, that of organizing religious and civil festivals, or levying taxes on baptisms and marriages, in which they interfered whether invited or not.[3]

Were they therefore political organizations? Perhaps Milano reads too much into the material. Certainly there are records of action by authorities to suppress both the associations and the festivities. For example, the annual St. Bartholomew's Fair, founded in 1133, and an occasion for happy excess, was shut down by the dour authorities of Victorian London in 1855. I doubt whether those authorities smelled revolution in the breezes of Smithfield, where the fair was held: more likely crime and indecency. That *I Stolti* were "an expression of liberty against theocratic and reactionary principles" is, I suspect, a view from the twentieth century. I do not think that *I Stolti* were out to change the seigneurial system under which peasants lived; they were just expressing resentment of authority, exactly in the manner of a Švejk; they were acting out disrespect, as the rank and file do everywhere; they were not revolutionaries. Nor is the heavy formality suggested by the phrase "levying taxes" convincing; the "treat" in trick-or-treat is not a tax, but a form of tradition-sanctioned mild extortion.

There is another theory—the "safety valve"—that marginally connects these customs with politics and power, since it implies that unremitting orderliness cannot be sustained without at least an occasional contact with the pleasures of disorder and irresponsibility. The theory links the behavior of *I Stolti* with Carnival and explains both as a necessary psychological compensation for having to live in a structured society. Carnival serves as a vaccination, so to speak, against chaos. The duties of everyday life, the responsibility that one has to take for others, the resentments that one may feel when submitting to authority, and the sense that there is a diminution of self, a lack of fulfillment, and a denial of creativity in every structured interaction—which is indeed the case—all contribute to an inner tension that can only be relieved by actions that negate structure and orderliness. In Carnival the revelers wear masks; they are no longer citizens with civic duties and held responsible for what they do, but anonymous and free to indulge in pleasures that in normal times are forbidden. All the inequalities of daily life—masters and servants, male and female, old and young—are put aside; so are enmities, because every person is, for the occasion, a new person and every relationship is a new relationship that does not carry the baggage of past obligations and resentments. This is the same Sesame Street psychology that we met earlier: People need to "get the silly out of them." It is also—once again—Heraclitus and the philosophy of "is" and "is not." For everything that is (structured institutionalized conduct) there has to be an opposite, an "is not," in this case the revelers' acting out unstructured, autonomous, rule-free spontaneity.

There is an oxymoron in this. The spontaneity is shaped by conventions; there are rules for breaking rules. Masks are worn. Revelers are required to enjoy themselves. Times are fixed; Carnival takes place over an appointed period; Mardi Gras (Shrove Tuesday) is the final day and on Ash Wednesday all the revelers return to the structured identity from which Carnival momentarily freed them. In a similar way *I Stolti* from time to time put off the mask of carefree mischief-making and take on responsibilities for public affairs and for the well-being of the community. They are its champions against other communities; they put up a ritualized protest when one of their women marries an outsider; they work to make their festivals better than their neighbors' festivals; at that level and in those fields (but not in all fields) they represent the body politic. Inside the community they are guardians of public morality, but not of its entirety—the church and the law and the state have the ultimate say in what is permissible and what is not. Murder, theft, assault, dangerous driving, banditry, disorderly conduct, failure to pay tithes or taxes, indebtedness, and the like are the concern of church and state authorities. *I Stolti* are the guardians not of the law that is on the books but of customs and traditions, which escape official attention. Henpecked husbands and scolding or turbulent wives, cuckolds, marriages or sexual liaisons between inappropriately aged partners, jilted girls—these are not the bishop's concern or the magistrate's worry.

Should *I Stolti* then be considered a political institution? On those occasions when the state or the church stepped into the arena to discipline them, they must have been reckoned a threat to public order and, at least locally, to the authorities themselves. That is the point that Milano makes. But, as in the case of Hobsbawm's social banditry, I think the claim misreads motivations and marks *I Stolti* as more concerned with public affairs than they probably were, perhaps because the writers—historians, anthropologists, political scientists—seeing injustice, project their own feelings onto the peasants and assume they must have been politically conscious of their own wretchedness. The history of peasant-based states is in fact replete with peasant rebellions, but rough music and all the other features that I have described in this section are not part of them, except perhaps for the slender link provided by mockery of official dignitaries.

I Stolti, however, were themselves authorities—of a kind—inside their own communities. Their jurisdiction was over matters, as I said, that the state and church chose to ignore. Nevertheless, a case can be made that they were in fact guarding tradition and upholding a normative framework. On the other hand, the list of transgressions is bizarre and it suggests that offenses were created and added to the list in order to increase the occasions for a payoff. But can that not itself be a political act? Each addition represents an increment of power. And *I Stolti* did it, as politicians do it in other places, under the cover of acting in the public interest.

I see a link between the activities associated with rough music and what (according to Caro) Lyndon Johnson did both at San Marcos College and when he was an aide in the House of Representatives: He found a vacant place and created a political arena where none had before existed. *I Stolti* can be understood in that way. Young men in peasant villages, at least until early in the twentieth century in most countries, were normatively excluded from the politics of state and church, and even from village politics (where the priest and the seigneur and the older men dominated). There was no regular arena in which they could compete for power. This seems to suggest that vacant spaces, where the jurisdiction of the state and other dominant organizations comes to an end, tend to be colonized by those excluded from the existing political arenas. It suggests also that in addition to "the silly" that has to be vented from the young, there is in many people, young and old, a need for political expression.

A case of that sort can be made for factions, which are examined in the following section.

Factions

Many words used in politics are prelabeled as good or evil. The master term itself—politician—now has such a negative connotation that practitioners refer to what they do not as "politics" but as "public service," and when they want to insult opponents and impugn their sincerity they accuse them of "playing politics," which is to say that they have lost sight of the general good and are promoting one or another kind of sectarian interest. The word "faction" has a similar negative connotation: It denotes a form of contest, which is coming near to stalemate or chaos. Its use, in most instances, is decisively pejorative.

For about twenty years, beginning in the 1950s, anthropologists made an attempt to bypass value judgments and give the term "factionalism" a scientific meaning. Guided by the reigning paradigm of the day, they investigated the structure and function of factions, using data mainly from village communities in India and Latin America. They defined factions as groups formed to contest for power and centered on a leader. Loyalty to the boss was more salient than adherence to an ideology or a program; in fact, there seldom was a program beyond beating the opponents down. Factionalism was considered an "irrational" form of politics, because squabbling seemed to be an end in itself. Again, in accordance with the then current theory, factional arenas were analyzed as equilibrium systems, each faction having its ups and downs, some vanishing and new ones appearing, but no single one winning so conclusively that factionalism came to an end. Nor was the system seen as entirely pathological; it had a function. Like the people who played rough music, the villagers of India and Latin America were normatively excluded from "real" politics, and the widespread occurrence of local factionalism was said to be their response to this exclusion: They created their own political arenas and disputed endlessly over issues that were trivialities, because all the important decisions were made for them in higher arenas from which they were excluded. They were, so to speak, like children playing at the grown-ups' game of politics. Looking back, these interpretations now seem patronizing.

The people of Bisipara, you will recall, were divided into two factions. They called them *dola*, and factionalism was *doladoli*. Even while they regularly practiced it, they professed to deplore *doladoli*, because it often led to an impasse in their *panchayat*'s quest to find consensus. Both factions were composed mainly of Warrior households, one being led by the Sirdar (the Bisoi) and the other by Jodu, the postmaster. The factions were kin-based; in other words, you were born into a faction. Genealogies showed that all but a few Warrior households belonged to a single agnatic lineage and that the factional division, with one exception, was exactly in line with a genealogical division. Households in both factions were more closely related to each other than to any household in the other faction. (The single exception was a man who had quarreled violently with his father and brother, and announced that he now belonged to the other *dola*. People said that he would sooner or later return to his natal *dola*.)

Faction membership was acted out in several ways. Mourning for a member of one's faction was longer than for someone in the other faction; contributions to funeral costs and marriage expenses and other ritual occasions were higher. I was told that several generations back, at the time when the Sirdar's lineage and Jodu's lineage divided, the Sirdar's ancestors had somehow tricked Jodu's ancestors out of the Sirdarship. No one knew the details and there was never a suggestion that the succession issue might be reopened. The Sirdar's faction seemed to have an edge, but not so much that Jodu's people could be prevented from routinely speaking against whatever the other faction wanted. On the other hand, a major crisis—such as the affair of Tuta and his *devata*, or various problems that the Warriors had with their politicized Panos—invariably caused ranks to close. In short, while the people of Bisipara for sure did not see themselves as having created a play-arena for politics to make up for their exclusion from larger arenas, there was an air of gamesmanship about *doladoli* that was wholly absent from the struggle for power between the clean castes and the Panos. *Doladoli* was play-politics; the Pano affair was serious issue-politics.

The clinical detachment of these structural-functional analyses of factionalism is generally not found in the work of historians or political philosophers, undoubtedly because what they categorize as factionalism is neither play-politics nor, in the end, issue-politics, but the most raw form of power-politics. "Faction" comes from the Latin noun *factio* ("doing" or "creating"), which also meant an association or an organization. More specifically it denoted the rival groups of politician-businessmen—we would see them as mobsters—who contracted to provide chariot teams for the Roman circus and who recruited street gangs to perform whatever violence was needed. The murdered Clodius and his assassin Milo, whom Cicero defended, were two such men (see Chapter 8). At that time, Rome was in political disarray; the Senate was in the process of losing its authority to military adventurers, principal among them Julius Caesar. The deadly encounters between Clodius and Milo and other Roman mobster-politicians have little in common with *doladoli*, other than the centrality of a leader. *Doladoli* was far from being shaped by the win-at-any-cost principle. Roman factionalism is generally considered to be a pathological condition of the body politic.

A very famous description of factionalism in the classical world occurs in the third book of Thucydides' *The Peloponnesian War*. It vividly conveys the moral void into which politics in the city-states of fifth-century Greece had descended. The war between Athens and Sparta had been going on already for five years. The city-state of Corcyra was a subordinate ally of the Athenians. A group in favor of joining Sparta indicted for treason a man called Peithias, the leader of the democratic party in Corcyra and a supporter of Athens; he was acquitted. Peithias then took his opponents to court on a charge of cutting vine poles from a sacred grove. They were convicted and fined, but immediately sought refuge in a temple and appealed to have the fine reduced. Peithias, an influential man, prevailed against them. Whereupon they broke out of the temple, gathered a raiding party, and murdered Peithias along with sixty members of the council. There followed a civil war. Athens and Sparta both sent fleets to intervene. The Spartans withdrew. The Corcyrean democratic faction, now victorious, took its revenge. "There was death in every shape and form," Thucydides wrote, "people went to every extreme and beyond it."

> What used to be regarded as a thoughtless act of aggression was now regarded as the courage one would expect to find in a party member; to think of the future and wait was merely another way of saying one was a coward; any idea of moderation was just an attempt to disguise one's unmanly character; ability to understand a question from all sides meant that one was totally unfitted for action. Fanatical enthusiasm was the mark of a real man, and to plot against an enemy behind his back was perfectly legitimate self-defence. Anyone who held violent opinions could always be trusted, and anyone who objected to them became a suspect. To plot successfully was a sign of intelligence, but it was still cleverer to see that a plot was hatching. If one attempted to provide against having to do either, one was disrupting the unity of the party and acting out of fear of the opposition. In short it was equally praiseworthy to get one's blow in first against someone who was going to do wrong, and to denounce anyone who had no intention of doing any wrong at all.[4]

That is a very lucid description of the factional style of politics—violence, fanatical enthusiasm, a mindless disregard for consequences, and a virtual absence of normative restraint. Most striking is the

absence of ideology. The factions are labeled democratic and oligarchic, but the ideological implications of those words vanished
under the overwhelming need to eliminate the opponent. Victory
became an end in itself, by whatever means; ideologies did not count.

The Corcyrean nightmare continued down the centuries to be the
boilerplate example of chaos for those who aimed to keep their politics civilized. *The Federalist*, a series of essays written by Alexander
Hamilton, James Madison, and John Jay and published in 1787 and
1788, has this at the beginning of Paper IX (written by Hamilton):

> It is impossible to read the history of the petty republics of Greece and
> Italy, without feeling sensations of horror and disgust at the distractions
> with which they were continually agitated, and at the rapid succession of
> revolutions by which they were kept perpetually vibrating between the
> extremes of tyranny and anarchy.[5]

This extreme chaos-producing instability was the outcome of factionalism. Paper X, by Madison, contains this:

> The latent causes of faction are thus sown in the nature of man. . . . A
> zeal for different opinions concerning religion, concerning government,
> and many other points [and] an attachment to different leaders, ambi-
> tiously contending for pre-eminence and power . . . have, in turn, divid-
> ed mankind into parties, inflamed them with mutual animosity, and ren-
> dered them much more disposed to vex and oppress each other, than to
> co-operate for their common good.[6]

So there will always be factions. But factionalism, a morbid condition,
The Federalist argues can be contained so long as there is a sufficient
number of contenders in the arena, because when any one contender
looks likely to become strong enough to dominate and exploit the
rest, they will gang up on him. The notion is not unlike that of a self-
regulating market, in which a natural order (an equilibrium) emerges
although no one intends it or designs it.

The midcentury structural-functional view of factions—a flexing of
political muscles that were denied entry to significant political arenas—is relatively nonjudgmental. So also is the idea of a system that
finds a balanced equilibrium. Thucydides, on the other hand,

denounced factionalism; so, generally, do those who write about the political chaos out of which Imperial Rome emerged. *The Federalist*, likewise condemning factionalism, at the same time offers a blueprint for a constitution that will control the effects of two inescapable human tendencies: to look after one's own interests first and, second, to go to extremes, even violent and self-destructive extremes, in order to do so.

The Federalist's model of factional politics contains an explicit notion of "normal" politics; the book has a subtitle, *The New Constitution*. Any model of factionalism must offer, at least implicitly, an idea of normality, which is in fact the civic view of politics: concern for the public interest; leadership by statesmen (not politicians); civility; no violence; readiness to give opponents a hearing; and a constant watch to control the natural tendency of political encounters to drift toward chaos. This drift occurs in conditions of unrest caused by the failure of a regime and the efforts of interested parties to replace it with a different one. This was the case in Corcyra and also in the longer historical perspective of the decline of the Roman republic and its replacement by a regime of emperors and military dictators. The United States of *The Federalist* was also at a turning point. Only Bisipara's *doladoli* fails to fit that picture; radical change there was being contested not in the *doladoli* arena but in the much more impassioned arena of caste politics. *Doladoli*, that is to say, is an arrested or incomplete form of factionalism.

How, then, should factionalism be understood? Factionalism and normal politics are not radically different: They both are composed of the same ingredients—normative designs put in competition by contestants who each have an ax to grind. This contest of ideas is a form of unintended experimentation that serves to adjust political structures to an ever-changing reality. It is a normal process; it is not pathological. It is not an experiment in the scientific sense, a rational, analytic redesigning of political institutions; it is rather a negotiation in which each side has to give in order to get. The negotiations are, by definition, a departure from the standards of normative purity in the direction of pragmatism, and the pragmatism serves to keep the adjustment process relatively orderly. Factionalism is a morbid version of the adjustment process, brought on initially by an unwillingness to make pragmatic concessions, and terminating in a condition of

total amorality when, as Thucydides wrote, "men take it upon themselves to begin repealing [the] general laws of humanity." In other
words, factionalism is, paradoxically, the outcome of excessive normative zeal, coupled with a determination to win at whatever cost.

The next chapter, which is about revolutions, will show that an
excess of normative zeal and a determination to win at all costs is often
less the reality than it is theater, a performance that serves to conceal
the actuality of compromise, confusion, and ambiguity.

12

Revolution

- The strategy that Gandhi used against the British shifted the boundaries by introducing religion into the political arena and rejecting notions of calculation, interest, and compromise. He risked chaos. But the doctrine and practice of non-violence diminished the threat of disorder and at the same time wrong-footed the British by confusing the line between seditious behavior and legitimate protest.
- Revolutionaries generally present their movement as clear and absolute, something that has not been marred by compromise; but this posture, like so much else in politics, has more to do with theater than with reality. Revolutionary processes are seldom clear-cut. To the extent that they are fuzzy and ambiguous, they are open to analysis by the same basic model—normative frames contested by people who have their own interests to serve—that is used to understand any political process.
- Both Mao's Cultural Revolution and Gandhian nonviolence were in essence a kind of theatrical performance that symbolized a normative design for the distribution of power that was itself quite unrealistic; but the dramatic presentation served both to intimidate the adversary and to call the faithful to action. Threats to take action are less costly than the action itself and they fall short of creating chaos. At the same time, precautions are needed to see that the drama of conflict and chaos does not itself escalate into the real thing.

Moving the Boundaries

In the contest between the Indian Freedom Fighters and the British, there was no overarching set of formally stated normative conventions agreed by both sides. (No one has ever done for revolutions what the Marquis of Queensberry did for boxing.) Indian independence was a revolutionary cause, potentially a bringer of chaos. Each side had its own version of what normative rules of government should prevail, and each developed a set of strategic rules to make its version dominant. The result was, as you will see, an arena with a delicately ambiguous combination of normative and strategic features. Each side, of course, would have labeled the other's tactics with whatever epithet they used at that time for "pragmatic."

None of the strategies Gandhi used against the British offended his own strongly held and clearly proclaimed normative principles. At the higher levels of their administration, the same might be said of the British. They were in fact handicapped by their own normative standards, because Gandhi practiced on them a kind of moral jujitsu, using two of their own rules to overpower them. One was an avowed normative respect for the rule of law. The other was a strategic rule about keeping religion and politics apart.

British policy in India, certainly in the twentieth century, was dominated by the idea that religion and politics make a bad mix, because from an administrator's point of view religion in India was an abnormally sensitive issue, potentially costly—even disastrous—because it so easily led to disorder. Except in instances where the imperial power felt it must follow an ethic of absolute value (e.g., the mid-nineteenth-century suppression of human sacrifice in the region where Bisipara lies or outlawing, in 1829, the practice of having a widow immolated on her husband's funeral pyre), the British imposed on themselves a rule of noninterference with the practices and beliefs of Hinduism and Islam. Some other parts of the world colonized by Britain—sub-Saharan Africa or the islands of the Pacific—did not pose the same problem because for the most part religions in those places were fragmented, were not religions of the book, and were not equipped, like Hinduism and Islam, with a scholarly apparatus and an institutional strength that resembled Christianity's own. In those other places, Christian missionaries could be let loose and even, in certain areas of the Pacific, allowed to become a virtual government. India was different. Certainly there were missionaries and some converts; there were also long debates, particularly in the early nineteenth century, about the part that Christianity could or should play in governing India, but by the late nineteenth and early twentieth centuries the administrators' rule was a very firm "hands off."

That policy did not, of course, remove the hostility that prevailed between Hindus and Muslims; local administrators in certain parts India spent much time trying to keep the peace between them, particularly on festive occasions, and the civil servant's folklore is rich with tales of resourceful district collectors preventing the mayhem that would have followed if the procession of Hindu (or Muslim) devotees had been allowed down the route they wanted to take. Peace, strategically achieved by keeping one set of fanatics apart from the other set, was the normative intent.

Indian nationalists saw that policy differently. They viewed it as more than crowd control. Rather, it resulted in institutional devices like separate electorates, which the British claimed to be necessitated by preexisting implacable hostilities. In fact the policy, supposedly a way of lessening disorder, heightened it. (The situation, mutatis mutandis, resembles that brought about by the Los Angeles Police Department's perspective on minority ghettos: Definitions create their own reality.) From that position it is only a short step to arguing that the policy was in fact a deliberate (and pragmatic) exploitation of religious differences, exaggerating and exacerbating them in order to maintain control through the Machiavellian strategy of "divide and rule." British policy worsened sectarian differences that were not inevitable; it deliberately widened the gap between Hindus and Muslims to prevent them from uniting against the ruling power. (President Roosevelt used a similar strategy to keep his entourage in line.)

The Congress Movement could point to itself as proof: From its inception until Partition and even afterward, the movement had both Hindus and Muslims within its ranks. On the other hand, Partition and the creation of Pakistan in 1947, at the cost of half a million deaths and more than four times that number of people turned into refugees, appear to demonstrate that religion does have its own explosively divisive power and needed no help from imperial pragmatics. The Muslims, moreover, had themselves, before the British arrived, conquered and controlled large areas of the Indian subcontinent, converting some of the Hindu population and making enemies of the rest. Whatever the truth of the matter, it was certainly the case that a strategic rule used by the British to guide their everyday administration in twentieth-century India was that politics and religion should on no account be allowed to mix; they should have a wall—a firewall—between them, because institutionalized religions have incendiary qualities.

One huge contribution that Gandhi made to the Freedom Fight, perhaps the decisive one, was to turn Congress into a mass movement. He did so by advocating a normative structure of politics that, far from excluding religion from the political arena, made it a foundation for political action. Given the situation in India, that was a perilous course, since neither Hinduism nor Islam, the main institutionalized religions, tolerated differences in the way that Gandhi himself did, and neither subscribed, as a first principle, to nonviolence. This is not to say that Gandhi's deployment of his own distinctive religion caused the terrible violence that killed five hundred thousand people at the time of Partition; that would have happened if Gandhi had never existed. Nor is it the case that the millions of ordinary people who lent their support to the Freedom Fight did so because they were converts to *satyagraha* and *sarvodaya*. They mostly were not; they were converts to Gandhi himself; they imagined him as a holy man, a person in touch with God (as he indeed said he was). The man himself, personifying asceticism, was the magnet, not the refined and abstract gospel that he preached.

Gandhi firmly (and in vain) rejected that kind of beatification: "Thank God my much-vaunted Mahatmaship has never fooled me."[1] The title "Great Soul," however, did fairly represent his image with many Indians and the image itself was a source of power not only because it gained the Congress a vast following, but also because it caught the British off balance. They were acutely sensitive to the dangers of offending religious sentiments and knew from experience that even small offenses against Hindu or Muslim sensibilities could quickly escalate beyond control. Imperial folklore had it that the Indian Mutiny of 1857 (more recently called "The First War of Independence") started because soldiers were ordered to crimp cartridges with their teeth, and the cartridges were greased with pig fat, which is polluting for both Hindus and Muslims.

The image of a holy man, even if Gandhi himself rejected the title, was firmly conveyed in his style of living, to both the British and

Indians, and it allowed him to operate, in British minds, as from the middle of a minefield. It made him formidable in a way that would not have been possible for Nehru or any other of the secular-minded Indian leaders who believed, as the British did, that politics and religion should not be mixed. When Gandhi fasted for six days (in the tussle with Ambedkar), the British did not fear mystically induced disasters, as an orthodox Hindu would have done; nor, for sure, would most of them have wept for him if he had died. What they feared was the very real threat of uncontrollable civil disorder if they let him die. From their point of view (and from Ambedkar's), fasting and other manifestations of religiosity were nothing but a kind of moral blackmail, an irresponsible breach of the rules of fair play in politics. For Gandhi, on the other hand, religion in politics was a normative requirement, a foundation without which the just society would not be possible. "For me politics bereft of religion are absolute dirt, ever to be shunned."[2]

In that way Gandhi shifted the normative boundaries of politics as the British defined them. Law and order as a mainly secular matter, enforced by the judiciary, was replaced in Gandhi's philosophy by "soul-force," that is, by religion and morality.

A normative regime is more easily displaced if it can also be shown to be ineffective, especially if it can be made to work against itself. That brings us to the second sensitive spot that Gandhi detected in the British Raj: its normative respect for the rule of law.

What actions go into one or another of the three categories (normative, strategic, and pragmatic) depends on who is doing the sorting. For a Gandhian, nonviolence was a normative rule, a physical acting out of *Rama Rajya* ("God's Regime," the phrase that set Nehru's teeth on edge). Noncooperation was a strategic rule intended to bring about *Rama Rajya* by expelling the British without violating the prime directive of nonviolence. The same noncooperation was defined by the British differently, but not in any unitary way. From one aspect— perhaps General Dyer's—it was simple insurrection and a plain defiance of the normative rule of obedience to the commands of a legitimate ruler. On the other hand, it was clearly not in the same category as armed rebellion or the assassination of a government servant or even the willful destruction of government property. It seems better described, from the British point of view, as a pragmatic device that allowed the noncooperators to cause chaos and make good government difficult, but shielded them from the full penalties that could legitimately be visited on armed rebels—in effect it was an overt form of recalcitrance. It prevented the government from doing what they would have done with plain rebels, which was to hang them or shoot them.

In this way Gandhi had introduced into the contest a strategy for which the government had no ready-made effective response. Nor is the point only that the strategy was new. Rather its strength came from its ambiguity; it did not fall into any well-established category of political action familiar to the British at that time. It involved religion, certainly, but it was nothing like a *jihad*, the Muslims' holy war, against which all those brought up in the same school as General Dyer would know, without hesitation, how to react. Against noncooperation there was no single tried and trusted counterstrategy.

We are back with Heraclitus: "We step and do not step into the same river: we are and we are not." Gandhian noncooperation was a defiance of the laws of British India; but it also was not defiance because it was a protest against injustice, and no law can forbid that. It was an attack on the forces of law and order; it also was not an attack on them at all, but an effort to win their cooperation and to educate them. Of course, none of these ambiguities stopped the British from putting Gandhi and his supporters in prison. But even there the categories were still confused: A person in prison is a criminal, but a political prisoner was not a criminal. The political prisoners were separated from ordinary criminals and, according to the stories I heard from them, were not as a rule subjected to physical violence, or to brainwashing—systematic attempts to "reeducate" them. Nonviolence was the instrument that created this ambiguity; nonviolence, at least so far as it concerned the Gandhians, prevented the struggle for freedom from being a war and preserved at least a substratum of cooperation.

The strategic lessons in this story, stated in general terms, are simple. First, to bring about a change of normative structure, one essential part of the process must be the blurring of hitherto firm categories, making it possible for people to say, at some stage, "they are and they are not" or "this is and this is not." When there is no ambiguity, nothing can be moved. It is an irony that Gandhi, for whom nothing remained ambiguous for long and who believed that every ambiguity could be resolved in the struggle to find the truth, should discover so powerful a weapon in strategies that promoted ambiguity by breaking down the firm barrier that the British built to keep religion from "contaminating" the political arena.

Second, to accelerate a change of normative structure, a good strategy is to make the target structure seem both meaningless and ridiculous, not simply by defying it but by using its own normative rules to make it unworkable. Gandhi was a lawyer and a tireless litigant, skilled in deploying the law as a weapon against those whose law it was. So were many of his followers; they went at the task with enthusiasm. Some of the Orissa politicians whom I interviewed had spent their years in prison in collaborative study of the immensely complicated land regulations; they had an eye to the land reforms they would introduce when they eventually came to power, and were readying themselves for the legal obstacles that could be put in the way.

Third, the politician's dilemma—how to surprise the enemy with a new strategy and yet still communicate effectively—was easily solved by Gandhi: He took a familiar part of Indian culture (asceticism as the symbol of the divine) and politicized it, and in the process mobilized people hitherto excluded from the political arena.

Finally, I want to draw a line that will make clear what so far has and has not been said in this chapter. Nonviolence is not the standard weapon that revolutionaries use. The philosophy that goes with nonviolence is, in a sense, profoundly apolitical (at least as I see politics—perhaps nonviolence is the civic variety of politics that I subordinated at the outset). Paradoxically, it enjoins cooperation and shifts the focus of a contest away from the battle between antagonists and toward the obstacles that stand in the way of "truth." I do not believe, however, that totally harmonious cooperation could ever have been the actuality, not even among the Gandhians themselves. They were contestants; there were winners and losers among them. Nor, except for Gandhi himself and a few of his disciples, did the Gandhians try to cooperate with the British to find truth; they pressured them into accepting as truth the right of Indians to rule their own country.

That being said, Gandhian nonviolence and nonviolent campaigns elsewhere do have distinctive features. One, admittedly, is a propensity to end up in violence. But that is not the inevitable outcome; nonviolent campaigns can remain peaceful and yet achieve their goals. They can do so for several reasons. First, they are contests to win people's minds, not to subjugate them or eliminate them. Second, nonviolence seems to be effective when there is at the outset a sufficiency of shared values between the antagonists with respect to what should and should not be done in order to win. There is an "If . . ." fantasy about how Gandhian nonviolence might have fared if Hitler had won the war and taken control of India. "I made the mistake," Gandhi said as he was led away by his German guards, presumably to be shot, "of thinking I faced a regime ruled by conscience, one that could at the very least be shamed into doing that which is right."[3] For nonviolence to work, there has to be some degree of collusion, some acceptance of the same ethic by the oppressing party. Here is a man from Orissa:

> This is how we did it. First write to the [Magistrate] saying what you would do; then publish it in all the newspapers. Police used to come and wait. The *satyagrahi* goes there with bag and baggage, knowing he will go to jail. He stands up and says, 'No one is to help the war effort; no one is to give a single penny.' Then the police approach and take you to jail.

Nonviolent campaigns generally are not remembered in the way that "dirty" wars are remembered; the legacy of shameful conduct is likely to be relatively small, perhaps because encounters between the antagonists in a short time become virtually ritualized, as if there was an unwritten and unspoken and unacknowledged equivalent of Queensberry's Rules presiding over the rule-breaking. It sounds very sportsmanlike. Pains are taken to break the rules according, it seems, to the rules for breaking rules; it is by convention forbidden to surprise an opponent; nothing secretive is done; no one makes a move that could be a cause for shame.

Fair play, obviously, is not found in every political encounter that is labeled nonviolent. Nor, for sure, does fair play characterize everything that was done in the struggle for Indian independence. Nevertheless, despite General Dyer and despite the mid-nineteenth-century atrocity-studded Indian Mutiny, India's "revolution" against British rule was relatively orderly. No armies took the field to win freedom. (In the virtual civil war that is called Partition—a war between civilians—the retreating colonial power participated only as a mostly ineffective peacemaker.)

The Fuzziness of Revolutions

What is a revolution? Definitions are contingent things, put together for a purpose; therefore the same word may cover a variety of situations, depending on what features the definer wants highlighted. *Revolution* generally denotes a radical and abrupt change, usually with violence, that involves a shift of regime; the new rulers and the old rulers come from different classes and/or profess different philosophies of government.

Some cases seem clear enough: The American Revolution of 1775–1781 ended British colonial rule; the French Revolution of 1789 and the Bolshevik Revolution of 1917 removed monarchies and purportedly gave power to the people. Castro's proclamation of a Marxist-Leninist program in Cuba in 1959 certainly represented a change of regime, and so did the Mexican Revolution that began in 1910, the Chinese Revolution settled by Mao's victory after the Second World War, the revolution in Spain in the mid-1930s that left Franco's Falangist party in power, and the civil war in England (1642–1648) that ended in Cromwell's Protectorate and the execution of Charles I. All of these were violent; all involved a change of regime.

The English Revolution of 1688 removed the Stuart dynasty (James II) and replaced it with the House of Orange (William and Mary) and was extremely violent. But in what sense was the regime changed? The monarchy, as an institution, was left intact, the principal difference being that the Stuarts were Catholic and their replacements were Protestant. Was that still a revolution? Yes, if you consider a change in religion to be radical; otherwise not.

Some revolutions did not involve violence. Communist Czechoslovakia in 1968, under Alexander Dubcek, had attempted radical reforms, which provoked the Soviet rulers to send in tanks and use violence to maintain the status quo. That was the "Prague Spring." In 1989, well-organized street protests in Prague forced the hard-line Communist government to resign. Vaclav Havel, who had been imprisoned by the Communists as an enemy of the regime, became the new president. This was the "Velvet Revolution." It was, relatively, nonviolent; but it still was called a revolution because it introduced a philosophy of government (a normative design) that was, arguably, radically different from the communism that had preceded

it. Under communism the legitimate political arena is the party itself
and only party members can compete for power; the mythology of
government is essentially civic—everyone cooperates for the public
good, which is identified with the Party itself (or, sometimes, with the
person of its leader). The economy has a similar one-piece quality,
assumed to be a single great enterprise organized to serve the common interest. The Velvet Revolution of 1989 brought in free elections
and free markets, a normative design that is radically different from
communism. Therefore it seems reasonable to call it a revolution.
But, as you will see, things are not always so clear-cut.

In 1985 Gorbachev became general secretary of the Soviet
Communist Party and initiated the programs of *glasnost* (openness)
and *perestroika* (restructuring) that led, in 1991, to replacing the
Union of Soviet Socialist Republics (USSR) with the Commonwealth
of Independent States (CIS). The Commonwealth is governed by a
council of presidents and prime ministers from the twelve member
republics; it coordinates policies on defense, economic affairs, foreign
relations, law enforcement, and other matters. The Communist Party
is still a presence in Russia and most other CIS states, but now there
are other parties in the arena and no CIS state is constitutionally a
one-party democracy. Given this radical change in the normative
design for government, and the proclaimed intention to replace command economies with free-market capitalism, these transformations
are generally summarized in the West as "the defeat of communism"
and considered revolutionary. The normative politicoeconomic frame
of communism (a one-party democracy and a command economy) has
given way to a different normative design, which is capitalism (a mul-
tiparty democracy and a free-market economy).

But normative frames are not the same as lived-in realities. "Frame"
is an apposite word: It suggests a neat boundary around a composition
that has unity—a consistent whole without ambiguities or equivocali-
ties. Thus Tsarist Russia was a monarchy with a class-stratified bour-
geois-capitalist economy; after the 1917 revolution Russia became a
Communist state with a command economy and a Communist society
in which all citizens were equal and there were no class distinctions.
Those are normative statements and are true, up to a point, but it is a
truth created by simplification. Underneath the command economies
in all the communist countries there flourished, as a pragmatic reality,
a black market that ran on free-market principles. Also unadvertised in

the classless society, there existed a privileged class of party functionaries, denounced by Milovan Djilas, a fervent but disenchanted Yugoslav communist, in his book *The New Class*: "The greatest illusion was that industrialization and collectivization in the USSR, and the destruction of capitalist ownership, would result in a classless society."[4] His democratic tendencies cost him his Party membership in 1954, and he went to prison in 1956 when he—correctly—hailed the swiftly suppressed Hungarian uprising as the beginning of the end of Communism.

Then, in the final decade of the twentieth century, there was another revolution that made free markets normatively respectable. Those who before were unscrupulous pragmatic dealers in the black market now, along with some ex-*apparatchiks*, became the vanguard of free-market capitalism. In Armenia, a member of the CIS, such people are called the New Armenians, and their activity, which before 1987 was the amoral pragmatism of black marketeers, a decade later had become normatively respectable free-market capitalism. Most recently those who prospered have begun to validate their power by entering electoral politics, bringing with them a mobster-style violence that before was rare. So there has been a change in the normative design that certainly is revolutionary. But the reality is that for a large part of the population the free market and its political entailments are anything but legitimate. They represent not a revolution, not a new normative design that might command respect, but a simple breakdown of public order and effective government. Nor has the Armenian revolution eliminated Armenia's "new class" from the arenas of power and privilege. Its members, one-time *apparatchiks*, still play a major role in public affairs.[5]

The end of British rule in India saw a similar set of confusions and ambiguities. Independence in 1947 can plausibly be presented as a clean sweep of the imperial regime and therefore revolutionary, but the reality is not so neat. India's communists certainly saw the outcome of the struggle for independence as nothing more than the substitution of one bourgeois ruling class for another, and therefore, according to the Marxist doctrine of social evolution, not fit to be recognized as *the* revolution, which would be the defeat of the bourgeoisie by the proletariat, the downfall of capitalism, and its replacement by communism. There were others, not from the left wing, who also had doubts. One of Orissa's post-Independence leaders, a devoted follower of Gandhi and firmly committed to nonviolence, allowed

himself to wonder (momentarily) whether it might not have been better to have had a violent struggle, even a civil war. That (he assumed,
I think optimistically) would have eliminated from the scene not only
the British but also the politicoeconomic institutions they had
imposed on India, in particular the bureaucracy, and along with it all
of those many Indians, persons of influence, who had supported the
British (or at least had not made the sacrifices that he had made when
he committed himself wholeheartedly to the Congress Movement)
and who nevertheless had remained in positions of power after 1947
because they were thought to be indispensable to the maintenance of
orderly government, and (perhaps) because Gandhi's philosophy
mandated loving forgiveness.

When one looks closely at any revolution that is considered successful, there are many continuities; many features survive from the old
regime. That is to be expected; the routines and rituals of everyday life,
including everyday politics, cannot be totally erased and replaced by an
entirely new set. Individuals, let alone whole societies, need time to
unlearn the old and learn the new—to be reprogrammed—even when
they are ready and willing to accept the changes. But this inescapable
conservatism—mind-sets surviving from the past regime—is not likely to be advertised. Those without power fear punishment from the
new masters if they make a parade of continuing to do what they did
before the revolution. The masters themselves are likely to be no less
discreet; a "new class" is naturally keen to conceal the hypocrisy of its
own position. Beyond that they are moved by the inescapable human
desire to pretend, both to others and to themselves, that the normative
design (by which, of course, their authority is validated) is closer to
reality than they know it to be. There is, as I said earlier, not just a
temptation but a *need* to play down the fact that normative codes
describe no reality other than themselves. To remove the façade and
expose the very confused actuality that lies behind the public-relations
billboards is to call for a new revolution and to reopen roads that lead
to chaos. That is a fair description of what Mao's Cultural Revolution
did to his Communist Party bureaucracy.

Stopping Short of Chaos

One could think of the Cultural Revolution as a drastic way to reform
a civil service, but the word "reform" does not convey the psycholog-

ical (and sometimes physical) violence that marked those three years. Mao's strategy was not to reform the bureaucracy by changing its rules, but to reconstruct the bureaucrats themselves—turn them upside down—by teaching them that, although they make decisions and give orders, they are the people's servants, not their masters. His technique was to induce a failure of nerve by shattering the high opinion they had of themselves. Roles were inverted; worker-peasant committees took charge; the bureaucrats were literally degraded.

It is an interesting experiment. A normative design, which is by definition not a reality, was forcibly brought as near to reality as possible, thus producing a kind of caricature of itself. The normative telos in the Marxist evolutionary myth is a society that needs no state apparatus because the people are the rulers and the state, as Engels put it, "withers away of itself." There are no classes; everyone has equal power and therefore no one has power. That normative design, of course, could never be realized, and if it were, the reality would be chaos. Meanwhile the party functionaries in China were given a taste of what life was like on the lower deck, no doubt with the expectation that, returning chastened to their offices, they would be humbler and better persons, no longer so contaminated by revisionist antidemocratic tendencies.

Looked at casually, the Cultural Revolution had an un-nuanced quality; it lacked restraint and promoted disruption; it was total and complete, a genuine, from-the-ground-up revolution. Control and rational calculation were seemingly absent, leaving room for a carnivalesque exuberance (symbolized by Mao's swim down the Yangtze) that would psychologically demolish revisionist institutions and clear the ground to rebuild the democratic structures that revisionism had destroyed. Apparently hearts and feelings ruled, not heads and calculation. But in fact the Cultural Revolution, although it certainly had a drastic effect on China's "new class," was not in the least a spontaneous emotional uprising. It was contrived and controlled. The disrupters—Red Guards dispatched to agitate the lives and institutions of the faux bourgeoisie—did not rise up of their own accord. They were recruited, presumably trained, and told what to do by Mao and his aides. This was not an impulsive protest by workers and peasants. Nor was it uncontrolled: When the Red Guards displayed more exuberance than the master wanted, soldiers were sent out to bring them to heel. Again, when the master—in this context deserving to be called a Lord of Misrule—decided that the job was done, the performance ended. Carnival makes an apt comparison, at least with respect to the controlled, purposeful, and time-limited deployment of chaos. It surely was not Mao's intention to have the peasant-worker committees remain forever in charge of institutions that could not function without professional expertise. The Cultural Revolution was staged; it was a performance, the enactment of a theme; it portrayed the normative design of an unranked society (including, as an irony, the chaos into which such a society would inevitably dissolve); but it did not convert—nor was it intended to—the normative design of citizen equality into a reality.

To say that politicians are putting on a performance, are play-acting, seems to cast doubt both on their sincerity and on the importance of whatever is being said or done. Politicians never describe themselves as performers; their enemies do. They might, however, admit to a trusted audience that what they were doing was intended not *directly* to change the institutional framework, but to send a message and create a shift in attitude. Consider Gandhi again (always remembering that we discuss the way his messages can be read, not what was actually in his mind). Gandhi, for sure, was a performer. The clothes he wore, his style of life, the Hindu values that he dramatized, the comments that Nehru and others made about his presentations, and other features described earlier amply demonstrate the public-relations aspect of his campaigns. Here I want to focus more narrowly on the messages that inhere in the drama of nonviolent protest.

Nonviolent protests—holding meetings and rallies, making speeches, blocking roads or occupying government buildings, refusing to pay taxes, and the like—transmit an ambiguous message about chaos. It is ambiguous because it rejects violence and yet at the same time holds out the possibility of escalation into chaos. (It also ensures that if chaos results, the opponent will be blamed and the nonviolent protesters can flaunt a clear conscience—no shame, no guilt.)

Nonviolent protests hint at a descent into the void because they convey, in a token form, the inability of a regime to keep order and to govern. The message, indeed, is the paradoxical one that they, the protesters, are the true guardians of order, justice, and good government. But at the same time the message contains a threat. Gandhi and his nonviolent followers opened a small window onto chaos, inflicting on the British civil servants, in a mild and more controlled way, the same traumatic lesson that Mao's Cultural Revolution visited on the party bureaucrats. Each case demonstrated to would-be masters that they could govern only with the consent of their subjects. Such a performance puts courage into the protesters and, if there is no violence, it has the benefit of being relatively costless. Recall the calculating young man who reckoned that more than one or two casualties from police firings could take the steam out of a nonviolent campaign. Recall also, however, that the young man's cynical cost–benefit calculations were anything but Gandhian in spirit. Nonviolence was a part of *satyagraha*, the struggle to find truth, and in that philosophy its purported intention was not to embarrass or frighten the British by a token display of what might happen if they remained uncooperative, but rather to give them the privilege of joining the struggle for truth and so to fulfilling God's intentions. This sounds far distant from the physical and psychological cruelties of China's Cultural Revolution, but the strategy and the goal are the same: to produce a change of heart in the opponent by means of the psychological shock that an experience of token chaos and the prospect of real chaos induce.

Both the Cultural Revolution and the many episodes of nonviolent protest in India's Freedom Fight were statements about normative designs for the distribution of power. They were intended to create attitudes and change people's minds; they were symbolic enactments—morality plays—about where power should lie; they did not directly redistribute power. The performances, however, did have a practical purpose, which was to provoke crises and to make it clear to everyone concerned that the time had come to make decisions and take action. Causes or programs, whether the withering away of the state or the moral regeneration of humanity, or, more specifically, beating back revisionist tendencies or ending imperial rule in India, come to the mind as empty things, that cannot be seen, or heard or touched, but only envisaged. Red Guards on the rampage, however, or the hunger-striker that I saw lying in the roadway at the entrance to the Orissa legislature in calm defiance of the police, catch the attention; they entertain or even fascinate in a way that the cause alone, merely stated and not dramatized, cannot do. But at the same time, performances are not only amusements; they say clearly that things are happening, that there is a crisis, and that it is time to make choices and take action. Political performances, in other words, are not intended merely to entertain (although sometimes that is all they do); they are calls to action, adrenaline-rousers, which shift the locus of experience from the realm of the intellect to the emotions.

Adrenaline-rousing is dangerous. I said earlier that when Gandhi introduced religion into the political struggle for independence by presenting himself as a moral savior rather than as a political leader he risked chaos. The same is true of nonviolence, when it is presented not as doctrine but as performance. Mao also risked a breakdown of the social order. No leader, however, who is not crazy wants genuine chaos, because it negates control; it leaves no room for leadership. A rational leader, therefore, when seeking to unnerve opponents by threatening them with chaos or giving them a taste of it, takes care not to let go of the reins.

There are two ways to control contrived chaos, corresponding more or less to the two basic strategies of leadership (captivating a mass or manipulating an entourage). The entourage strategy is to maneuver in such a way that the opponent (which is, so to speak, chaos itself) never has access to more than a part of the total arena. That is a version of Machiavelli's "divide and rule" tactic or of President Roosevelt contriving enmities within his entourage. Red Guards are sent out to initiate the chaos; the Red Army is not, but stands ready, throughout the three years of the Cultural Revolution, as the ultimate police force. Alternatively, one can think of chaos used to intimidate opponents or seditious followers as a form of controlled burn that takes place within firebreaks; those outside, safe from the conflagration, watch and learn that it is better not to be a revisionist, or whatever it was that offended the leader. Inflicting chaos indiscriminately and without keeping a sufficient reserve of disciplined support is to risk setting the whole forest on fire. The trick is to make sure that the chaos-makers themselves do not get burned and that nothing is done to alienate their supporters. The obvious suitable targets are those institutions (or groups) that are sufficiently out of favor to make attacks on them popular. Mao and Gandhi both directed their disruptive campaigns at authoritarian bureaucracies, which are not loved by anyone except the bureaucrats themselves. President Clinton's Republican opponents, attempting systematically to disrupt his programs, misread the public, misread his popularity, and did not anticipate the cost to themselves of trying to shut down the U.S. government. Union leaders everywhere, when they call a strike, take the potential fallout into account. It is a necessary calculation: A strike that causes no disruption does not move management; one that creates all-round havoc will cost the strikers whatever support they had with the general public.

The second way to control contrived chaos is to have (and make well known) a code of conduct for the protesters that by its very nature symbolizes order and restraint, and disassociates them from the idea of chaos. Protesters then present themselves as bound by conscience and principle to order and discipline. In one aspect this strategy is quite self-contradictory: It is both a fight and a nonfight. First, the protesters are conducting what appears to be a contest that lacks the master strategy of any adversarial encounter, which is to make a surprise move. Gandhian nonviolent encounters were highly ritualized, as the brief description given earlier showed—"First write to the [Magistrate] saying what you would do; then publish it in all the newspapers." How can a contest that is ritualized be considered a contest at all? One answer might be that winning it is less important than avoiding chaos, because chaos leaves behind it a wasteland. Second, Gandhi's campaigns were about issues that were heavy on symbols— the salt tax, the status of Harijans, indentured-labor emigration, the plight of textile workers—but in themselves, whether separately or in aggregate, were not likely to deal a mortal blow to the regime. They did not close the government down; they made life inconvenient for its bureaucrats. The deduction, once again, must be that order takes precedence over victory; these were token attacks, public-relations exercises intended more to draw attention to the cause than to inflict heavy and direct injury on the opponent. They were propaganda, shows of strength, perhaps sometimes bluff, not committing resources to a battle but sending messages about resources that could be deployed if it became necessary. That interpretation focuses on the strategic payoffs of veiled threats. Gandhi himself would surely not have admitted entertaining such thoughts. His own proclaimed view discloses no self-contradiction in the idea of nonviolent struggle and as a strategy it was entirely self-consistent: His stated intention was not to destroy opponents but to change their hearts, and hearts are changed by debate, persuasion, and symbolic behavior.

In this section I have examined manifestations of restraint in apparently disruptive revolutionary strategies and have linked them with an earlier claim that all revolutions are incomplete; no revolution is total. The ground is not cleared; there are always continuities; a total revolution is something imagined, whether wished-for or feared, but never achieved. More generally, there is no situation (political or otherwise) that does not contain contraries.

In the concluding chapter I will ask what the gap between a proclaimed normative ideal and the experienced reality, here exemplified by continuity and orderliness in purportedly radical and revolutionary change, signifies for our understanding of political processes.

Conclusion

The Normative Façade

Reality is directly experienced and in that way is directly known. To *understand* reality—to explain why things happen or to forecast what will happen or even to identify one's own experience or describe it to other people—it is necessary to construct models that represent the patterns that one has perceived in (or imposed on) experience. Let me paraphrase what I said earlier:

> The way to make sense of complexity is, paradoxical though it sounds, to pretend that it does not exist and to assume that matters are more simple than you know them to be. This is done by translating raw experience into ideas, which are elementary categories stripped clean of the complexities that in reality cling to them. These elements are created through a process of abstraction and then put together in a model that will reveal patterns hidden in the confusion of the raw experience.

Models accommodate reality's complexity in varying degrees. The simpler the model, the further it is removed from any particular reality and the better it is for making comparisons (as when I compared mafiosi and Swat Pathans or Tuta and Dukakis), but the less useful it is as a guide for investigating the particular realities. I now want to construct, as a summary and as a tool to apply to political events anywhere, a general model of political processes and strategies, built around the notion that political process is a pattern that emerges when self-interested individuals compete to make one or another normative frame prevail in a political arena. I will build the model stage by stage, beginning at the simplest level and progressively adding complexities.

Stage 1

The simplest model is that of an arena in which competition for power is regulated by a single normative code. The code spells out what the prizes are, who may compete, what tactics may and may not be used, and so forth.

In Bisipara, the normative code that clean castes favored excluded Panos from the competition for power by excluding them from the *panchayat*, which regulated public affairs in the village. There are no complexities in this description because it merely states what ought, according to the clean castes, to be the case; it pays minimal attention to reality. Reality includes, in addition to the normative rules and the conduct they justify, conduct regulated by strategic and pragmatic rules (Stage 2) and—a further level of complexity—conduct justified by rival normative codes (Stage 3). To model political action as the product of incompatible normative codes is to transform a *simple* arena into a *complex* one.

Stage 2

The first step in the direction of complexity is taken when the single-normative-code model is expanded to encompass strategic and pragmatic behavior. All normative designs leave unnoticed and unregulated tracts of social interaction ordered by strategic rules, including some that are pragmatic evasions of the regnant normative code. Individuals, seeking to gain advantage, seize opportunities in these domains and acquire power in ways that either have been neglected by the regnant code or sometimes are violations of it.

Švejk, presenting himself as the humblest soldier in the Austro-Hungarian army, ran rings around its regulations and made himself a life that suited him. Therefore he had power; but he did not want his power recognized, because publicity would increase the risk of the authorities deciding to rein him in. Pragmatic power depends on *not* being formally acknowledged.

Hašek's book describes a system in equilibrium; there is one arena and one normative code, and plenty of pragmatic action. Švejk's strategy, other things being equal, would have let him continue to play the game of outsider/insider indefinitely. He is a rebel but not a revolutionary; he is a force for conservatism, content to have things stay as they are. (Švejkism is yet another form of safety valve: It relieves frustrations that might otherwise lead to open normative protest.) Hašek's tale unfolds without any hint that the military code might be changing, or that the depredations of Švejk and the thousands of others who flanneled their way through military service might cause change or might themselves be a response to changing conditions. The novel does not address the historical dynamics of organizations. It cannot, since it presents only the single, fossilized version of the military mind. Hašek conveyed, with great élan, organizational inertia—the blinkered unresponsiveness of Colonel Blimps who reject whatever is not covered by the regulations.

In other words, he describes a process but does not put it into an explanatory context (other than the psychological context of human stupidity) or into a context of alternative normative designs.

Stage 3

The next step is to feed into the model the presence in one arena of alternative normative codes. All normative codes are designed (and evolve) to fit a particular context, which can change independently of them. When the context changes, it may do so in a way that increases the scope for strategic and pragmatic actions that, whether the agents are initially aware of it or not, are a potential threat to the legitimacy of a regnant normative code. The potential threat becomes real when agents try to have their actual power normatively recognized. In making those claims, they transform a simple arena into a complex one.

Change forces its way into the real-life narratives about Bisipara. The Bisoi, dealing with Tuta and the Distillers and the Panos, was coping with the political uncertainties of a caste structure that was being progressively destabilized both by pragmatic actions and by the invocation of rival structures. The Distillers, cashing in on the windfall opportunities provided them by a maladroit administration, challenged the rank order of Bisipara's castes but did not question the fundamental role of caste in village politics, wanting only to rewrite the "small print" so as to give themselves a more exalted position. They were out to amend the code, not to put a different one in its place. The

Pano story began in the same way; individuals acquired power in new domains that were unregulated by caste and then tried to revise their standing in the caste hierarchy. When that failed, they adopted a strategy available to them in the state and national political arenas and openly challenged the caste system as the regnant normative design for village politics. Let me expand and generalize this brief analysis, which recounts the various claims people made but does not sufficiently fill out the history of how they came to be able to make them.

Consider again the Pano Untouchables and their attempts to stage a revolution in Bisipara. Their strategy was, in its main features, Gandhian. The protesters were avowedly nonviolent; they did not attempt to seize power directly but, like Gandhi, they put on a performance. They went in procession to the village temple and demanded admittance, in accordance with a law passed some years earlier in the Orissa legislature. Admittance would have been a normative statement that Pano ritual status was equal to that of the clean castes. There would then have been no reason to continue excluding them from the *panchayat* on the grounds that it met in the *mandap*, a sacred building.

The procession and the troubles that followed happened in 1953. To make sense of those events requires one to go back along two paths. One leads to the 1920s, to Gandhi and his campaigns, which intensified in the 1930s, to remove the stigma that marked Untouchables. The laws that, around the time of Independence, mandated admission to temples for all Hindus, whatever their caste, had their origin in Gandhi's preaching. So also did the many "headstart" ordinances passed at that time. The second path goes further back, to the 1860s when the British decided to annex the Kondmals, the region in which Bisipara lies. The incursion was violent and the region was not pacified until the mid-1870s. Since the place was remote and promised little revenue, the British did not do much, intentionally, to promote economic development or to change the indigenous social order. They built some roads and established markets, they built some schools, their administration provided some jobs, and, significantly, they built jails and law courts and policed the area. Nevertheless, despite their conservative intentions, they began a revolutionary process that profoundly modified the existing structure of power. Blundering over prohibition (see Chapter 2), they inadvertently made the Distillers rich. The Distillers became major landowners. Likewise, as the years passed, some Panos prospered through trade or through jobs with the administration and a few of them became substantial landowners. They were the men who led the agitation for admittance to the village temple; they were the ones who sought office in local and state government and asserted political equality (as citizens) with members of the erstwhile dominant castes.

Without the politicoeconomic changes that broke the dominant caste's exclusive control over land, which was the main productive resource, there could not have been an effective protest against its political dominance. Land ownership by members of other castes, especially Panos, was a pragmatic departure from the regnant normative design. But the Panos had in fact gained some power and the 1953 agitations were an attempt to have that power validated, first within the normative scheme of caste and, when that failed, by the normative scheme of citizenship. The actual distribution of power, however, had already been substantially altered before the Panos made their bid to have the change normatively recognized.

The earlier stage of this process of change was carried forward by individuals who were not politically motivated (except in the private sense of wanting control over their own lives); the later Gandhian stages were overtly political. When the Panos made their bid for ritual equality and then for political recognition as citizens, their goal was *public* power, the right to have a say in determining what normative design would regulate village affairs. The campaign was not waged for any particular individual's benefit, but for the whole Pano community. That its later stages were so explicitly and self-consciously political was certainly the consequence of Gandhi's Harijan crusade; that it took place at all in Bisipara, however, was the result of a normatively unrecognized redistribution of power that had been going on for more than half a century.

Stage 4

Having explained how more than one normative code comes to exist in an arena, the next step is to work out what different uses actors make of this complexity.

That brief history of political and economic change in Bisipara outlines a process in which the actual distribution of power and the regnant normative model became progressively disparate. A simple arena became complex; the new arena contained competing normative models—the model of caste and the model of citizenship. People in Bisipara then had the opportunity to reach across from one normative domain into another, and did so for a variety of purposes and with a variety of consequences. These are "bridge actions." Here are some examples.

A simple form of bridge action was used by the Panos when they chose to define the situation as the Indian government mandated it should be defined: Untouchability does not disqualify anyone from competing for public power. Crossing that bridge subverted caste as a regulator of village political action in a most direct way. In fact, excursions of that kind were an ever-present reality in village politics. The *panchayat* lived always in apprehension that some disgruntled litigant (like Tuta) might go over their heads and appeal to the judiciary. They used to add a muddle-headed rider to their decisions saying that anyone who appealed to the government court against the *panchayat's* decision would have to pay the *panchayat* a fine for doing so. There was, in short, a clear awareness that they were living in a complex arena: Some normative structures were in contradiction, and to choose one was to diminish the other. The potentiality for that kind of arena shift had in fact existed, in a formal way, since the mid-1870s. Normative political sovereignty over village affairs belonged to the British administration and its courts of law. But the villagers were reluctant litigants and the administration, for reasons outlined earlier, had a policy of letting things be whenever possible; the result was that the many discrepancies between these two quite different normative designs, for example those concerning caste, came into the open only when strategies and/or a normative push from outside motivated lower-caste people to use their status as citizens.

A more complex type of bridge action is the one used not to subvert but to sustain an imperiled normative design. Tuta the Washerman, hard-working, fairly astute, and lucky in his business dealings, unintentionally put himself in a position where (in the Bisoi's judgment) he constituted an affront to the normative order of caste. Tuta himself did not openly defy caste codes and in fact everyone, including Tuta, conducted themselves as if there was no other issue than his *devata*. I am unsure, as I made clear earlier, about the Bisoi's motives. He could have been concerned with public safety and the need to punish anyone who kept a malevolent *devata*. He could have been after Tuta's money. Or (the possibilities are not exclusive of each other) he could have instigated the witch-hunt in order to restore the hierarchy of caste by humbling a low-caste person who had become a man of substance. But at no time during the inquiry did he make the case that Tuta was out of line for a Washerman; instead he used the normative frame of witchcraft. Whatever his intention, the effect of what he did was (in a small way) to restore caste as the defining normative framework for village politics. He did it indirectly, using a different set of normative conventions that had nothing directly to do with caste. Why? I think it was because by 1953 it was no longer politic ("politically correct") for a public figure (the Bisoi was technically a government servant, as well as being the traditional headman) to say openly that a low-caste man had no right to be rich.

The Bisoi's strategy (assuming it was that) used the values of one normative system (witchcraft is evil) to buttress another normative system (position in the caste hierarchy as an index of political rights). The fact that he did so did not enter into public discourse and therefore did not testify to the growing weakness of caste as the regnant normative frame for village politics. Moreover, the domain of witchcraft and its associated beliefs is not in itself a political domain, and a bridge action that makes political use of it is very different from the bridge action that invoked citizenship, which did directly contradict the regime of caste.

Stage 5

I have so far outlined four things that may be done or not done when political practice strays from a regnant normative code. The first, briefly described earlier in the relatively straightforward case of Švejk, is to leave matters alone. Second, the code's details may be changed, leaving its principles intact; that was the Distiller choice. The third possibility is to remove the code and put another in its place; the Pano strategy evolved into that. The fourth is to use the resources of a different normative code to support the failing code by bringing practice back into line with it. The second and third maneuvers are, in different degrees, revolutionary in intent; they promote change. The first and fourth are conservative, the fourth designedly so, the first by default.

I now come to a fifth possibility, which is the most complex. It too is conservative, but not by default, as in the Švejk case; nor is it a clear use of one normative code to make up for the deficiencies of another, as in Tuta's case. It is the use of pragmatic maneuvers to accomplish ends that are normatively desirable in the regnant code but are beyond its capacity; the pragmatism does what the normative code is supposed to do but in fact does not. I will argue that this strategy paradoxically makes the normative designs, which are being violated, appear to be authoritative; it protects their legitimacy by concealing their failings. It is not merely a matter of definition to say that without pragmatic actions normative codes could not survive. Think about Sarojini Naidu's ironic comment: "If only Bapu knew the cost of setting him up in poverty."

The supreme pragmatist in this book, after Švejk, is Lyndon Johnson operating in the gigantic void that the normative codes of representative democracy in the United States and most other nations leave for strategic and pragmatic action. His case is complicated and the motives for his actions can be differently interpreted; their effects, however, are less ambiguous. I will begin with some comparisons.

Johnson, as he appears in my sources, has some Švejk-like features. Both figures are unstoppable and beguiling raconteurs. Švejk has no scruples about breaking normative rules; neither does Johnson. In Caro's books, he is unencumbered with principles that would prevent him from using whatever pragmatic device would get him what he wants. There is, as I mentioned earlier, an impressive trail of electoral fraud and a no less stunning account of political influence used to make a personal fortune—what Plunkitt calls "honest graft." But there is one fundamental difference: Švejk hides, Johnson wants the limelight; Švejk looks for the kind of power that comes from evading powerful others, Johnson wants normative recognition as a leader and is a far from reluctant public figure; Švejk's doings are unequivocally and exclusively pragmatic, whereas Johnson's are both normative and pragmatic, and many of them are ambiguously Heraclitean, being simultaneously normative and pragmatic.

Johnson had a normative agenda, partly inherited from President Kennedy, which he enhanced and expanded as the Great Society program. These were goals—voting rights, welfare measures, educational reform, and the like—that were publicly declared and therefore were given unambiguous normative status. They also commanded public support, but not enough to have them passed into law on their intrinsic merits. In any case, leaving aside intrinsic merits or demerits, the way representative government works in the United States gives every legislator a motive, whether or not he agrees in principle with a particular measure, to first find out what market value his support or his opposition would have. I intend "market value" to have the whole range of meaning, from earning a quid pro quo credit with someone in power who will help later when a favor is needed for constituents to screwing money out of businessmen who think they might be hurt or helped by the measure and are rich enough to invest in the political game.

Johnson was an extremely skilled operator in this market. It is also clear that without these skills he could not have outmaneuvered the Dixiecrats and accomplished the changes in voting, welfare, education, and other areas. But those enabling deals were never given clear normative status. Why not? Why is it left to biographers and investigative reporters to dig up the details and report them as semiscandals? In this particular case I cannot imagine that many of those who approved of the Great Society reforms would line up with Gandhi and argue that what could not be done openly and honestly should not have been done at all. The pragmatism, in other words, gets qualified approval, if the question is put; but people prefer not to be asked.

Johnson did other things (outlined in Chapter 10 and described in loving detail in Caro's two books) that he certainly did not want made public for the obvious reason that they either broke the law or offended the conventions of fair play that people still demanded (but mostly did not expect to get) from politicians. Stealing elections would be a cause for shame, people agree; it steps over the line because it breaks the law. But accepting contributions from Herman and George Brown and other businessmen is different because in practice it is quite difficult to distinguish that kind of money (at least in a way that would be lawyer-proof) from money legitimately given by people who are ideologically committed to the party's program. I suspect that these payments too would get approval—probably reluctant and tacit—from Ordinary Jane and her spouse, not because the graft links directly to some particular meritorious end (like the Great Society) but because it is believed that without it the system would not run at all. Money contributions to politicians and their parties are inevitable, it seems, virtually a fact of nature. They are the rain that irrigates the political crop, and without the rain there would be no harvest for the special interests, and life for everyone would become solitary, poor, nasty, brutish, and short. Again, if this is the case, why keep quiet about it? Why not argue that this *is* a natural system—the political equivalent of a free market—and say that invoking morality is like moralizing about the movement of the tides? But that argument is not made in open political debate; it has about it an air of heresy. The money that Johnson extracted from the Brown brothers to help finance his party and himself, and the government contracts they got in return, are *res tegendae*—things to be kept covered. Why?

The answer comes from two directions. One seems obvious: It helps no one's reputation in politics to be unashamedly manipulative; to brag about operating behind the scenes is to put a weapon into your opponents' hands. But that still begs a question: What is wrong with manipulation? The answer, though hard to pin down, involves a collusive lie about how all our social systems, including our political systems, work.

They work at two levels, the ideal and the real (which is another way of saying that they can be resolved into two sets of rules, normative rules and strategic/pragmatic rules). This model fits a variety of contexts. It may be the individual who keeps one eye on what is right and good and the other on what is to his or her advantage, and tries not to go too far in either direction. It may be whole societies or, more often, institutions within societies passing through alternate phases of political sin and civic redemption. The sin phase is when officials or politicians attend to their own wants and ignore the public weal. When the Chinese party bureaucrats began to behave too much like Djilas's New Class, Mao administered a dose of anarchy and purged the body politic, so to speak, for a return to Communist purity and the rule of the people. Then the process begins again: Pragmatism reemerges and flourishes until once more cut short by a bout of civic-minded enthusiasm.

This two-level model also works for revolutions. At the ideal level they have the utmost normative clarity: An evil regime run by evil politicians is uprooted and in its place is planted Maoism or Castroism or Leninism or, as the wheel turns, *glasnost* and *perestroika*, regimes that purportedly replace with good the evil that was there before them. The muddled hybrid reality and its ambiguities, however, go carefully unremarked. A similar startling clarity and consistency, also distant from reality, can be claimed for Gandhi's strategy of nonviolence. But this, as I said, is theater, a play put on not to reveal but to hide reality.

The collusive lie in all of this is the pretense that the normative pattern is the reality, and that pragmatic departures are temporary deviations. The scriptural account of the way political systems work is protected by the commandment that whatever pragmatic things are done out of sight should be kept out of sight. If the Brown brothers' money wins an election for Johnson in Texas, that fact should not be allowed to openly contradict the canonical statement that Texas voters, freely exercising their rights as citizens, determine who will be elected. But again, why do politicians—or the rest of us in our own lives, which follow a similar pattern—think the lie is needed? Why the ideal?

The ideal sells itself because it is simple, clear, unambiguous, and reassuring. There is a psychological payoff to simplification: It is good for morale. It provides a sense of security, a feeling that someone—or some creed—is in control; there is a center; things will not fall disastrously apart. Certainly political persuaders exploit that feeling. Albert Hirschman's three categories of reactionary rhetoric, which are perversity, futility, and jeopardy, minister to it.[1] Naysayers argue that the proposed reform will do the opposite of what it intends (perversity), it is impossible anyway (futility), or it will wreck some of the good things we have now (jeopardy)—all three arguments appeal to the fear that we may not be in control of our lives. In a similar way, what might seem very new and anxiety making, for example self-government for India and the expulsion of the British, Gandhi makes familiar and acceptable by spreading over it the cloak of his well-known and accepted holiness. Radical proposals may be dressed up as "nothing really new," not departures from existing principles but only minor procedural adjustments that are in accordance with established values. (This rhetorical strategy prompted F. M. Cornford's enigmatic advice: "Nothing should ever be done for the first time."[2])

The art of practicing politics is not the same as a scientific understanding of political systems. I suppose any successful politician must have some grasp of both, but power over people by defining situations for them is not gained by offering them a full and balanced analysis; it is gained by presenting simplifications of selected goals and situations and, correspondingly, obfuscating not only their true complexity but more especially their variance from acceptable normative codes. Lyndon Johnson was notoriously reluctant to enter into debates about principles. Perhaps he knew that the price of allowing any normative system to intrude too strongly into the *Realpolitik* domain of strategies and pragmatics would be to substitute actual chaos for the imagined sociopolitical order that curtains off a wheeler-dealer political reality.

This reality—prudently concealed—is an evolutionary mélange that emerges from simplification, self-interest, moral compulsions, mindlessness, and, of course, acts of God.

"*What is truth?* said jesting Pilate, and would not stay for an answer."[3] It may be, as he implies, that the only truth anchored in eternity is that none exists. Plato would disagree; so would Gandhi. Heraclitus saw things differently: Things both are and are not. Politicians say they stand with Plato and found their actions on the truth that is there to guide them. But to make sense of what politicians actually do, one has to stand further back, with Heraclitus, look for the ambiguities, know that truth has many versions, and focus the inquiry on the strategies that politicians use to make and unmake competing definitions of truth.

Notes

Chapter 1

1. Foucault 1991, 102–103.
2. Weber 1948, 155.

Chapter 2

1. Barth 1959.
2. Tyler 1987, 96.

Chapter 3

1. Burns 1979, 410.
2. Adams 1931, 373.
3. Moraes 1973, 37.

Chapter 4

1. Fox-Davies 1913, Vol. 2, 49.
2. First 1974, 121.
3. Andrews 1952, 60.
4. Lacouture 1970, 256.
5. Weber 1978, 241.
6. Fest 1975, 279.
7. Leites 1977, 104.
8. Urban 1971, 139.
9. Nehru 1962, 129–130.
10. Ibid., 373.
11. Ibid., 73.
12. Moraes 1973, 245.
13. Walter 1969, 134.1
14. Ibid., 165–166.
15. Tugwell 1957, 359–361.
16. Burns 1956, 204.

Chapter 6

1. Nehru 1962, 371.
2. Ibid., 72.

3. Mahtab 1965, 4.
4. Weber 1948, 120.
5. Nehru 1962, 81–82.
6. Fischer 1954, 103.
7. Fischer 1954, 121–122.
8. Nehru 1962, 371.
9. Avard 1962, 24–25.

Chapter 7

1. Bondurant 1965, 20.
2. Kripalani 1960, 74.
3. Ibid., 88.
4. Ibid., 129.
5. Kripalani 1960, 136.
6. Ibid., 132.

Chapter 9

1. Goodwin 1976, 226.
2. Riordan, 1963, 25.
3. Goodwin 1976, 230.
4. Goodwin 1976, 224.
5. Ibid., 182–183.
6. Goodwin 1976, 228.

Chapter 11

1. Scott 1987, 426–431.
2. Hutson 1973.
3. Milano 1925, 90; my translation.
4. Thucydides 1972, 242–243.
5. Beloff 1948, 36.
6. Ibid., 42–43.

Chapter 12

1. Bose 1953, 201.
2. Kripalani 1960, 90.
3. Turtledove 1990.
4. Djilas 1957, 37.
5. Ishkanian 2000.

Conclusion

1. Hirschman 1991.
2. Cornford 1953, 15.
3. Bacon 1909, 7.

References

Adams, Henry Brook
  1931 [1918] *The Education of Henry Adams*. New York: Random House.
Andrews, P.
  1952 *This Man Nixon*. Philadelphia: Winston.
Avard
  1962 *Panchayat Raj as the Basis of Indian Polity*. New Delhi: Avard.
Bacon, Francis
  1909 [1597] "Of Truth," in *Essays or Counsels*. Harvard Classics, Vol. 3.
    New York: Collier.
Bailey, F. G.
  1969 *Stratagems and Spoils*. Oxford: Basil Blackwell.
  1994 *The Witch Hunt*. Ithaca: Cornell University Press.
Barth, Fredrik
  1959 *Political Leadership Among Swat Pathans*. London: Athlone Press.
Beloff, Max (ed.)
  1948 *The Federalist, or, the New Constitution*. Oxford: Basil Blackwell.
Bondurant, Joan V.
  1965 [1958] *The Conquest of Violence*. Berkeley: University of California
    Press.
Bose, Nirmal Kumar
  1953 *My Days with Gandhi*. Calcutta: Nishana.
Burns, James MacGregor
  1956 *Roosevelt: The Lion and the Fox*. New York: Harcourt, Brace and
    World.
  1979 *Leadership*. New York: Harper and Row.
Caro, Robert A.
  1974 *The Power Broker: Robert Moses and the Fall of New York*. New York:
    Knopf.
  1982 *The Years of Lyndon Johnson: The Path to Power*. New York: Knopf.
  1990 *The Years of Lyndon Johnson: Means of Ascent*. New York: Knopf.

Cornford, F. M.
1953 [1908] *Microcosmographia Academica*. Cambridge: Bowes and Bowes.
Djilas, Milovan
1957 *The New Class*. New York: Praeger.
Evans-Pritchard, E. E.
1940 *The Nuer*. Oxford: Clarendon Press.
Fest, Joachim C.
1975 *Hitler*. New York: Random House.
First, Ruth
1974 *Libya: The Elusive Revolution*. Harmondsworth, England: Penguin.
Fischer, Louis
1954 *Gandhi: His Life and Message for the World*. New York: New American Library.
Fortes, M., and E. E. Evans-Pritchard
1940 *African Political Systems*. London: Oxford University Press.
Foucault, Michel
1979 *Discipline and Punish*, translated by Alan Sheridan. New York: Random House.
1991 "Governmentality," in *The Foucault Effect*, edited by G. Burchell, C. Gordon, and Peter Miller. London: Harvester Wheatsheaf.
Fox-Davies, Arthur Charles (ed.)
1913 *The Book of Public Speaking*. London: Caxton.
Gandhi, Mohandas K.
1972 *An Autobiography: The Story of My Experiments with Truth*, translated by Mahadev Desai. Boston: Beacon Press.
Goodwin, Doris Kearns
1976 *Lyndon Johnson and the American Dream*. New York: Harper and Row.
Hašek, Jaroslav
1973 *The Good Soldier Švejk*, translated by Cecil Parrott. London: Heinemann.
Hirschman, Albert O.
1991 *The Rhetoric of Reaction*. Cambridge, Mass.: Belknap Press.
Hobbes, Thomas
1946 [1651] *Leviathan*. Oxford: Basil Blackwell.
Hobsbawm, E. J.
1959 *Primitive Rebels*. Manchester: Manchester University Press.
Hutson, Susan
1973 "Valloire," in *Debate and Compromise*, edited by F. G. Bailey. Oxford: Basil Blackwell.
Ishkanian, Armine
2000 *Hearths and Modernity: The Role of Women in NGOs in Post-Soviet Armenia*. Ph.D. thesis. University of California, San Diego.

Kautilya
1951 *Arthasastra*, translated by R. Shamasastry. Mysore: Sri Raghuveer Printing Press.
Kripalani, Krishna (ed.)
1960 *All Men Are Brothers*. Ahmedabad: Navajivan Publishing House.
Lacouture, Jean
1970 *The Demigods: Charismatic Leadership in the Third World*. New York: Knopf.
Leites, Nathan
1977 *Psychopolitical Analysis: Selected Writings of Nathan Leites*. New York: Sage.
Machiavelli, Niccolò
1950 [1531] *The Prince* and *The Discourses*. New York: Random House.
Mahtab, Harekrushna
1965 *Lectures on Gandhian Philosophy*. Annamalainagar: Annamalai University.
Milano, Euclide
1925 *Dalla Culla alla Bara*. Borgo San Dalmazzo, Italy: Bertello.
Moraes, Frank
1973 *Witness to an Era*. New York: Holt, Rinehart & Winston.
Nehru, Jawaharlal
1962 [1936] *An Autobiography*. Bombay: Allied Publishers.
Riordan, William L.
1963 [1905] *Plunkitt of Tammany Hall*. New York: Dutton.
Robert, Henry Martyn
1978 [1907] *Robert's Rules of Order*. New York: Bell.
Scott, James C.
1987 "Resistance Without Protest and Without Organization: Peasant Opposition to the Islamic *Zakar* and the Christian Tithe." *Comparative Studies in Society and History* 29: 417–452.
Thucydides
1972 *The Peloponnesian War*, translated by Rex Warner. Harmondsworth, England: Penguin.
Tugwell, Rexford G.
1957 *The Democratic Roosevelt*. New York: Doubleday.
Turtledove, Harry
1990 "The Last Article," in *What Might Have Been*, edited by Gregory Benford and Martin Greenberg. New York: Bantam.
Tyler, Stephen A.
1987 *The Unspeakable*. Madison: University of Wisconsin Press.
Urban, George
1971 *The Miracles of Chairman Mao: A Compendium of Devotional Literature, 1966–1970*. London: Stacey.

Walter, E. V.
  1969 *Terror and Resistance*. New York: Oxford University Press.
Weber, Max
  1948 "Politics as a Vocation," in *From Max Weber: Essays in Sociology*, edited by H. H. Gerth and C. Wright Mills. London: Routledge and Kegan Paul.
  1978 *Economy and Society*, edited by Guenther Roth and Claus Wittich. Berkeley: University of California Press.

Index